Creative Communications for a Successful Design Practice

Creative Communications for a Successful Design Practice

By Stephen A. Kliment, AIA

WHITNEY LIBRARY OF DESIGN
an imprint of
Watson-Guptill Publications/New York

Copyright © 1977 by Whitney Library of Design

First published 1977 in New York by the Whitney Library of Design
an imprint of Watson-Guptill Publications,
a division of Billboard Publications, Inc.
1515 Broadway, New York, New York 10036

Library of Congress Cataloging in Publication Data
Kliment, Stephen A
    Creative communications for a successful design
practice.
    Includes bibliographical references and index.
    1. Communication in architectural design. 2. Com-
munication in design. I. Title.
NA2750.K54 1977   658.4'5   76-56257
ISBN 0-8230-7133-2

Manufactured in U.S.A.

First printing, 1977
Second printing, 1977
Third printing, 1979

For Felicia

Foreword

In the early 1960's, after half a decade of intense professional work, and a lifetime of personal preparation, the day came for planner Edmund N. Bacon to present the first Comprehensive Plan for the City of Philadelphia to his client—the very top echelon of the City's municipal and civic leadership. For more than two hours, Bacon and his staff, using words, drawings, models, photographs, and slides, presented their recommendations for the future development of Philadelphia. Those who were present say that it was a profoundly moving experience. When Bacon finished, everyone in the room sat silent while the then mayor, Richardson Dilworth, rose to respond. He said only one word: "Amen."

I have often wondered: Was this a response to the design, to the communication, or both?

Ed Bacon is a master at communication and at his design discipline. So by all accounts were Wright and Draper, as are Nervi, Loewy, LeMessurier, Noyes, and so many of their peers.

Is it possible there is a correlation between the talented designer and the ability to communicate? Really, what is the principal skill necessary in order to:

• Get the opportunity to design.

• Establish a bridge of understanding with the client so the needs of the assignment generate an outstanding design.

• Persuade the client to embrace and support the design solution.

• Convince public officials, citizen groups, donors, and others to support the implementation of the design.

• Have the result understood and recognized so that further opportunities will come to the designer.

This book, for the first time, discusses in a comprehensive way the communication skills necessary for successful design practice.

Stephen Kliment is uniquely qualified to address the relationship of communication to design practice. As an architect, he is trained in design and understands fully the need of the designer to communicate. As an architectural journalist, he demonstrated personally the compatibility of design and communication. His exposure to the state of the communication art as practiced by his peers worldwide, his subsequent work in hands-on marketing of design services, and his wide experience as a consultant have given him a perspective on communication in design practice that is without equal.

This book gives practitioners, educators, and students a completely comprehensive outline of the communication skills that are necessary for successful design practice. In doing so, it also raises the underlying question: why is it that the most successful designers are often the most skillful communicators?

The finite answer must await future research on all the intangibles that make up a talented designer. Meanwhile, there is abundant empirical evidence that there is, indeed, a vital correlation.

Design is an act of communication. This book should help make every designer a better communicator and, thereby, a better designer.

Weld Coxe, Hon. AIA
Philadelphia, December 1976

Acknowledgments

I owe a debt of gratitude to many inside and outside the design professions for their help in bringing this book to birth. Bradford Perkins, Stephan Geissbuhler, Charles Redmon, and James Brett looked over key chapters, and their sharp, frank comments have made this a better book.

By generously sharing with me communications experiences from their own practices, the following people provided invaluable information: Frank Orr, Harry Weese, Fred Bassetti, Emanuel Pisetzner at Weiskopf and Pickworth, Roy Allen and Ann Landreth at Skidmore, Owings and Merrill, Peter Piven at Geddes Brecher Qualls Cunningham, Ann Hardeman at Syska and Hennessy, Edward Agostini and Ann Wilson at Hellmuth Obata and Kassabaum, Robert Campbell at Reid and Tarics, Harry Schwartz at Abeles and Schwartz, Gerard Valk at Valk and Keown, and James Cagley at Martin and Cagley.

Conversations with John Jansson, Weld Coxe, Larry Coppard, and Alan Stover yielded important facts on the management side of communications, and gaps in my knowledge on the production aspects were ably filled by Vic De Nino of Scanlan Press, Robert Beal and Lauren Sinclair at Stone's, Steve Lohrius at Atlantic Blue Print, and various technical representatives of the major producers of phototypesetting equipment.

George Finley, chief editor of *Industrial Design*, has kindly allowed me to use those parts of my article dealing with advertising communications.

Unique thanks are due to Susan Braybrooke, Susan Davis, Jim Craig, Frank De Luca, and Ellen Zeifer at the Whitney Library of Design for their rare skill and patience in shepherding this manuscript through the publication process and to John Cordes, Bob Ballek, and Paul Scicluna for their help with the artwork.

I owe a special debt to my former partners at Caudill Rowlett Scott for the unique challenges and opportunities to tackle communications problems first hand on a big scale; to David Hagenbuch, publisher and salesman extraordinary; and to my students in the continuing education program at Harvard University, for stretching my mind in new directions.

Finally, a great measure of gratitude goes to professors Jean Labatut and the late Donald Egbert, who, while I was a student at Princeton, placed before me standards of excellence in design and verbal expression that I have yet to match.

Stephen A. Kliment AIA
New York, 24 January 1977

First Professional: "What we need is to communicate better."
Second Professional: "What do you mean by that?"

Quote courtesy of Wallie E. Scott, Jr., FAIA

Preface

The purpose of this book is to help architects, planners, engineers, interior and industrial designers, and other building professionals communicate more effectively with present and prospective clients, with the media, and with the public. It is for the small firm gearing up for growth, the middle-sized office seeking to improve the overall quality of its communications products, and the large organization intent on imposing a greater consistency on its communications effort.

As competition tightens, communications skills are becoming vital ingredients of successful practice. Day in and day out, professionals are called on to provide prospective clients with office brochures, to compose letters of interest, and to write proposals, articles, and reports. They take part in interviews requiring slide presentations, and they often need to develop slide shows that the client himself then uses to "sell" his own constituency. They regularly submit project folders to design award juries, prepare exhibit panels for display at conventions of prospective clients, make speeches, and, in larger firms, even issue news releases and publish newsletters. And chances are that soon they will also be permitted to advertise.

I have over the years reviewed many, many examples of communications products developed by the nation's design firms, large and small. Many of the products were of high quality. Many others were replete with the kinds of oversights and even blunders that alienate clients—pictures of school buildings without a child in sight; floor plans so reduced you could not read the titles; report covers so overinked that they showed up every thumbprint; fancy language the client could not understand; and material quite obviously geared to the wrong audience.

The aim of this book is to identify the elements of good communications practice and to show how to produce what one writer has called "paper work that sells." The first two chapters describe the specific objectives of all communications programs and introduce the tools at hand. The third chapter takes up the "end products" of communications one by one—the brochures, the reports, the proposals, the design award submittals—and points up the unique requirements of each.

Certain ingredients cut across the board and apply to all of a firm's communications. How to write for impact (Chapter 4) and how to use graphics creatively (Chapter 5) deal with those ingredients and provide tips and methods for improved communications performance in those areas.

The components of the good audiovisual presentation are given in Chapter 6. Design professionals are often required to serve on panels or address various audiences (including designer selection committees), so Chapter 7 offers some guidelines on how to prepare for this sometimes nerve-wracking experience. Chapter 8, while not a primer on photography, shows when outside help is needed and how to get the best results.

How to approach the press with good prospects of publication has always been an unnecessary mystery for the design professional. Chapter 9 identifies the various types of media and suggests some proven ways for the professional to attract the eyes of the press

None of this effort stands much chance of success unless it is coordinated and managed. No matter whether the firm has six employees or 600, it needs a consistent, organized approach. How to do this is what Chapter 10 is about.

Every firm, not just the large or the well to do, should be able to tap the abundance of technical information and specialized consulting talent available. Yet most offices cannot afford to add to their staffs specialists in writing, editing, graphics, press relations, photography, and audiovisual.

What this book does is to identify sources of assistance (consultants and such trade suppliers as typesetters and printers) and shows how to evaluate and select them. It highlights basic procedures in those specialties, and introduces the vocabulary to help the reader discuss his problems intelligently with them; it lists printed sources to consult for more detailed information; and it offers ideas of all kinds that the reader can develop on his own.

Contents

Creative Communications for a Successful Design Practice

1

Good communications: who needs it?

Good communications is good business. Poor communications is an unnecessary drag on your marketing effort. In an ever-tightening competitive market for the design professional, the ability to communicate capably and forcefully with your various target audiences may spell the difference between stagnation and reaching the goals you have set for yourself and your organization.

CHANGING BACKGROUND

Both the business and ethical climate in which professional design firms have practiced for generations are in a great state of flux.

The business climate

In the last few years, much has happened to change the professional business climate.

• The recession of 1975 further taxed the smaller firm's ability to survive in competition with the better financed larger offices that were more able to weather the economic pressures.

• The huge capital resources of the oil-producing countries coupled with their large-scale domestic industrial, cultural, and health care development needs have captivated many western design firms against a background of intense competition.

• With growing sophistication client-owners are insisting on efficiency from design firms in the areas of cost and schedule control, and in the ability of facilities and products to perform efficiently over their planned life spans.

• Many firms, to meet the demands of owners wishing to deal with a single firm that will provide all the required professional services—even delivery of the final facility or product—are merging with, or acquiring, other firms to balance out their arsenal of services.

• Some of these firms, to strengthen their long term capitalization, have sold stock to the public, thereby acquiring a whole new family of eager watchdogs—stockholders, outside directors, financial analysts, and the Securities and Exchange Commission.

• And the trend toward bringing the public into the decision-making process in areas that shape the fate of the built environment is adding still another target audience to the array of "clients" the professions must reach and cultivate.

All these developments will place a growing premium on good communications with the traditional owner conscious of (and no doubt happy with) the fierce competitiveness among firms anxious to do business with him; with prospective overseas clients bringing language as a new barrier; with the public, who is the final beneficiary of the professions' skills.

The changing ethical climate

By opposing fee schedules and requiring greater price competition among design firms, law enforcement agencies are, more and more, hoping to lower the cost of design services to the nation's public and private clients. More recently, the federal government sought to dislodge another stone in the wall of professional ethics by questioning the proscription on self-laudatory advertising found in the codes of most professional societies. This could open up a whole new range of opportunities for design firms, especially in the way of advertising and direct mail to prospects not personally known to the firm.

REACHING YOUR AUDIENCES

The public relations and advertising practitioners have a word for the sum total of the various types of audience you must reach with your communications message: *publics* (see 1-1). Not all of them are excited by the same content or format. Identifying each public and tailoring your message to bring each one around to your way of thinking is what is meant by good communications.

Four groups make up the design professional's publics: the *client-prospect*, the *media*, the *general public* (in the conventional sense of the word), and *peer-fellow professionals*. What kind of strategy and tactics should you devise and carry out to reach each of these publics?

The client-prospect

The point of your communications to the client-prospect is simple: commissions. All the means at your disposal— the brochure (or, as we shall also call it, the portfolio), proposals and proposal correspondence, your communications with current and past clients, and the means you use to tell clients (past, present, and future) about your victories and recognition—*must be geared to the client's motivations, and not yours.* This is one of the simplest, yet most often neglected principles of good communications. Client communications is the striking arm of marketing, which is the art of promising the client-prospect that his needs will be met, and that your firm is the one to do it.

What, then, will make the client respond favorably to your overtures?

1–1 Gear your message to your audience.

The client has capital to spend. Mostly, today, it is someone else's money—the taxpayer's or the stockholder's. You must assure him, therefore, that you are qualified to obtain for him maximum value in facilities (or planning quality or product performance) for his outlay; that the money he pays you will provide him in part with an early and accurate estimate as to what the project will cost him; that the solution you propose can be carried out and completed by the time he needs to use it—and that you are prepared to see to it that this in fact happens; that the facility (or plan, or product) will perform in line with his needs (which include such criteria as occupant and user satisfaction, reasonable operating and maintenance costs, high productivity, and energy thrift); that you are easy to work with during the often tempestuous course of planning, design, and construction; that you yourself are capitalized enough to pay your designers until the first fee check comes in; and that the building (or urban design, or landscaping solution, or interior design, or industrial product) will be visually pleasing to the client, his superiors, and employees.

To convince him of your worth in all these areas, you need to reach deep down into your professional track record—to your training, internship (those first few years as an employee), and growth within the firm, or, in due course, independent practice. Line up the strong points and the successes—evidence of jobs built on time and within the budget and of deft solutions to difficult problems, the design awards, the articles in the journals. Translate these into communications messages, and see to it that they reach his ears.

How to do it is what this book is about.

The media

The media are a second target public of your communications. The information to send will differ, depending on whether you send it to the professional press (the kind read by your peer-colleagues), the so-called business press (the kind most likely to be read by clients), or the general media. As noted in Chapter 9, the professional journals are interested in breakthroughs in design, technology, and practice. The business press—the journals read by the hospital administrators and the city officials—wants information that will help their readers do a better job. The two are not necessarily the same. That hospital design breakthrough that fascinates the editor of the professional journal will not always captivate the reader of the hospital journal unless the story is turned around so the implications to that reader stand out clearly.

As for the general press—the city dailies and national weeklies and the broadcast media—it is concerned with news that will cut the widest swath of interest among its audiences. Hence its need is for information from you in simplistic, human interest, and often superficial terms. Furthermore, its market impact, with the few exceptions pointed out in Chapter 9, is usually neither very direct nor very great.

Since the goal of your communications is new commissions, your media effort should be directed mainly to the business press segment of the media community.

The general public

This may not be a prolific source of job leads, but it is a fast-growing factor in either upholding, extending, or damaging the reputation of your practice, especially if a big part of it is in the public sector. Most federal legislation in the 1960s and 1970s involving facilities planning or the environment includes strong and explicit provisions for citizen participation. With revenue sharing, the same requirements are being written into state and municipal laws and ordinances.

Moreover, community groups in the 1970s took on an increasingly vocal, activist line in seeking to protect historical, cultural, or esthetic landmarks from disfigurement or ruin. Any professional firm whose practice touches upon these areas should concern itself with reaching those groups. The communications effort needs to be geared less to brochures and press releases than to taking an active, direct, and verbal part in neighborhood and community activities and to polishing up your techniques of audiovisual presentation and public speaking.

Peers

Recognition by your peers is satisfying, and evidence of it can be turned to good marketing advantage. Every firm should review the opportunities for publication in the professional press and for professional design awards—Chapters 3 and 9 explore this subject in depth. As to the design award programs, the effort required to prepare materials often takes up time and dollars that can swiftly become exorbitant. You should, therefore, screen any opportunities with a shrewd eye as to time, cost, and benefits, and proceed to focus your resources on a modest number of such programs where your prospects of success are sharpest. Do not forget the architectural schools as an important segment of this peer-group public.

COMMUNICATIONS: YOUR IMAGE AND PERSONALITY

Sooner or later every professional practice is faced with reconciling two goals that often conflict. One is the need to present to each public the face likeliest to succeed. The other is the urgent need not to dilute your own image and personality. Your communications program is tangible evidence of how you have approached this dilemma.

Every so often, a firm takes stock of itself: Where are we heading? What is our philosophy towards design, management, and professional ethics? What segment of the market is most promising? In which segments are our qualifications strongest? Are we an old-line firm with a long tradition of performance among large corporate clients? Are we a young firm that plans to make a strong involvement in local civic and community affairs our life's work? Are we a regional, medium-sized firm with aspiration to national practice, acquisition, and possible public ownership?

The answers to such self-questioning can be translated into communications terms by the way you choose the location and design for your office, by the attire and attitudes of the office staff, and by the graphics and writing/editorial image of your communications products.

This book deals with the written and graphics aspects

of your communications efforts. For sure, bright colors, open planning, supergraphics, pants suits, open shirt collars and rolled-up sleeves, and a poster at every desk spell informality and an absence of precedent-worship. Stratification by rank, enclosed offices and a subdued layout, time clocks, and four-in-hand neckties bespeak a more traditional mindset. No value judgment is intended here, and infinite combinations of styles are possible. *But the issue of identity and image must be faced*; and it must find its expression through the graphics and writing that are the chief face your firm presents to its several audiences.

It is possible, as shown in Chapter 5, to develop a *formal* graphic image through classical typefaces, engraved stationery, subdued paper stock, standard page sizes, and other aspects of conservative design without compromising your promotional approach to a more informally minded client. Most clients will respect a professional firm with a personality that does not quite match their own, as long as the firm's qualifications are sound and it is prepared to assign to the job personnel in tune with the client's needs.

At the other end of the scale, the *mod, trendy* practice with a colorful portfolio in odd-sized pages may be acceptable to a staid corporation in search of innovative ideas or to a bank planning a branch facility in a suburban location where a fresh, trendy solution is desirable.

The real issue

The need for readable writing and clear graphics applies no matter what personality the office wishes to project. A pompous, long-winded writing style, made obscure through unneeded jargon, will make no new friends in any quarter. Graphics design that draws attention to itself through self-conscious, flashy arrangements and makes no effort to observe what should be its first aim—to help the reader get the message—fails no matter if the client is Bell Telephone or a local theater group.

ON BEING CONSISTENT

Good writing quality and good graphics are not themselves enough. The occasional brilliant planning report produced with the help of a prestigious outside graphic designer will not only fail to outweigh, but may actually embarrass, the balance of your communications.

Be prepared, therefore, to develop at the start an overall set of graphics and editorial guidelines that are clear to anyone in the firm concerned with communications—from the marketing principal to the secretary who types his letter on the stationery.

Next, insist on controls that will insure compliance. These should not be elaborate or time consuming. As noted in Chapter 10, a small quality control group can meet several times a year to review the most recent batch of brochure fact sheets, printed reports, formal proposals, design award submittals, exhibit panels, and samples of correspondence; judge them for individual quality and overall consistency; and take management action if any of them fail to make the grade.

Clear purpose, the right aim at the proper target, good graphics and writing, and consistency are the foundations for the successful communications program.

2

Means of communications

The various parts of the communications package only have value in so far as they are part of your firm's overall marketing program. The characteristics of this marketing program—the type and size of target client-prospects; the present and hoped-for size of your firm; the emphasis on one building type or on many; the offering of services over and beyond those considered as typical or basic—each of these will have a direct bearing on the number, variety, and nature of the communications products developed by your office.

An overall listing and appraisal of possible means of communications is contained in 2-1. The following six-point yardstick is used:

1. Initial marketing impact.

2. Long-term marketing impact.

3. First cost of developing the item.

4. Probable lead time required to develop the item.

5. Ease of updating.

6. Probable shelf-life of the item, i.e., how long it will be good without updating.

The table may be used in two ways. *By reading down*, the table provides at a glance a general comparison of the relative strengths and weaknesses of the various means according to first cost, ease of updating, and so on. *By reading across*, each individual communications tool may be assessed across the whole range of the six criteria.

SUITING THE MEANS TO THE TASK

Each office will tend to break its communications down into three areas of effort—printed, audiovisual, and the spoken word. The classifications are taken up in detail in Chapters 3, 6, and 7, respectively.

Printed communications

These are by far the most common form. It is still the staple medium for most kinds of contact between professional offices and clients, client-prospects, and media editors, despite a rising volume of audiovisual and spoken contacts.

As 2-1 indicates, the printed communication has the advantage of being easily aimed at the intended audience. The immediacy of the impact also is good, as is its duration. Most individuals by nature tend to retain what they have *read* for a longer time than what they have *heard* from a lectern or *seen* as a fleeting image on a projection screen. Preparation costs, too, are usually quite

modest compared to other methods, as is the lead time required.

Ease of updating varies: the right kind of brochure system (see Chapter 3) can by updated very simply; to update the other kind, the solidly bound, single package brochure, is far more difficult.

In sum, printed communications are flexible, require no very large investment in materials and equipment, are simple to update if properly planned, and may in most cases be developed at very short notice.

Audiovisual (A/V) communications

Wherever a strong, immediate response is required and where you are able to justify the somewhat greater investment in time and first costs, audiovisual communications come into play. The slide presentation, for example, aside from its value as a marketing tool with prospective clients, also has its uses for reaching public agencies and community groups whose support you may need to see a project through; professional school audiences through lectures describing your firm's work; civic groups and luncheon clubs; conferences of your own professional society; and magazine editors considering a story on your project or firm.

A/V does have its drawbacks. The equipment needed to prepare and project a packaged show is costly and often elaborate to set up, and specialized consultation is commonly required if it is to rise above minimum technical and dramatic standards. Yet the duration of its impact is not great, and if sound is synchronized, the slide show is by no means simple to update. By far its strongest asset is its ability to make a powerful, immediate impact on the listener, an impact that the seasoned professional marketer can then exploit orally and through printed means.

Often neglected is one variation of the audiovisual presentation that substitutes simple means such as newsprint, wrapping paper, and large index cards for slides and film. In lieu of a cut-and-dried slide presentation, the professional who uses these simpler means can work jointly with the audience in developing a concept before their eyes. Yet the low cost and close involvement of the audience is offset somewhat by the small size of the audience that can be accommodated within visual and oral range of the presenter, and by the difficulty of reusing the materials.

The spoken word

This third category of communications likewise covers situations where a strong, direct impact is desirable. For-

		MARKETING IMPACT		PREPARATION/ DEVELOPMENT			
Legend: ● GOOD, ◐ FAIR, ○ POOR; N/A Not applicable, V Varies, 1 In reprint form, 2 Through reuse, 3 Cost paid by client, 4 Submittal package		INITIAL	LONG-TERM	FIRST COST	REQUIRED LEAD TIME	EASE OF UPDATING	SHELF LIFE
PRINTED							
Advertising (in client-read media)		●	○	○	◐	N/A	○
Article (journal read by client)		●	●	●	◐	N/A	◐
Article (professional journal)		◐	●[1]	●	◐	N/A	◐
Brochure/portfolio (modular)		●	●	◐	◐	●	●
Brochure (one-part)		●	◐	○	◐	○	○
Construction site sign		◐	○	◐	●	●	V
Design award		◐	○	◐[4]	○[4]	●[4]	●[4]
Direct mail promotion		●	◐	●	◐	◐	◐
Exhibit panel		●	○	○	○	◐	●[2]
General news story		◐	◐	●	●	N/A	N/A
Letter of interest		●	○	●	●	●	○
News release		●	○	●	●	○	○
Newsletter (to client prospects)		●	●	◐	◐	○	◐
Newsletter (in-house)		○	◐	●	◐	●	○
Poster		V	V	V	◐	○	◐
Proposal (format prescribed by client)		●	N/A	○	◐	◐	N/A
Proposal (open format)		●	N/A	◐	◐	◐	N/A
Report for client (planning, feasibility, etc.)		●	●	3	V	○	V
Standard form 254		◐	●	●	●	●	◐
Standard form 255		●	N/A	●	●	N/A	N/A
Yellow pages telephone entry		◐	◐	●	●	○	●
AUDIOVISUAL							
Flip charts (pre-drawn)		●	○	V	◐	●	◐
Model		●	◐	V	V	V	◐
Newsprint, brown paper, chalk board (write as you talk)		●	○	●	●	●	○
Rendering		●	◐	V	◐	◐	◐
8 mm. film (silent)		●	◐	◐	○	○	V
16 mm. film (sound)		●	◐	○	○	○	V
Slide show (self-narrated)		●	◐	◐	◐	●	●
Slide/sound tape package — single projector		●	◐	○	○	○	V
Slide/sound tape package — 2 projector, single screen		●	◐	○	○	○	V
Slide/sound tape package — multi-projector, multi screen		●	●	○	○	○	V
SPOKEN WORD							
Client conference		●	◐	V	V	N/A	N/A
Client interview		●	◐	◐	○	N/A	N/A
Community presentation		●	◐	◐	◐	N/A	N/A
Interview (press)		◐	◐	●	●	○	N/A
Interview (radio)		○	○	●	●	○	N/A
Interview (television)		○	○	●	●	○	N/A
Lecture (professional audience)		○	○	●	◐	○	N/A
Panel moderator (client audience)		●	○	●	●	N/A	N/A
Panelist (client audience)		●	◐	●	◐	●	N/A
Speech (client audience)		●	◐	●	◐	◐	N/A
Speech (general audience)		○	○	●	◐	◐	N/A

mal interviews with client-prospects; service as moderator of a discussion panel; acting as a panelist or formal speaker at a convention or conference heavily sprinkled with members of a client organization, such as school or hospital administrators; or an interview on local or network radio or television—all serve to project your personality and, by implication your firm's, strongly and directly on the audience you are courting.

A talk requires relatively little by way of preparation time and cost, and, once it is delivered on a given topic, it is a simple matter to update and adapt it to the next audience.

On the other side of the coin, the spoken word has as perhaps its greatest challenge the need to develop new skills—those of the public speaker. In the process of developing the printed piece, there is usually time to proofread, edit, and correct; and the taped A/V presentation allows for corrections to be made before the package is "frozen" for showing. But the spoken word carries the greatest risk of costly slips of the tongue and alienating an audience through the speaker's lack of skill in phrasing and delivery.

In broadcast interviews with the media, the speaker is especially vulnerable, since in most cases the listener/viewer is under no compunction to hear the speaker out and if displeased will merely switch off the set.

These few generic conclusions are an introduction to detailed coverage in the ensuing chapters. In the final count, each design professional must make his own assessment based on his objectives, his communications talents, and his resources.

2-1 Comparison of communications media. Read *down* to compare all media by individual yardstick. Read *across* to trace each medium across all yardsticks.

End products of communications

Until he gets to see, touch, or walk through the concrete results of a firm's design efforts, the prospective client or editor has mainly one visual yardstick by which to judge your firm. That is the look of your brochure, stationery, commissioned reports, written proposals, and the various other products of your communications. To strike the proper note, these items should be consistent in image and of high quality without seeming extravagant, flexible for varying categories of client, and up-to-date.

Just as crucial to good client impact is the quality of the writing. Obscure trade jargon, passages short on facts but long on philosophy, super-long sentences, and a slant geared less to the client's interests than to the professional's ego are all pitfalls that the shrewd writer will sidestep at any cost.

This chapter takes up, one-by-one, the various printed end products of the professional firm's communications. It points up each product's special features, its advantages and limitations, and sets out the methods and techniques for carrying them from concept to fruition. A special section on advertising is included at the end of the chapter.

All these products have in common certain elements of good writing, editing, and graphic design. Accordingly, a special chapter (4) is given over to the topic *Writing for Impact* and another (5) to *Graphic Format: Choice and Execution*. Writing and graphics are discussed in this chapter, under each product, only where they vary from practices recommended in Chapters 4 and 5.

THE BROCHURE/PORTFOLIO

The term *brochure* is not a good one. It conjures up visions of a thick, glossy, permanently bound volume with much color, many photos, and novel-length text. But is this the right way to approach clients? Ask yourself these questions:

• After six months or a year, is it up-to-date in terms of services, projects, and people?

• Will the prospect of having to read a book lead the client to put it off in favor of your competitor's less formidable materials?

• If you are promoting a college science building, why take up space (and the committee's time) with detailed descriptions of your residential, hospital, and office building projects?

• What is the real, immediate purpose of the brochure? To close the sale or to whet the committee's interest and pave the way for a more detailed presentation?

What follows is aimed at placing the approach to brochure-making in its right perspective.

Why a brochure?

As mentioned above, the principles of good writing and good graphics are covered in Chapters 4 and 5. This section takes a close look at the brochure itself, its purpose, its value, and its preparation.

Purpose and content. Before a client retains your firm, he needs to know ten things about you. These are:

1. Do you have experience in solving his kind of problem—hospital design, a land-use study, campus planning, modernization, product packaging design, and so on?

2. Do you have a good estimating and cost control record in bringing projects in within a budget?

3. Have you managed projects so they were completed on time?

4. Have your completed projects stood the test of time and use?

5. Are your esthetics and the client's visual perception of his project in harmony?

6. Do you have professional staff of high caliber?

7. Are your partner-in-charge and/or project manager compatible with the client's in-house staff?

8. Can he pay your fee?

9. Are you solvent?

10. Are you available?

Clearly, the answer to these marketing requirements is not necessarily a brochure. Some, indeed, such as Nos. 7–10, cannot even be put in a brochure. If you are very well known, the client will already have many of the answers before he ever contacts you. And if you are small or new, you may have so few projects to show that you would produce a printed piece of embarrassing scantiness. If you specialize in several building types and services, you may want to approach each type of client in a different way—some with a brochure, some without.

Making a brochure, therefore, cannot be a conditioned reflex, but must be thought out carefully as a part—but only a part—of your overall marketing effort. Some clients are best approached with a two-page letter and a listing of past clients and projects. Others prefer to get their information by visiting you at your offices, looking over your facilities, and meeting your staff. Others still, especially in the public sector, have specialized questionnaires that tell them what they need to know and discourage a weight of printed materials.

What, then, is the best way to balance the clear but occasional need for printed promotional materials with the risk of overdeveloping these and then watching the materials gather dust on your shelves?

To avoid the false impression made by the term *brochure*, we prefer to use the term *portfolio*, which avoids the aura of permanence implied by *brochure*. Since the latter term is largely accepted, however, we will use both terms interchangeably to make the alternative term more familiar.

Four steps in evolving a portfolio

To come up with a brochure/portfolio that meets your objectives, try the following procedure:

Step 1. List your firm's marketing and management objectives. If you are a new architectural firm, for example, the options might include the following:

• General practice, no specialization

• Institutional emphasis (educational)

• Institutional emphasis (health care)

• Commercial emphasis

• Public sector emphasis

• Research studies and investigations

• Outside engineering, planning, landscape architecture, interior design

• In-house engineering, planning services

• Special services (programming, construction management)

• Growth to a 15 (30, 45)-person office

• Limit to a five-person office

• Overseas expansion

If you are a medium or large-sized, established office, add these typical criteria:

• A one-city or multi-city practice

• Interdependence or autonomy of separate offices

• "Departmental" or "project team" organization

• Acquisition of, or merger with, other, complementary offices

• Intent to issue and offer stock to the public

If you are an engineering or specialized consulting firm, does a high proportion of your work come to you through referrals from the prime professional?

Step 2. Prepare a written statement or profile of your firm in terms of the foregoing objectives. A close look at such a statement will quickly tell you certain things; for example:

• If much of your work (as a consulting engineer, for instance) stems from being included in "team proposals" coordinated by an architect or developer, you will want to downgrade emphasis on other architects as clients and focus instead on the projects themselves.

• If you specialize in two or three areas (such as health facilities, construction management), you will want to assemble materials in each such area at short notice, without having to prune away unrelated materials from a general brochure. If you are a conglomerate, made up of acquired firms with a broad array of services (like water resources, underground construction, construction management, land development), you may need a two-tier package—a detailed one when each office promotes alone, an umbrella one when two or more of the units promote jointly.

• If you intend to remain small and develop a practice with a strong focus on supertailored design—with construction documents, bidding, and construction contract administration by and large carried out through an associated firm—your needs may be limited to heavy emphasis on illustrations and listings of design awards and prestige clients.

• If your image rests (or you hope it will rest) on a reputation for tight control over costs and schedules or on the systems approach to design and construction, you may want to focus your efforts on a special piece on those themes. This could include a tabulation of projects showing *budgeted* and *actual* project costs and time schedules, along with brief project descriptions.

• If you have a strong, loyal senior staff, you may wish to develop a printed piece with pictures and biographies. If you have average or above average turnover, this information is best confined to sheets typed on good paper but without elaborate printing.

Step 3. With this type of analysis in mind—from Steps 1 and 2—you are now ready to plan your portfolio. Remember that since all your clients are different, it is foolish to try to make one brochure do for all. To tailor the portfolio to the prospect, develop a series of printed and/or typewritten components or "modules"; a method to assemble them and keep them assembled in the desired order; and a personalized transmittal. A typical checklist of components is given in 3-1.

Step 4. To create the portfolio, review carefully the guidelines to good writing and editing given in Chapter 4. Then follow the detailed procedure for graphic design, layout, and production described in Chapter 5.

As you work, make sure that the text and graphics are consistent. Internal "family" resemblance among the components of a portfolio is as vital as the overall graphic consistency of your firm's communications program. This means consistency of type faces, control over page design, color, paper stock, titles of drawings, and design of the container. Even reprints should be imprinted with a distinguishing symbol, such as a logo or numeral, to tie it into the system. Remember also that a container of loose fact sheets risks being reassembled by the client in the wrong order or not at all, once he has studied the contents. The checklist of components (3-1) shows ways to prevent this.

The search for consensus

The office portfolio is the most sensitive of any of a firm's communications elements, because it embodies the outcome of difficult choices by the firm's principals as to outlook and marketing strategy. Strong arguments often mark the process as partners (and departmental heads, in the larger firms) debate *purpose*, *image*, and *audience*.

3-1 Checklist of components for a brochure/portfolio system. Each firm must tailor its effort to resources and growth objectives.

1. The firm's basic descriptive module. Includes such information as a general summary of how you organize a job for good client liaison, giving the pattern, flavor, and scope of the firm's professional experience. Include illustrations of a project or two—for atmosphere, not to illustrate the project (that comes later). The basic firm piece should rarely exceed four to eight pages. You may include photos of your office showing staff at work, but do not overdo the facility angle unless you manufacture widgets and want to impress a customer with the size and cleanliness of your plant.

2. The project fact sheet. Develop one fact sheet for each project you elect to include. Topics for a project fact sheet could be new buildings, master planning, furniture design, historic preservation, feasibility studies, research projects, special investigations (such as a campus facilities inventory and evaluation), graphics and signage, product design, and building system develop-

ment. Limit fact sheets to two to four pages per project.

The project sheet is the area in which to concentrate the bulk of your photography budget (color, if necessary) and to exercise great care in writing. Fact sheets can be very dull if written from the firm's and not the client's viewpoint. Therefore, the fact sheet text should always consist of two parts: a detailed statement of the *problem* as assigned to you and the *solution*—how and why you arrived at it, how it was carried out, and, if you can obtain it, a statement of approval from the client and/or an excerpt from a flattering review in a magazine or newspaper. Also have available basic statistics (materials, construction method; structural and energy systems; areas and costs), but do not automatically include them since they are often subject to misinterpretation. Some firms place this information in a simple printed supplement, and include it with the project fact sheet when appropriate. Clearly caption all photographs, even at the risk of repeating what is also said in the text.

3. The services fact sheet. Develop one fact sheet per type of service, de-

pending on the volume of business you hope to generate through it. The service fact sheet could be geared to building type (planning of health care facilities, educational facilities, commercial buildings, and industrial buildings), or it could focus on "process services" (programming, construction management, computer software, systems development, public relations services on the client's behalf). Unless the service is expected to generate a great deal of its own income, it is better merely to list it in the basic firm modules. On the other hand, if it is on such a scale as to have its own staff and management (such as construction management, engineering management, materials handling), it should probably have its own basic descriptive firm piece.

4. Staff biographies. Develop one sheet per staff professional. This should include *all* professionals, since many clients make a practice of reviewing the biographies of all team members who may be assigned to their project. Do not include photographs (every viewer draws different conclusions, for better or worse), but have unposed, informal glossy prints available if required. Due

Examples of general firm "anchor" pieces that stand alone or may be combined with supplementary materials.

3-1 (Continued.)

to turnover, biographies may be simply typewritten and mimeographed. Each member should be asked to update the information twice a year. Biographies may be done as a brief *narrative*, or as a *listing* showing education and experience.

5. Listings of past clients. Past clients always intrigue future clients, so list them on a separate fact sheet. You need not include contact names, addresses and telephone numbers.

6. Listings of past projects. Include location, dates, and one-sentence descriptions. Project costs may mislead—are they total project costs, or construction costs only? Do they include design fees? permits? fixed equipment? furnishings? Some firms prefer to omit costs to avoid confusion.

7. Listings of published books, articles, lectures by partners and senior personnel. This has merit chiefly for very large firms with long histories who can assemble an impressive listing. Most clients do not care, but it is useful to have in reserve in case of a close contest for a project, where it could swing a more academically inclined client board member to your side. Also,

it may impress technical panels reviewing proposals for government-sponsored research contracts.

8. Article reprints. Prospective clients are interested in what the professional and business press has had to say about you and your work. The value of reprints is high, for it is third-party endorsement and worth almost any amount of self-praise. It helps to assemble all such mentions of any substance—especially articles by you or about your firm—as reprints in a uniform format. Journals will usually furnish you with a few tearsheets but not enough to use for promotion. You can always get a lower rate by ordering reprints before the publication goes to press, and many magazines are geared to providing this. If not, a good offset repro house will run off good quality reprints if you give them clean, original tearsheets, including black and white photographs. If the article has four-color materials, try to order an "overrun" from the magazine; if the magazine refuses, it will perhaps lend you the original plates.

9. Divider sheets. Divider sheets identify the various modules of the portfolio (basic firm description; project and

services fact sheets; biographies; lists and reprints). High-intensity colors may be used for these dividers as a change of graphic pace, and they may be printed on stiffer paper stock and even tabbed for easier reference.

10. The letter of transmittal.

11. The container. Components may be assembled in any of three ways. One method is a *folder* made of stiff paper stock and provided with die-cut pockets or flaps in various configurations. Inserts are placed on the right, the letter of transmittal on the left or as the top sheet on the right (in which case the left side may be imprinted with such information as the name(s) and address(es) of your firm's office(s) or other permanent information). Large firms may develop a container for each self-sufficient division or department, such as health facilities, computer software services, or transportation planning. The container should be carefully designed for the anticipated number of sheets, so when folded it is neither too full nor too empty. The folder has the advantage of fast assembly and the drawback that an outside user (such as the client) may not bother to reas-

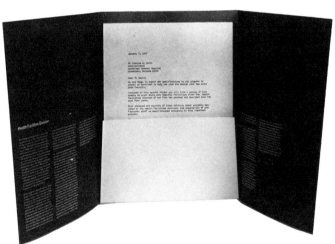

Container (right) is designed to hold an array of project and other fact sheets and listings, as well as the basic services piece. Larger firms with many specialties (above) may print long-term information directly onto folder.

semble it correctly (or at all) once the pieces have been removed. To forestall this, the order of modules should be clearly marked with a numeral.

A second option is *mechanical binding*, using commercial plastic or metal, spiral or ring binders. This will require a simple cover sheet, possibly topped with a sheet of transparent acetate. This method makes it possible to bind in a letter of transmittal, and it lacks the drawback of wrong reassembly.

A third option is *permanent binding*, with a hard or soft cover. Selected portfolio components are assembled for each use and for each occasion. Arrangements are made with a bindery to keep on hand an inventory of loose portfolio components and preprinted or embossed covers. The binding operation may take from two to four days. This method has the advantage of strong client impact ("You mean, you printed all this for me!"). On the other hand, the apparent extravagance of the process may disturb the client. Also, the three-day binding time and the actual cost (which can reach $20 for a ¾"/1.9 cm "book" with cloth covers) may steer you toward one of the first two methods.

Project fact sheets (above right) have high graphic consistency and lively headlines. Stiff 8½ by 11 sheets folded twice make for a compact, fact-filled basic information piece for each of many specialties of a large firm (above left). Individual fact sheets (top) are simply bound into a tailored brochure using a mechanical binding. In the open brochure by Harry Weese & Associates, applicable sheets are often passed around individually at interviews or mounted in plastic for permanence.

The path can be made smoother by establishing a process in advance. After each approval stage (i.e., statement of purpose; review of of concept; review of text and preliminary graphics; review of final graphics), partners should agree to abide by the results to date, and resist the temptation between those dates to add, subtract, or alter materials. Equally crucial is the designation of a single individual through whom all suggestions are channeled.

The tactics of selecting content

Which photographs, descriptions of projects and services, and lists of past clients will do the most good and should be included?

Consider the following five-point yardstick:

1. Was the project bid and built within its budget, and, in the case of an industrial product, was it manufactured within its budget?

2. Was the project completed on schedule or with all delays justifiable?

3. Has the project performed in line with its program from the viewpoint of productivity, operating cost, and occupant or user satisfaction?

4. Was your working relationship with the client a happy one, and is he likely to state so when asked?

5. Do your firm's qualifications and personnel résumés testify to experience with the building type, as well as to general problem-solving ability?

Views differ as to photographs. The schoolhouse that seems to you a gem of contemporary design may strike the school building committee as an eyesore. The best solution is to focus the entire photographic effort on illustrating a project *in use*—with people, bustle, informality, thriving landscaping, and unobtrusive parking. This will attract the client's attention to what is to him, after all, the main concern and will play down the strictly esthetic aspects that may be controversial.

Portfolio/brochures and the small office

The small one to eight-person office may not have the time, funds, inclination, materials, or even the need for a printed brochure/portfolio. The planning, design, and production of even a relatively modest 16–32 sheet) printed portfolio with container can run easily to $5000 when in-house labor, outside editorial and graphic consulting, typesetting and printing costs for minimum economical quantites of 500 to 1000 copies are included. And 500 copies may take forever to use up.

A young firm whose record of performance is tied to the partners' experiences as former employees in other firms should build a communication program in which the printed portfolio plays a reduced role in the overall marketing plan.

It is not within the scope of this book to cover marketing—two good works on the topic by Coxe and Jones are listed as references. Yet the $5000 (approximately) of a portfolio program is often better spent on such tactics as stepped-up "bird-dogging" of sources; greater reliance on longer, more detailed letters of interest and letters of proposal (see pages 42–45); stepped-up writing of magazine articles for reprint value; and greater efforts to be in-vited to speak at conventions of potential clients. In many of these situations, you will need to leave some reading materials on the client-prospect's table.

Short reading material. One method is simply to type neatly (and reproduce offset on a high-quality rag bond) the following:

1. A listing of services. Include as much detail as you can fit on a single page.

2. A listing of previous clients and projects (include those under previous employers, but indicate it). Give a brief description and the nature of your involvement (project manager, designer, and so on).

3. A biography of each principal.

4. A cover piece, consisting of a letter of transmittal on your firm's best letterhead.

5. Reprints of articles, where relevant. Articles are usually copyrighted by the publication—be sure you obtain written permission to reprint.

6. Selected project photographs, printed on 8½ x 11 paper. This costs a little more than 8 x 10, but it keeps your format uniform. Add a half-page description defining the problem and its solution.

Assemble and bind these components in any of several handsome but inexpensive methods described in Chapter 5. Few of these bindings cost over $3 each, and most come in a variety of acceptable colors. Note that for architectural or engineering firms seeking government work, much of this information must be supplied on *Standard Form 254: Architect-Engineer and Related Services Questionnaire*. Use it with discretion as a basis for providing background information to private-sector clients also.

The essence of this low-budget approach is to pay for a minimum quantity of any component at one time. For example, photographic prints may be ordered singly, and so may bindings. A hundred high-quality offset reproductions of typed pages from an 8½ x 11 original rarely cost over $5. Article reprints cost the same (slightly more when printed on 11 x 17 stock and folded).

More elaborate reading material. You can invest in one four-page printed piece that includes the more "permanent" parts of the same basic information and attach separate photographic prints as needed. The problem of keeping such a piece up-to-date is handled, for a time, by identifying client and project lists as "representative." Such a piece, including typesetting and printing in black and one other color, could be produced (in 500 copies) for little more than $250, providing easily a two-year supply.

Keep portfolio costs modest

Whether your firm is large or small, multi-disciplinary or single service, think of the portfolio as a closely integrated part of your overall marketing program. Such a portfolio need not be cumbersome. Simply produced fact sheets describing your firm or department, staff, and projects can reach high quality with good design and are easy to update, without paying for the cost of printing and storing a large, bound brochure that is soon out of date.

Two practice exercises are provided at the end of the book, one involving a small firm and the other a larger one.

THE PROPOSAL

The line between a Letter of Proposal (see p. 42) and a full-fledged proposal is often a matter of degree and circumstance. In many cases, especially in nongovernment work, the briefer, more informal proposal letter follows up an interview and commits the design professional to a certain scope of work, time schedule, and compensation. A formal proposal does about the same, but usually in far greater detail.

In some proposals, scope of work is defined by the client. In others, the professional is required to develop the scope himself, often in a high degree of detail. This occurs especially in research and development proposals addressed to government agencies in response to Requests for Proposals (RFP's) and in grant or contract award applications to foundations. Some firms leave a proposallike document with client committee members after an interview—it outlines the presentation and furnishes support matter.

Proposal formats fall into two categories: *open* and *closed*. In the closed format, forms and questionnaires are supplied by the client to be filled out in line with instructions. In the open format, the professional himself determines the arrangement of the materials.

The open and closed formats have much in common in terms of communication strategy, wording, graphic criteria, and recourse to supporting materials.

The purpose of all proposals

They should tell the client the following:

Awareness of his problem. You must convince the client that you thoroughly understand his problem, whether it is a consolidation of school facilities in a district with dropping enrollments; the development of an energy retrofit system for a medium-sized campus; or the development of a building and packaging system for service stations, gasoline pumps, and oil product displays for a large oil corporation. In grant applications on self-chosen subjects, the foundation-client must be convinced as to the *need* for the project.

Scope of work. This differs from problem awareness in that it is highly specific; in some cases it is broken down into many tasks and sub-tasks, each one building on the one before. This section should *always* be preceded by a statement describing the concept, or "parti," you plan to follow in solving the problem.

Staffing and joint ventures. The client needs to know who will be assigned to the project, whether full or part-time; how and by whom the team will be led and managed; the organizational linkages with other members of a joint venture or association; and the contact persons with the client.

Work product. What will the client receive at the end? (A report? A manual? A building? A model?)

Qualifications. These should cover both the firm as a whole and the individual team members, focusing both on experience in the project type and on evidence of general problem solving or management talent. For a proposal (usually to a government agency) that is to be reviewed first by a technical panel of scholars and scientists, it helps to list academic credentials and published work.

Schedule. This should include interim milestones.

Compensation. Depending on the client, this may need to be provided in detail, including direct labor and indirect costs, percentage of involvement of listed team members, and itemized estimates as to direct and reimbursable expenses.

Affirmative action. Most government clients now also require evidence of an affirmative action plan that describes the firm's hiring practices as to minorities.

Developing the parts

Some of this information must be developed fresh for each proposal. Other parts, such as qualifications, lists of clients and projects, and illustrated fact sheets and reprints, may be adapted or used directly from material prepared for the brochure/portfolio.

A summary statement describing the project's objectives, methods, organization, time schedule, and cost to the client should come at the start of all proposals. Most government RFP's require it, although costs are usually submitted separately. You cannot spend too much time on honing this summary statement, because it sets the tone for what follows and often is the only part of a proposal read with any care. For a good example, see 3-2.

The following procedure may be followed to organize this information, with variations to suit special circumstances.

Step 1. After a thorough analysis of the intent of the RFP—or after carefully reviewing the minutes of prior interviews with a prospective client (including, if necessary, additional clarifying questions addressed to the client's representative or contracting officer)—develop a consensus within the team as to how to approach the problem.

Step 2. Develop an outline. Typical outline sections are listed in 3-3.

Step 3. Make writing assignments—proposals are usually developed under intense time pressure, and as many staff as can be spared should be enlisted for writing and preparing diagrams. Alert typists and obtain résumés and qualifications from joint venture members. At the same time, prepare the first-draft diagrams of the proposed organization and the activity flow-chart.

Step 4. Review first drafts, adjust, and return to author(s). Review and revise diagrams.

Step 5. Prepare a thumbnail layout of pages. Unless the proposal is very long (150 pages or more), plan to type on one side of the page only, as it simplifies collation and binding.

Step 6. Review and edit final text drafts; select typing format and assign final typing.

Step 7. Design for simplicity and impact (see samples, 3-4), and assign draftsman or graphic artist to prepare camera-ready art.

Project objectives

The purpose of this study is to determine environmental standards in manned space facilities over a 1973–1990 time period, for use by individuals with a wide range of physical and professional backgrounds and for a wide variety of mission durations.

We will develop a handbook of human engineering data for lighting, acoustics, temperature, and color (along with a rationale for the choices made); a handbook containing drawings and analytical data to illustrate concepts developed in the interior space utilization part of the study; and three-dimensional models and other materials as needed to document the output.

Conduct of the study

We will conduct a two-part development and documentation effort (Lighting, Acoustics, Temperature, Color; and Space Utilization). These will proceed in parallel, with interchangeable personnel, but under single project management and with at least two points of formal contact: 1. Initial research; and 2. The proposed Systems Integration Conference, which will test the final group of standards and concepts, and explore their integration.

Organization

The architectural, engineering, interior environment, research, documentation, and management expertise of Adams, Brock and Carter will be combined into a collaborative team with the expertise of Dayton, Eward and Ford, Inc. in the disciplines of lighting, acoustics, and behavioral science; Garrison and Hamlin in the discipline of comfort control; and Inman Computing Systems, Inc. in the area of systems analysis. The team will place major stress on a constructive relationship with the appointed NASA—Manned Spacecraft Center (MSC) Technical Manager, and, through him, with the immense technical expertise available at MSC.

Schedule

The study will require seven months to complete, of which the final month will be devoted to documentation.

Compensation

We propose overall compensation in the sum of $100,000.

3-2 Summary portion of a proposal submitted to a federal agency by a joint venture of firms including the disciplines of architecture, environmental control, and systems analysis (firm names fictitious).

1. Cover (text and titles)

2. Letter of transmittal

3. Table of contents

4. Summary

5. Statement of understanding of problem *and / or*

6. Documentation of need

7. Statement of concept or approach

8. Scope of services—include tasks and subtasks if complex project, and identify major responsibility for each task. Be sure to spell out assumptions as to services and needs to be provided by client.

9. Organization and liaison

10. Qualifications: firm or firms; individuals

11. Time schedule

12. Compensation (include man-hours where required)

13. Charts and diagrams: organizations; activities or precedence diagram

14. Index of supporting materials

3-3 Typical proposal outline. Note that the following items may be grouped and visual dividers provided in front of items 4, 5, 9, 11, 12, 13, and 14 for reading convenience.

Step 8. Proofread typed copy. *Do not downgrade this step.*

Step 9. Assemble supporting materials and send camera-ready pages to repro house and bindery for printing and binding. Order extra copies for your records.

Step 10. Mail, ship, or hand deliver the finished proposal. Most proposals are very costly in their demands on high-priced professional time, with the equivalent of one or even two-person months not unusual. Therefore, the penny-wise-pounds-foolish axiom applies. Some services, such as *Federal Express*, will ship a package the weight of an average one to three-pound proposal to any part of the country for about $16. And, if all else fails, $400 is a small amount to invest in a cross-country flight to deliver a proposal that may have cost $10,000 to prepare. Do not tempt fate by putting your trust in cheap but unreliable mail or express services.

Writing proposalese

The writing of proposals is no different from writing a letter, yet most proposals are written in a style that combines that of a production specification for a spacecraft with the more recondite clauses of an insurance policy. Why say "The Contractor shall implement and finalize the project within a time frame of 14 months," when "We promise to complete the project in 14 months," says it better? "Proposalese" is both awkward to write and awkward to read. Plain English, as advocated in the next chapter, can be made to serve at many levels—at the level of the scientist reviewing a research proposal, and at that of the vice president for facilities who will select a firm to develop a prototype structure for a fast-food chain outlet.

The proposal in most cases is not a contract document. If accepted, its provisions are converted into a legally airtight contract. Where signing or initialing the proposal constitutes the contract, have your legal counsel look it over first. But while such a case does not excuse loose language, neither does it justify pseudoscientific jargon.

Writing an effective proposal does take a little practice, and for that reason it is a good idea to assign the task to the same individuals time after time.

The parts and the whole

An easy thing to lose sight of when organizing the various parts of a proposal under pressure is concern for its organic unity. Every sentence, every diagram, and every piece of supporting matter must contribute to the controlling concept established at the start.

This organic whole is achieved by careful cross-checking of text drafts, lists, and activity flow charts. Just as a product or a building has its artistic unity, so must a skillful proposal hang together as a single, cohesive example of professional marketing.

THE NEWS RELEASE

The news release is perennial grist to the mill of the media. It gives editors topics for their news columns, ideas for longer articles, material for their *people, forthcoming events*, and *book review* departments. And it is one of the cheapest, most effective forms the design firm, whether it has five employees or fifty, can use to reach its various publics.

3-4 This proposal format (above) has colored dividers and bold lettering at the start of individual sections. In lieu of a formal proposal, a written record of presentation (below) may be simply assembled and left with client.

Preliminaries

There are several things to consider as you prepare to issue news releases. These are:

Subject matter. Not all happenings lend themselves to a news release; some do not justify a news release at all. News releases are used to announce a single event (usually) to a carefully picked audience. You may want to announce a merger with another firm; the promotion of a staff member to partnership; a major award; a new, large, or unusual commission; an address change; or the opening of a branch office.

A news release would probably not be the best vehicle for: announcing an internal management reorganization; the completion of an interim phase on a project; a transfer of personnel to a branch office (except to the local press). These activities or events are of far greater interest to you than they are to anyone outside the firm. A news release is also not in order for complex or continuing activities, such as a job in progress or the workings of your financial management system.

Frequency. It is possible to overload editors with news releases. If you do, like the child who cried "wolf" or the Fifth Avenue trinket stores that go out of business once a month, no one will take you seriously.

Timing. Timing depends on the audience. If the main purpose of the release is to have it picked up by the media (press, radio, or TV), keep in mind publication &dates. A monthly journal usually cuts off all but earth-shaking events about three to five weeks before the publication date—although some are arranging more and more for what is called a "late-closing form" to accommodate late-breaking news.

Weekly magazines, which tend to have a strong news orientation, are more flexible and will process news up to the last minute. Daily papers do so even more, especially large urban dailies with several editions. Consult *Bacon's Publicity Checker* for deadline information. If the news release is intended chiefly to inform your list of past and present clients—or stockholders, if you have any—of new events, *timing* is less of a factor than *appropriateness.*

Who should receive it? Whom to put on the list is one of the primary considerations. Begin to develop a mailing list no matter how brief. You may use it at different times to disseminate other products, such as new brochure fact sheets or, in the large firm, a client newsletter. Larger firms may break names down into the following categories:

- Past clients
- Current clients
- Client-prospects (under current ethical practices, these prospects must be known to some member of the firm before they can be mailed self-serving literature)
- Friends of the firm
- Media
  Press
      Professional (local, national)
      Business
      General (local, national)

    Broadcast
        Radio (local, network)
        Television (local, network)
      Wire services
- Financial (if publicly owned firm)
  Stockholders and directors
  Analysts
  Regulatory agencies
  Press
- Employees
- Clipping bureau (if retained)

If you are an architectural or engineering firm, and your firm consistently covers or intends to cover several building types, lists of the first three categories above should be broken down by building type, or type of service.

If your market is, for instance, chiefly residential, you may want to break that category down into single family, multi-family, renovation, and so on. Once you have the breakdown, it is no trouble to assign names of new or prospective clients to their proper slot. This allows you to concentrate rather than scatter releases across the whole spectrum of clients. A quick inspection of your list may indicate at once that the audience you expect to dazzle with the development is too small to make the effort worthwhile. In that case, some other format is in order, such as a special announcement with a personal covering letter, or no announcement at all.

Try to keep very short lists (up to 100 names) updated on individual file cards, typing new address labels or envelopes for each mailing. You could also cut stencils for each name and print via an addressing machine. Medium-sized lists are best handled by typing them on standard commercial 8½ x 11 master sheets, each containing space for 33 addresses, 1 x 2¾ in./2.54 x 7 cm. Use masters to run off self-adhering address labels to attach to the mailing pieces. To update, merely paste a corrected 1 x 2¾ in./2.54 x 7 cm label over the old name and address on the master.

Lists over 1000 or so are handled more smoothly if put on a computer. Any local computer service bureau will help you set up and maintain the system for a modest fee. You need only complete coding sheets to enter new names and addresses and any revisions. Printout comes in the form of straight lists, or as heat-applied or self-adhesive address labels. Break down the lists into categories as noted earlier for easier targeting of mailings.

Do in-house or get outside help?

There is no mystery in developing a news release that cannot, with a little practice, be mastered within your organization, whatever its size. The one advantage of retaining public relations counsel is the contacts such a firm may have with the editors who can give the event proper play. If the general public is your target, by all means contact outside counsel. Unless your organization has on staff someone with a broad public relations background *and many contacts among the general media*, going outside is about the only way your news release will be acted upon by the press, radio, and TV.

Monitor outside public relations counsel carefully. One story has it that counsel for three rival design firms sent out an identically worded new project announcement on behalf of the three firms, changing only the firm's name and location of the project.

Chances are, however, that the bulk of your news releases will concentrate on a professional and client audience, in part because of current ethical constraints. This picture may well change if the constraints are done away with, allowing design professionals far greater freedom in promoting themselves routinely to prospects unknown to them.

Coordination. There is no sadder sight than a firm that painstakingly prepares and issues a news release, only to find that the client, with far greater resources and usually better press contacts, has done or is about to do the same.

Always—where your agreement with the client doesn't already mandate this—coordinate publicity with the client, general contractor, supplier, and any consultants. It will save trouble and make a bigger splash. For information about press-conferences and when to hold them, see Chapter 9.

Preparing the news release

The news release should be made up of the following parts (see also 3-5):

- Title
- Contact information
- Release date
- Date line
- Text
- Supplements (such as photographs)

All are important—an error in any one part is enough to frustrate the entire venture.

Title. The most crucial element is the title or headline, which should be informative, active, specific, and dramatic without being coy, cute, or corny. Below are examples of incorrect and suggested forms—as in all examples in this book, the incorrect version appears on the left and the suggested correct version on the right.

ENERGY CONSCIOUS DESIGN	ARCHITECTS DESIGN 30% ENERGY SAVINGS INTO 1000-STUDENT HIGH SCHOOL
MERGER OF TWO FIRMS	ARCHITECT, ENGINEER MERGE TO FORM NATION'S LARGEST DESIGN FIRM

Contact information. The news release cannot contain enough information to please everyone. Therefore, a contact person is essential, along with a telephone number. Some contact persons also list their home telephone, but this seems to carry service too far. The arbiter, perhaps, should be the person to be called after hours, if anyone. The only justification would appear to be in cases where the news value crosses several time zones, making it easier for a Los Angeles editor to call a New York contact during the former's afternoon office hours when eastern offices are closed.

Release date. The point in putting a release date (or "for immediate release") at the top of the release is to give everyone an equal start and to control to some extent the breaking of the news. It is a sanguine office that believes all editors will observe the date, and it is safer to assume that at least one will break it.

Therefore, avoid including in the release information that would be harmful if printed prematurely. Or, said another way, wait until all the contents are cleared for immediate release.

Some firms stagger the mailing of the release to first reach the monthlies with their longer lead times. This is not foolproof, as there is nothing to stop the news editor of a monthly from sharing the release with a friend who works on a weekly journal put out by the same publishing house. The road to good press relations is riddled with such pitfalls.

Date line. Placing the date and place of release at the start of the first paragraph is a convenience, but the practice is often ignored, with little harm. It helps your firm's records to know when the release was mailed, but this can be done with a coded entry at the end, such as "041877-4" (for "Release #4 of 1977, April 18").

Text. The art of writing for impact is covered in Chapter 4. What distinguishes a news release text from conventional word organization is sequence and emphasis. Place the main point in a short first paragraph. Although the rule taught journalism students—to include the what, who, when, where, and why—is more appropriate to a kidnapping or a drug raid than to a story on your recently completed water treatment plant, there is much common sense to it, and it is worth following within reason.

The second and successive paragraphs should then take up the event in more detail, including some back-up rationale; a *quote* or two on the event by a principal (optional); *relevant* background on the firm and its principals; and information on other *relevant*, recent, or current projects. Double space the text and leave generous margins for use by the editor.

Supplementary materials. No news release should go beyond two typewritten pages. The aim of a release is to stimulate and to whet the appetite, not to cover every possible angle. If there is so much to say that it cannot fit into two pages, you need to either rewrite it or select supplementary information the reader can consult.

These supplements can consist of one or two photographs of, for example, new partners or of a facility—include a site plan and typical floor plan for the professional journals. If the subject is a far-reaching planning or research report, include a copy for the editor. Or tell him he can get one by calling for it. But eschew anything that might induce the editor to lay your release aside for further study. One such inducement is length.

Production. Your firm's basic letterhead is often adequate for producing the news release, with the word *NEWS* typed and underscored. If you plan to issue more than two or three releases a year, develop a special news release form. The words *news* or *news release* should be prominent; for the rest, the design should be consistent with your firm's other graphic elements (see Chapter 5).

Jones, Jones and McRae
Architects, planners, engineers
35 Blount Street
Stoneyport, Ill. 66666

For immediate release

For further information,
contact Egbert Heatherton
Telephone: 312-681-0000

ARCHITECT LAUNCHES EXPANSION
PROGRAM WITH FIRST MERGER

STONEYPORT, May 17th-- Jones, Jones and McRae today acquired the Jamesburg, Pa. firm of Higginbotham and Brown, JJM principal Reginald Jones announced. The merger, which climaxed several months of negotiation, combines the commercial practice strengths of JJM with Higginbotham and Brown's nationally recognized expertise in the planning and design of health facilities.

The Jamesburg, Pa. firm will now be known as the H+B Division of Jones, Jones and McRae.

The merger is the first step in JJM's expansion program, which was approved by the partners at their annual meeting last January.

"The needs of the modern building client are too broad, complex and varied to be handled adequately any longer by specialized local firms, such as ours," Jones told a staff meeting of the two firms. "Accordingly, we have started on a program which will, we hope, eventually offer clients a broad-based network of offices with in-depth experience in commercial, institutional and residential design, as well as in-house engineering support."

John Higginbotham and Arthur Brown will remain partners in the surviving firm, which now will have a combined strength of 75 professionals.

The Jones, Jones and McRae firm has designed $300 million worth of construction since its founding 15 years ago. Two

3-5 News release and distribution plan.

projects, the 400-family low-income housing project at Donner
Park and the Circle Shopping Center at Jockeyville, were given
coveted design honor awards by the American Institute of
Architects in 1968 and 1972.

Higginbotham and Brown were architects for the well-known
St. Olav's Medical Center at Jamesburg. The center is the
subject of several cost-saving breakthroughs in health facility
planning, including the use of systems building for the acute
bed care and ambulatory units of the Center.

Jones said his firm was negotiating with additional firms and
expected to announce a further acquisition in the fall.

-30-

News release 051777-7

Distribution plan

A. Complete client lists of both firms (with informal covering
    note from the partners).

B. Press list

    a) Professional

        Architectural, engineering and planning.

    b) Business

        Institutional

        Hospital, school and university administrators.

        Commercial

        Building developers, owners and managers.
        Real estate firms.
        Bankers.

        General business journals (e.g., Business Week).

    c) General press

        Local and regional papers in both cities.

    d) Broadcast

        Local and regional radio and TV stations in both cities.

3-6 Fruitful topics for client newsletter.

It is rarely worth setting the release in type. It costs more money and dilutes the sense of immediacy that the typewriter face imparts. The original should be clean, black, and sharp. Reproduction is best by photo offset for any required quantities within reason. Costs are about $5 per hundred per original.

THE CLIENT NEWSLETTER

In recent years, the newsletter has moved swiftly to the forefront as a printed medium geared to people who are short on time. The newsletter is fast and economical to produce, versatile, and lends itself to simple but effective graphics.

The large design firm should accordingly consider the newsletter as a useful medium for keeping in touch with clients. For the firm with 40 employees or less, other means—such as releases—may be more appropriate in effort and cost. No firm should ignore this medium, however.

General considerations

Whether your firm is large or small, you should consider the following with respect to client newsletters:

Subject matter. Subject matter must be linked closely to your firm's objectives. These, in turn, will depend to a great extent on your assessment of the current market for professional design services. If you are a larger firm and your main thrust is health facilities and other institutional building types combined with special stress on cost and schedule control plus concern for energy retrofitting of facilities, this will quickly dictate which subject areas to extract from your inventory of projects.

Newsletter stories should not be confined to completed projects. Stories about newly won commissions reflect just as strongly the client's faith in your ability to solve his problem (see 3-6 for diverse topics).

To avoid filling the client newsletter with irrelevant matter, apply this suggested five-point yardstick for establishing news value to the client reader:

1. Does the story reflect evidence of a high level of performance on a completed project in terms of such factors as maintenance and operating costs, user satisfaction, and productivity?

2. Did the project meet the owner's construction budget?

3. Did the project meet the owner's construction schedule?

4. Does the news item show evidence of a high degree of good rapport with the client?

5. Does the subject reflect an attitude and evidence of your firm's growth, such as into new areas of practice, new locations, or new personnel?

Frequency and timing. Unlike commercial or professional society newsletters, there is no major need to put a client newsletter on a regular schedule. Three or four times per year should be enough to update clients and prospects on your accomplishments. After all, he is not getting a publication that is essential to him in his work (except perhaps indirectly), and, as his time is valuable, there is no point in burdening his mailbox with too much reading matter.

On the other hand, you can safely assume that if what he is sent will help him make up his mind next time the matter of engaging a design professional comes up, he will read it and even, with luck, drop you a line of appreciation.

Some firms issue a technical letter of high quality, centered around a single topic. Journal editors often print such letters intact, making them an excellent publicity tool (see 10-6).

A good idea is to include, on the first or last page, a listing of the contents with a box next to each item that the reader can check off and return if he wants more information from you on that topic. It is one good way to uncover the client's future plans that may possibly require your services.

Recipients and coordination. See page 36 for an examination of the matter of mailing lists. By and large, every category on the list should be sent the newsletter, except in cases where you issue more than one newsletter (for example, planning, architecture, and engineering). In most cases, only the very largest firms can justify such a program and your firm is not, after all, primarily in the publishing business.

Coordinate the mailing lists carefully with the news release program. As noted, not everyone on the mailing list should be sent a news release that deals with a simple event. At the risk of oversimplifying, the news release is for the press and *may*, at your discretion, go to your clients; the newsletter is for your client and *may*, at your discretion, go to the press. The newsletter does have its uses in giving the editor a quick update on the firm's activities over the past few months.

The financial newsletter. If your firm is publicly held, its activities are exposed to three whole new classes of interested individuals—stockholders, members of regulatory agencies, and financial analysts. These groups are concerned somewhat less directly with the way your projects and people are performing, and rather more with whether all this will lead to increased earnings. It is not a good idea to try to mix the two approaches in a single newsletter. If the stock is traded widely enough (that is, if there is a large enough number of brokerage firms making a market in the stock and enough independent analysts following the stock's performance), and if there are enough nonemployee stockholders, it may be worthwhile issuing a quarterly newsletter aimed directly at these two groups.

As noted, the two newsletters should be kept separate. The suggested editorial slant of a client newsletter was reviewed earlier. The slant of your firm's financial newsletter should brutally weed out any story that does not directly imply short or long-term *financial* advantage.

This suggests such subjects as: new commissions; acquisitions; openings of new offices; elections or resignations of directors and officers; reporting quarterly earnings (accompanied by a news release); and any event that makes the firm more competitive in the marketplace. Less newsworthy are personnel changes at the subsidiary levels, project progress reports, references to the firm in professional journals, and personal honors.

The announcement of financial information must be handled with great care, as it is subject to strict regulation by the Securities and Exchange Commission (SEC) and other agencies. Regulations apply to the timing, format, and dissemination of information, especially in the matter of annual reports. The topic is too complex for discussion in these pages, but you may refer to a number of excellent guides on the subject (see the reference section).

Produce in-house or with outside help? As in the case of the news release, the planning, and development operation of a client newsletter is usually best handled in-house. Only in the beginning, when matters of format and editorial standards are established, should you consider outside consultation. Rarely should your newsletter exceed four to six pages. On a three to four times a year frequency, there is not enough work to farm out. Besides, the kind of delicate news sense needed to decide which items are suitable and how prominently to feature them is best left to in-house people.

Preparing the newsletter

The essence of the newsletter is its freshness, spontaneity, and informality. This applies whether it goes to clients or serves as a house organ. Its style should be reflected in its format and writing, which should be lively without being breezy. The following steps may be used in taking a newsletter through the stages from planning to dissemination. Focus is on the client-type newsletter. For the in-house letter, discussed later in this chapter, follow the same sequence but simplify it whenever possible.

Step 1. Planning. Assemble all possible topics that have accumulated in your file since the last issue. In addition, list other ideas and developments that have come to your attention. *Arrange these in order of importance*, and, to do this, hone your news sense to its sharpest, bearing in mind the five criteria noted on page 36. Contact sources that will help fill in the details. A useful tool is to develop a simple, typewritten, one-page questionnaire. Circulate this to principals, office managers, and department heads about ten days before you begin final planning. The questionnaire should allow these individuals to check off areas of possible editorial interest, and could follow the lines of 3-6 and 3-9.

Since these individuals, due to time pressures, will tend to give your request a low priority, design the questionnaire so it requires no more than a checkmark and a single line per item checked off. Follow up promising items by phone or in person.

Another fertile source is the project status report that most offices generate routinely for management control purposes. Also, if the firm subscribes to a clipping service—some firms do this to identify job leads—it is a simple matter to instruct the service to include in its coverage any mention of your firm in the media. Such references, too, are good for a brief mention in the newsletter.

At this stage, take a quick glance at your lists of topics, make an estimate as to the number of words required to do justice to each, take a critical look at available photographs, and then match these against available space in your four to six-page format.

If your assessment of news priorities is sound, you can swiftly sort the items into *ins, outs,* and *spares*.

Step 2. Writing. The style should be simple and informal. Eliminate any material not germane to the client's interest in your firm. Follow the eleven rules of Chapter 4 (see pages 62-64). If some materials were submitted already written, then edit along the same lines.

Headlines should be active and specific. They may be set off in a larger type face (see 3-7) or woven into the text, from which they are set off by using capitals, by underscoring, by adding a graphic accent (such as a bullet), or by using all three of these techniques (see 3-8). Chapter 4 lists various headline writing formulas in 4-3.

Photographs and other artwork should have complete captions. Do not place on the reader the burden of sleuthing out the description in the body of the text.

Step 3. Design. The principles of graphic design and layout are given in Chapter 5. What separates the newsletter from most other forms of printed communications is its simplicity. Select a page size. Any size other than 8½ x 11 (8x10½ for many federal government agencies) should be used only in extraordinary cases. Select a one, two, or three-column format. By and large, a one-column, single-space style is best for a typewritten newsletter, with a blank line between paragraphs. If the text is set in type, two columns are in order.

Three columns to a page tend to be harder to work with and lead to excessive hyphenation. This applies especially to typewriter type, which in the narrow, three-column format is impracticable.

Select a column width and adhere to it throughout—avoid mixing column widths, which takes away the flexibility of shifting a column from one page to another, or from one issue to the next.

How to measure the amount of type, translate it into an equivalent number of page lines, do a preliminary layout, and do final layout and mechanicals using a printed grid is described in Chapter 5.

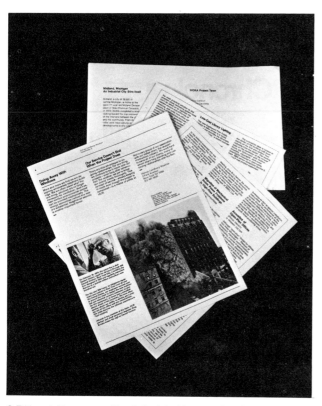

3-7 Newsletter pages with relatively bold typeset headlines.

■■■■■■■Have you read?

●CONSTRUCTION MANAGEMENT NEWSLETTER, as its name implies, each month covers the emerging professional discipline of construction management, and is completing its first year of publication. Publisher W. Marvin Ferrell tells us that sample copies are available to subscribers of KR. Write to P.O. Box 2612, Columbus, Ohio 43216.■

●PLANNING FOR HIGHER EDUCATION, a bi-monthly journal hitherto published free of charge by the Society of College and University Planners, will now cost you $15 or the price of SCUP membership. For details, write to SCUP, 3 Washington Sq. West, New York, N.Y. 10012.■

■■■■■■■Did you notice?

●"AIR-SUPPORTED STRUCTURES -- a faster building for less cost" is the name of a down-to-earth, case-study replete article in the February issue of Building Design & Construction. Author (and BD&C editor) Rob Cuscaden points to the fast mounting experience with these light, cheap, sturdy and safe structures. One case study shows an air-structure able to cover the 10-acre, 80,400-seat Pontiac, Mich. stadium

3-8 Underscoring and graphic accents enliven the typewritten text of newsletter.

Step 4. Reproduction. If a firm's mailing list exceeds 200 to 250, printing should be handled by a regular printer rather than on an in-house or outside photo-offset duplicator. This is especially true if the newsletter contains photographic half-tones.

It is possible, by very careful quality control and the selection of a good grade of paper, to obtain high quality work using such equipment. For the in-house newsletter, such methods are indeed satisfactory. For the client letter, however, where dependable quality is vital, choose a printer with more sophisticated equipment (see pages 121–123 for a discussion of printers and printing equipment).

A festive touch is possible by printing in two colors. This will raise your printing costs by some 50%. Restraint is in order, however. The most effective use of a second color is for the logotype, major headlines, and for any rules and boxes.

Step 5. Dissemination. Many printers will mail the newsletter out directly when provided with an original mailing list or labels. On the other hand, a mailing of this kind can easily be handled in-house by any office eager enough to run a newsletter program.

THE IN-HOUSE STAFF NEWSLETTER (HOUSE ORGAN)

The in-house staff newsletter bulletin or, "house organ," is a publication whose usefulness has been more assumed than proven. It is at worst harmless and at best a handy medium for the firm's management to confer with its staff, boost employee morale, and reinforce team spirit.

The in-house bulletin organ—at least in its more polished forms—has a place in the large (over 40 employee) firm or in a firm with several branch offices. In that case, it serves as glue to cement the disparate parts of the office structure.

The newsletter may, at the discretion of the principals, be carried on at several levels. One is the "Mary-from-the-typing-pool-had-twins-over-the-weekend-and-all-three-are-doing-fine" level. It carries reports of company picnics and the firm's performance in the bowling league. And it serves a useful object in telling employees about changes in benefits, in the firm's policy on overtime, and on the use of personal automobiles on company business.

The house organ newsletter should be written simply, designed simply, and produced simply. Even though it is part of the firm's overall communications image, it will get you no new clients. Its writing should strictly follow the eleven reminders of Chapter 4 and the graphic tenets of Chapter 5. It can be easily produced in-house, using the firm's logo and/or letterhead and a straightforward, typewritten format. Contents should be arranged into logical categories (see 3-9), each with a clearly legible, identifiable head, and should include at some point an invitation to the staff to contribute news. A staff newsletter need not follow a regular schedule. An eight to twelve times a year frequency should be enough to serve its purpose, with more urgent announcements circulated when needed or posted on a bulletin board.

In sum, the house-organ is not a top priority weapon in a firm's communications arsenal, but it is helpful where the size or dispersal of the firm justifies it.

1. **Staff news**
- Promotions, inter-office moves
- Professional licensing
- Graduation with advanced degrees, continuing education programs, and so on
- Honors and appointments
- Marriages, offspring, obituaries
- Out-of-the-ordinary travel

2. **Company policy announcements**
- Insurance
- Working hours and overtime
- Use of personal automobile
- Access to office during off hours

3. **Projects**
- New work
- Completed projects

4. **Publication**
- Articles about the firm or its projects

5. **Miscellaneous office activities**
- Performance of firm's bowling, baseball, and other athletic teams

6. **Photographs**
- Projects
- People
- The office, inside and out

3-9 Useful categories of topics for an in-house newsletter or "house organ."

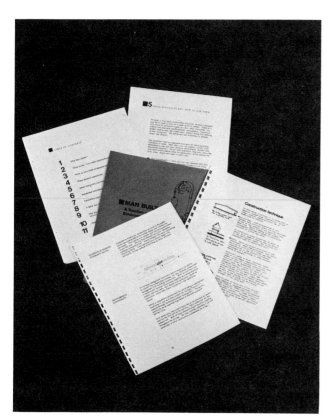

3-10 Typewritten reports may be made more attractive visually by a good arrangement of blocks of type and the use of press-on letters and symbols.

THE REPORT TO THE CLIENT

The formal report written for clients, whether geared to the feasibility or programming phase of a construction project, to research, or to planning, has a marketing value to your firm over and beyond its immediate usefulness to the client. It is an important portfolio enclosure for project promotion and an eloquent emissary of your firm as it rests on your client's desk or shelf or is forwarded to his associates and friends.

Special considerations

One feature that singles out the report from other parts of a firm's communications program is that it is commissioned and paid for by the client. Accordingly, you can arrange at little cost (due to the economics of printing) to order additional copies for later use in your marketing program. Always clear this with the client, since contents may include classified materials.

Reports come in a wide range of formats. Interim and even final reports are often acceptable in a typewriter format. Titles on covers and dividers and key text heads may be set in type or with press-on letters and symbols (see 3-10). Printing and binding may be done in an offset repro shop.

Reports of a more formal nature—those which the client himself will use to do a job of convincing *his* constituency as to a course of action, such as a campus master plan or a hospital merger facility study, or a research report requiring action by a company's top management—may call for typesetting, color, and more expensive paper, work-press printing, and more elaborate binding.

The style of the client report

After reviewing the procedures for developing a readable manuscript and the steps in designing and producing a publication for graphic excellence in Chapters 4 and 5, note the following special conditions as they apply to the client report.

Format. In many reports, artwork must be seen next to text. A horizontal format, while an advantage in that respect, is somewhat more costly to produce—also, with anything but a stiff cover, it tends to become floppy. Note that horizontal reports are also harder to file. Contents should be laid out with generous white space to allow for on-the-spot notes and comments by the client. Reports are often mailed individually; therefore, avoid a format that requires specially made envelopes, unless the quantity is enough to offset the premium cost. Any of the paper manufacturers whose books are listed in the reference section will supply a list of standard envelope sizes, as will local paper and printing salesmen.

Type size. Specify as large a typeface as space allows. 10 pt. type on a 2 pt. base is a minimum, especially when using a sans-serif text type. You never know under what conditions of lighting and fatigue the client will be reading the report.

Writing style. The reader should not have to search for meaning in a sea of turgid prose. The type of audience is, of course, a factor. A research report on energy use to the National Science Foundation can get away with a far more technical level of discourse than a similar report developed for the Department of Housing and Urban Development for distribution to local developers and housing sponsors. But a technical style is not an excuse for obscurity. Even an office with modest resources should find a way to have a technical text edited for clarity.

Credits. Triple-check the list of organizational and individual credits the client wishes to be included in the report, for sequence, prominence, and spelling. This is always a sensitive issue and merits special care.

Covers. There is a wealth of paper cover stocks and finishes from which to choose. Any local paper salesman or printer will show you smooth, rough-textured, metallic, and other finishes for inspection. Dark-colored, smooth covers should be plastic-finished or covered with a sheet of acetate, so they do not show smears through handling. Covers may be imprinted, silk-screened, stamped, or embossed with the title and other images at modest extra cost. They may also be die-cut to disclose the title printed on the next sheet beneath, but the effect is stilted. For binding options, see Chapter 5.

Color. The cost of printing in colors may sometimes be reduced by designing the report so all color falls within a single printing form (see Chapter 5).

Schedule. While a brochure fact sheet delivered to you late from your printer is at most an inconvenience, the consequences of a report delivered late to the client can be far more serious. Prepare a schedule as you would for any other client project and monitor it closely. Such a schedule is best developed by assigning an estimated duration, with a starting date and a completion date, to each of the steps shown on page 109. Obtain typesetting (if used) and printing and binding times from your suppliers. If this is your first report, obtain estimated times for in-house tasks by calling a friendly colleague or graphic designer in another office. Carefully record actual times as you proceed with your report, for use on future reports. A log will help you keep track of progress on complex reports (see 5-39).

LETTERS AND MEMORANDA

The letter—its purpose, its planning, and its organization—is one of the most extensive yet least understood components of a design firm's communications. Whether the aim of the letter is to influence a prospective client, to inform or request enlightenment from a lawyer, accountant, supplier, consultant, or professional colleague, or to communicate with associates or subordinates in the firm, the task of writing a letter or memorandum—unlike the brochure, planning report, or news release—is likely to fall to any member of the firm.

Common faults

Flaws found in letters are these:

1. Too long a lead-in before getting to the point. This ex-

ample (on the left) is taken from a letter to an engineering colleague.

Dear Jim:

A good many months have gone by since we last had any correspondence. In the course of this period our firm has been pretty busy— a commission for an industrial plant; a consulting agreement to provide mechanical engineering services to an architect designing a large new hospital in Pittstown, and design for an offshore oil platform in the Gulf of Mexico.

What prompted me to write to you is an idea that has been bouncing around in the back of my mind. The idea is to develop a series of workshops which our society would sponsor on the subject of retrofitting older buildings with energy-conserving materials and systems. I wonder, therefore, whether you would . . .

Dear Jim:

It has been a busy winter, but I didn't want to wait any longer to suggest this idea to you. As you know, energy conservation in buildings is a complex subject, and many of us could use updating in the area of retrofitting older buildings. Why not organize a series of workshops? We could . . .

With 56 words as against 114 and no wasteful lead-in, the second version gets straight to the point and saves time for both writer and reader.

2. Excessively formal, even archaic phrasing, as demonstrated in the beginning and end of the letter on the left below. As to the beginning of the letter on the right, even that first sentence is unnecessary. If you hadn't received the letter, you wouldn't be responding to it.

We are in receipt of your correspondence of July 9, 1976 and wish to advise you that we have taken the contents into account. . .

We thank you again for your letter and beg to remain

Respectfully yours

We have your letter of July 9 . . .

Sincerely

We live in a brisk, no-nonsense age and have outlived such formal phrasing, of which perhaps the most notorious example is the elegant (and, in France, still quite common) closing sentence, "We beg you, Sir, to accept the expression of our most distinguished and honorable sentiments."

3. Length of letter out of proportion to the message.

4. Conclusion of letter too drawn-out.

5. Faulty or illogical arrangement of contents.

6. A style that is too colloquial or out of character with client's or your firm's image. Some firms cultivate a deliberately folksy profile, even to the point of omitting the

"Dear . . ." in the opening address, saying merely "Mr. Jones: . . . ." Other firms prefer to convey a more formal or austere impression.

The matter of image, discussed in the first chapter, especially concerns the writing of letters, the most frequent form of communication that most of your staff will use. Therefore, the management controls over the firm's style of communications (see Chapter 1 and Chapter 10) are especially vital in the writing of letters.

Categories of letters

Letters and memoranda from the design professional usually fall into one of three categories: the letter to a client or prospect; the non-client outside letter; and the internal memorandum.

The client letter. Letters to clients and prospects fall into several groups. They include the letter of interest, written upon hearing of a potential commission; the proposal letter, usually written in response to an invitation; and the follow-up letter.

The letter of interest. Of all the kinds of client communication, this requires the most delicate touch from the writer. It is likely to be the first formal contact between you and the client.

Imagine this situation. You have learned that Jack Pratt, a major out-of-town developer, is planning a large shopping center on your city's outskirts. Mr. Pratt, you have also learned, will shortly be looking for a design-build team to plan, design, and erect the center. He is known as quality-conscious but a stickler for time and cost ceilings. Your experience is strong in all these areas, and you know several reputable in-state and out-of-state general contractors. Pratt has completed his market studies but has not yet chosen among three candidate sites. You have decided to write to Mr. Pratt indicating your interest in being considered.

The first step is to look into Mr. Pratt's motivations. He clearly will need an indication as to:

- Your interest in being considered.
- Your track record in the field.
- Your ideas as to joint arrangements with a builder.

On the other hand, he will not expect, in this first overture, a great deal of detail as to potential fees or definitive joint arrangements with a builder.

Your approach, therefore, should be to structure the letter in such a way as to project an aura of confidence; a sense of awareness of Mr. Pratt's main concerns (costs, schedule); ease of liaison and rapport; and, last but not least, an indication of strong interest in the job. The letter should be short—not over a page or two—and leave a unique flavor of you and your firm.

One way in which such a letter could be written is seen in 3-11. You may add support materials to a letter of interest, but they should be few at this stage (probably no more than your basic brochure and a few fact sheets of similar projects, if any). The point here is not to anticipate and try to consider all Mr. Pratt's questions, but rather to get him interested enough in you to invite you to submit a more specific, detailed proposal.

The letter in 3-11 contains a mere 350 words—not enough to fill two single-spaced pages—yet it gives the prospective client a clear picture of your performance, priorities, and interest.

The letter of proposal. This type of letter is one big step closer to an agreement than the letter of interest. It assumes that you have been given a fairly detailed set of requirements issued to the competing firms, or else a first interview. It is now much easier to respond to particular client problems with appropriate items drawn from your firm's background and experience (for handling a full-fledged proposal see page 33).

The letter of proposal differs from the letter of interest chiefly in that it allows you to think the client's problem through and to indicate to him in writing that you indeed understand it. This awareness is the first, and perhaps most crucial, element of your letter. The others are:

- The listing of scope, tasks, and (on a large project) sub-tasks, and—so far as you can determine at this stage—who will be responsible for each item (client; your office; consultants).

- Your qualifications—this time in detail, including references to attached résumés of proposed staff.

- A proposed schedule, broken down by phases and tasks.

- Estimated compensation.

- When you can start work.

Proposal letters vary widely in the amount of detail required. There is, accordingly, no rule as to length. It is important, in any case, to make it easy for the client to find his way without risk of confusion, by means of arrangement of type or by use of supporting graphics.

A good example of clear organization is shown in a letter in 4-4. This letter is closer to a letter of interest than a proposal letter in that it stops short of a fee estimate. It was sent by a principal in a large firm in response to an invitation from the superintendent of schools in a fair-sized suburban county. The circumstances the partner was responding to had these features:

- An *urgent* need for classroom space.

- A commitment to team teaching and instructional television.

- An inventory of outdated schools.

Study this letter, as it is a model of the direct approach. Especially worthwhile is the way in which it echoes the writer's awareness and understanding of the client's problem.

Proposal letters, unlike formal proposals to government agencies, cannot fall back on elaborate proposal forms and questionnaires that spell out precisely what materials to put in and how to organize them. The proposing firm is, therefore, obliged to rely on its own ingenuity in making the greatest impact on the client.

The follow-up letter. This requires tact, firmness, and pluck. At least three kinds of situations may call for a follow-up letter.

In one case you have returned from an interview and wish to record your satisfaction (presumably) prior to the final selection by writing to the chairman of the interview committee. A second case arises when more than enough time has elapsed (in your opinion) since the interview

Dear Mr. Pratt:

We understand you will shortly be interviewing design-build teams to help you develop a new shopping center on the out-skirts of Bread City. We are most interested in being retained for this challenging assignment.

We have had a general architectural, planning, and engineering practice in Bread City since 1960. During this time, we have been responsible for design of a number of commercial projects. These have included a 300,000 sq. ft. commercial complex downtown that includes a department store, branch bank, and large food retail outlet with appropriate parking and landscaping. We have also designed an 80,000 sq. ft. rental office building; medical office building; and a facility for the manufacture of novelties linked to its own retail outlet.

On most of these projects, in addition to providing traditional services, we prepared predesign feasibility studies and developed the program jointly with the client. In one case, we also carried out a post-construction, in-use study of the building which showed high productivity, a high level of staff and retail customer satisfaction, and operating costs that are in line with budgeted costs.

You will be especially interested to know that on the commercial complex, we worked as a team with Smithson Builders, Inc., a highly qualified general contractor with an excellent record of performance throughout the state. We and Smithson are prepared to collaborate again on your project.

All these projects were completed on schedule, in part thanks to our use of phased construction; all were built at or below the owner's budget.

Our staff includes specialists in planning and design. In addition, we have long-standing working relationships with several local structural and mechanical/electrical engineering firms, the well-known graphics consulting firm of Bread City Five Associates, and with Four Dollars Inc., the economic consultants.

To tell you more about our firm we attach a basic brochure and 4 project fact sheets.

We look forward to meeting with you to discuss our qualifications in more detail.

Sincerely

3-11 Letter of interest to an out-of-town developer planning a large shopping center.

Dear Mr. Singleton:

Three weeks have gone by since our interview, and we have
been unable to reach you to enquire as to when you may
expect to reach a decision in the matter of the proposed
new sewage treatment plant.

We are concerned about not hearing from you because of
other pending commitments for which we will need to assign
personnel and time.

We were delighted to have been able to present our
qualifications, and we look forward to hearing from you.
We will gladly send you any additional information if you
require it.

Sincerely

3-12 Follow-up letter for a difficult circumstance.

Dear Mr. and Mrs. Jolyon:

A brief note to thank you for last night's fine dinner and
lively talk. It was kind of Jack to suggest the idea and
gracious of you to ask me.

It was especially considerate of you to encourage me to
talk about our firm, of which we are very proud.

If a trip should bring you to Bread City, I would be delighted to show you our offices and ask you to join us for
lunch.

Sincerely

3-13 Follow-up letter after a promising social occasion. On social occasions such as these, do
not oversell. At the same time, do not lean over backwards not to talk shop. Jolyon is a man-of-
the-world and expects it.

was held or the proposal submitted. There is no word from the client, and telephone calls are not returned. A third case covers situations of a generally social nature in which a member of your firm may have had occasion to meet with an individual who could some time in the future influence the hiring of your firm.

The post-interview follow-up note—always a good move—can simply be a one sentence letter offering to provide more information if needed and saying you are looking forward to the result. There is no need to re-enact the interview.

Following up a nonresponsive prospect requires not only tact but firmness. There is, after all, little to be lost by going on the offensive. The client has no doubt not responded because the decision is out of his hands and he is averse to admitting it; or the decision is not yet made; or the project has been put off; or the commission has gone (or is about to go) to another firm. If a telephone conversation is able to dig up the root of the delay, the task of the letter writer is made easier. All that need be said then is: "We are still interested and look forward to your decision," or "We are sorry not to have been chosen this time but look forward to another opportunity."

If the client's silence leaves you in the dark, though, a less restrained letter will be required, perhaps along the lines of 3-12.

For the third situation, there are no specific rules, but certain suggestions are in order. One is to be brief. Another is to keep a light touch. Take the following situation. Last night, as part of a business trip, you, a principal of a 12-person office, enjoyed a fine dinner in Cartersburg, a distant city, at the house of Mr. and Mrs. James Jolyon, friends of a junior designer in your firm who has suggested the idea to the Jolyons. Jolyon is chairman of the Cartersburg National Bank and a trustee of Cartersburg College, a well-endowed private liberal arts college, and is otherwise well-connected in this 100,000-inhabitant city. A follow-up letter is obviously in order—but so is a measure of delicacy, since the border-line between the dinner as a social occasion and as an occasion to promote your firm is a rather fine one. One way to write such a letter is shown in 3-13.

Letters to clients and prospects require of the writer a subtle feel for the rub of each situation. The guiding rule should always be to couch the language in terms of the client's perceived needs—costs, schedule, quality, esthetics, flexibility, rapport with his consultants, and innovation. And since the time of prospective clients is dear, letters—especially important ones—should be edited and re-edited, if need be, to convey the most punch in the least amount of space.

The non-client, outside letter. Any letter from your office that has a purpose other than market development should follow the basic rules of writing and editing as covered in Chapter 4 and earlier in this chapter. Such letters, whether oriented to projects (for example, to contractors, sub-contractors, suppliers, or consultants) or to office management (like letters dealing with insurance, legal, accounting, and similar matters) do not have a "selling" function. This does not in any way, however, reduce the need for brevity, logical build up, and getting swiftly to the point.

If you suspect that the letters emanating from your firm are not up to a quality you think adequate, appoint an individual or, in larger firms, an informal committee to review correspondence quality along the lines suggested in Chapter 4. Review those principles, and arrange to have letters edited and rewritten whenever necessary. When consciousness about the quality of letterwriting itself grows in the firm, the battle is usually half-won.

The internal memorandum. The internal memorandum—within your office or between branch offices—is a vital vehicle for communications. It is used as a tool to manage the flow of a project and/or to conduct the internal business and personnel management of the firm.

The format of memoranda should be of the utmost simplicity and designed to reduce to a minimum the staff input required. A standard memo form should be preprinted with the firm's letterhead and carry the following information (see 3-14):

• Principal recipient

• Sender

• Subject

• Date

• Number to be copied

• File number

You may find it useful to prepare a routing slip bearing the names of personnel arranged either alphabetically, by rank, or, in larger firms, by department. Due to inevitable turnover, there is little merit in producing these slips elaborately. A plain, typewritten listing with a box or line next to each name can be updated five or six times per year. It is simple to assemble the slips in pads for ease of use.

When composing memoranda, a resolve to assign numbers to the various points or paragraphs of the message is often a useful discipline for clear structuring of the memo. The same method may be used for outside letters, but take care that in the process you do not cause what may be an informal style to take on the tone and appearance of a legal document.

The letter and memorandum are two of the most vital and all-encompassing arms of a firm's communications program. They seep into every aspect of marketing, project management, and business operations. You cannot invest too much time to ensure a high quality of content, style, and format.

THE DESIGN AWARD SUBMITTAL

Many types of organizations regularly sponsor award programs which offer design professionals fame, prizes, and the opportunity to impress clients and prospects (see 3-15). These programs, most of which recognize projects (some, like the AIA's Firm Award, focus on the long-term record of a firm), should not be confused with competitions. The latter are normally used to select a firm to carry out a commission. The design award program, on the other hand, recognizes caliber of work already performed. Success in competitions depends chiefly on the ingenuity of the solution, while design award programs often rely on a firm's ability to select an appropriate past

MEMORANDUM

TO	CHARLES JOHNSON
FROM	GEORGE ALLEN
SUBJECT	AASA COMPETITION
DATE	14 NOVEMBER 76
COPIES	BOOTH, KLEIN, GHERMEZIAN
FILE	A76-32

We have been notified that three out of the four projects submitted to the American Association of School Administrators will be exhibited at AASA'S two conventions this year. They are:

1. Plainsville Community School, Plainsville, Ore.

2. Beaver Community College, Melton, Mont.

3. Madison Elementary School, Pacific City, Calif.

Also, two of the projects entered, Plainsville Community School and Beaver Community College, have been selected for inclusion in the 1978 filmstrip (each year a filmstrip with guidebook is prepared with the best entries, for sale to school administrators).

We deserve a pat on the back -- we did about as well as was possible to do.

3-14 Internal memoranda should be simple in content and format.

---

1. Societies of design professionals
- National
- Regional
- Regional, with finalists eligible for national
- State
- Local

2. Professional journals

3. Trade associations of product manufacturers.
(Usually, but not always, of basic materials; rarely, individual product manufacturers.)

4. Associations of buyers of professional services
- Institutional administrators
- Federal construction agencies
- Manufacturers of industrial products (who retain industrial designers)
- Residential, commercial, and industrial developers

5. Local civic groups and chambers of commerce

6. Environmental improvement groups

3-15 Typical sponsors of design award programs.

project and to organize the materials into an outstanding submission package.

Early reflections

Only the most relentless firm will enter every award program. Such a policy would quickly push company overhead through the ceiling. The shrewd firm will size up the advantage and limitations of each program, and center its resources on the handful each year that may do it the most good. Several criteria should be borne in mind. These include:

Prospects. As in roulette and blackjack, the odds favor the house, not you. Therefore, limit submittals to programs where you have a variety of projects from which to draw, unless there is strong evidence, from prior publicity, that the only marine cofferdam sheet pile foundation you have ever designed is a winner. Your chances at the local or regional level will tend to be higher than at the national, but then look carefully at the caliber of the sponsors.

What happens if you win. A successful submittal package is often not the end of the road. Often, you must prepare exhibit panels, order supplementary photography, and write or design additional project descriptions. This usually calls for a sizable extra outlay of time and funds and should be taken into account when choosing among award contests.

Marketing value. Some programs will make more points with clients than others. Top ranking goes to programs sponsored by client or user groups, such as school or hospital administrators, residential developers, federal construction agencies, and, for industrial designers, product manufacturers.

Close in second place are national design award programs sponsored by the national professional society and by the top professional journals in your field. And lest there be any misunderstanding, this second category is good not because of the self-respect and peer recognition it brings, but because it is nearly always accompanied by effective publicity arranged for by the sponsor.

Indeed, always look for this "prestige conversion factor" before entering a contest. An ugly duckling among contests may suddenly acquire swanlike qualities when there is the prospect of big publicity and, perhaps, media advertising for the winning project.

Prize money. Few contests offer monetary prizes. One of the largest, the R.S. Reynolds Memorial Award program open to buildings using aluminum innovatively, carries with it $25,000. (One story heard in architectural circles relates that one year the award was actually higher than the architect's fee on the winning project.) Some awards also provide an extra premium, such as a piece of sculpture.

Preparedness and resources. This criterion is placed last for emphasis. It is far easier to enter contests when a firm's communications resources are geared to the effort required (see also Chapter 10). If sufficient black and white photographs and slides are at hand on all candidate projects of the firm, if project descriptions are up-to-date and staff time is available to make the minor changes often required to adapt written resources to contest rules, then entering contests becomes a routine staff operation rather than a hasty, feverish undertaking.

The number of contests varies from year to year, and any listing in these pages would soon be out-of-date. Most professional societies maintain an updated listing of award contests open to their members. Moreover, most sponsors make special efforts to publicize contests.

Preparing the submittal package

As noted, the task of preparing a submittal package is made immeasurably easier if the firm, no matter how large or small, has functioning, up-to-date resource files. The process, by and large, follows these steps:

Step 1. File entry form and fee. In many cases, the sponsor will mail you a required binder in which to insert the submittal after you have entered the competition.

Step 2. Prepare and select materials. This is where gamesmanship comes into play. Assuming the necessary photographs have been taken (Chapter 8 covers the subject of photography), the half dozen or so 8 x 10 pictures prescribed under most contest rules must now be selected. If a building or plant is involved, a view of each side is usually called for, along with a view of the immediate environs and one or two interior shots. If the job is a renovation, there are also before-and-after views.

Several candidates *for each view required* should be laid out on a table and compared. Is the character best conveyed by a hard, sharp contrasting print or by a soft, flat shot? Should people appear, and, if so, should they be used sparingly to help indicate scale, or freely to show the building in use or the plant in operation? In pictures with a strong interior or furnishings theme, do people tend to conceal the furniture, or give it life? Should pictures be all horizontal or all vertical for ease of turning the pages of the binder, or is a mix in order? Should a white border be used to fill the margins between the customary 8½ x 11 sleeve and the 8 x 10 print, or should you go to an 8½ x 11 print? And should you try for a kind of "theme sequence" from general views to details, or merely select your technically best shot in each required category?

These questions must be asked, even though there are no absolute answers. Judgment and intuition are the best guides. A marketing principal should always take part in this crucial early selection process, as well as in reviewing (but not necessarily composing) the written parts of the submittal package.

35mm color slides need an even more rigorous selection process. Slides can be used to advantage in showing a sequence of spaces. Some contests discourage slides because most are not easy to convert to black and white prints for publicity shots. They are still, however, the best way to show color, which often is a major ingredient of a project. As discussed in more detail in the chapters on slide presentations and photography (6 and 8), use only "first generation" slides made from the original. Each successive generation loses some 5% in overall quality.

Drawings showing site plan, floor plans, elevations, sections, and, in some cases, construction details will not, at 8½ x 11, be able to show much detail. It is a mistake to take a large drawing that was used for a client presentation and try to reduce it to page size: closely spaced lines will fill in, titles will become illegible.

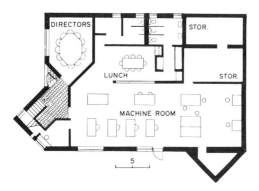

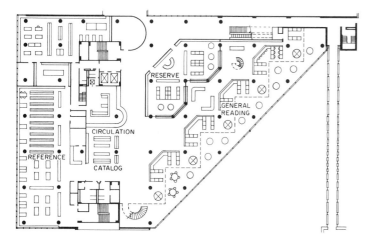

3-16 Though simplified, drawings show all the client needs to know.

3-17 Design award judges are set to tackle a large volume of submittals. Standard folders with acetate sleeves make their task easier.

The best and—unhappily, costly—solution is to prepare special drawings. This takes time and should be done well ahead of due dates—many weeks of lead time are usually needed for a competent office draftsman to fit this assignment into his normal, fee-paying, project-oriented drafting schedule. The draftsman should be instructed to eliminate ruthlessly any information on the base drawing that doesn't help explain the plan, elevation, sections, or detail. Door swings, excessively fine crosshatching, any but basic furniture—none of these belong on a drawing whose prime task it is to tell a harassed juror at a glance the gist of the concept. Study the drawings prepared by the delineators for the major professional monthly journals: they are models of "selective exclusion." (See also 3-16.)

Identify all photographs and drawings, but keep titles to a minimum. The amount of lettering that clutters up a drawing can be reduced by using numerals and a legend. This, however, is less convenient for the reader, whose eyes must move continually back and forth between number and legend. Always indicate scale *graphically* rather than *numerically* (i.e., ½ in. = 1 ft.), since any reduction will destroy the value of a numerical scale. And remember the north arrow.

The last part in this step is to select the data and write the descriptive text. Most contests limit the number of words or number of pages—understandably, since jurors sometimes must review several hundred projects. Accordingly, check and recheck the text to make every word or phrase count. A sequence, from problem-statement to problem-solution, is a useful one in catching and holding the juror's interest. Avoid generalized statements (such as "the district's high school enrollment was rising"), and instead give facts, figures, and rates of increase. Similarly, eschew jargon (see Reminder 4, Chapter 4), as many jurors may be laymen who will rightly resent any effort to impress them in this manner.

When typing the final draft, do not crowd the page, preserving ample (1½"/3.81 cm) margins. The container will normally be supplied. Where it is not, a versatile binder is the CB-10 Ful-Vu 8½ x 11 binder or its equivalent. This binder has ten transparent window sleeves separated by black paper, enough to show twice that many exhibits back to back. There is usually space to include one or two 8½ x 11 holders for 35 mm slides in the back. It is sturdy and simple to use (see 3-17).

Step 3. Clearances. Some sponsors will require clearances from you so they can use texts, drawings, and photographs for publicity and other purposes. Obtain any permissions and clearances from the client, consultants, and photographers *before* you submit the project.

Step 4. Credits. Policies as to credits vary from firm to firm. Some firms limit credits to the firm's name, along with any outside consultants. Others include any individual who had a professional connection with the project.

Step 5. Concealed identification. Often a project is so well known that concealed identification is futile. In any case, check your whole submission with great care to make sure that the firm's name has not remained on a drawing, letterhead, or photograph. There is no easier way to be disqualified.

Step 6. Final review. Conduct a final review, with a marketing principal present. Leaf through the binder as though you were a juror. This is the time to make a last-minute adjustment in the choice or order of inserts or in the wording of the description. After all, it takes at most 20 minutes to retype a page or replace a picture. This is a very crucial step.

Step 7. Mailing. If the sponsor is serious about delivery dates, put your trust in one of the private express services. Sometimes the sponsor will accept the package as long as it is postmarked by the prescribed date; this reduces the risk in using the U.S. mails.

Conclusion

Design awards are a fruitful channel for bringing the products of your professional practice to the attention of potential clients. The choice as to which contests to enter should be made with care, as the preparation of a strong submittal requires much painstaking effort. Consider only those programs with a high marketing advantage. Since the preparation of materials requires so much time and effort, it should not be left to the last moment. Assemble a year-ahead schedule of known contests, and see to it that the processes of writing, drafting, and photography get underway with plenty of time in hand.

Finally, keep the message short and simple.

THE EXHIBIT PANEL

Like the design award submittal package—to which it is often the sequel—the exhibit panel is an important communication tool for the design office.

The exhibit panel has many uses. If the annual national or state convention of an organization of potential clients contains, as it usually does, a concourse area for professional and product exhibits, you have an excellent forum in which to display your firm's accomplishments.

In some cases, payment of a stiff fee will reserve display space. More usual, and more desirable from the professional's standpoint, is a screening process that subjects submittal packages to certain criteria established—and sometimes announced ahead of time—by the sponsoring organization's selection jury. These criteria are not always limited to quality of architecture, engineering, planning, landscaping, interior or industrial design; they often include elements like geographic balance, safety, and use of innovative concepts in such areas as energy conservation and environmental control.

Firms that submit winning packages are then invited to prepare exhibit panels, pay the exhibit fee (that can range as high as $150 for a two-panel exhbit), and crate and ship the panels to the convention hall. Fees are returned to unsuccessful entrants, or to those whose panels arrive too late for hanging—minus a sizable charge for processing and handling.

Other forums for exhibit panels of a firm's projects include public display at community gathering places, such as suburban shopping malls, local schools and colleges, and museums.

Special considerations

The guiding principle when planning panels for an exhibit is, above all, uniqueness. Your firm's panels, whether displayed at a convention of school administrators or at a museum show, will be competing, side-by-side with many other exhibits, for the attention of men and women who are busy and moving in crowds.

Imagine the usual setting in space and time. There is a two-hour lunch break between morning and afternoon convention workshop sessions. Conventioneers pour from the auditòrium, and decide, after a glance at the program and prodded by convention staff, to take in the exhibits after downing a quick sandwich. A dense line of people files past closely spaced exhibits arranged in tight aisles or along the walls.

This is no time for a fine-stroke exposition of your project's features. Nor is it the occasion for subtle refinements of graphics and heavy flights of literary composition. Time is short. The project's design concept either grabs the viewer's attention at once, or you have lost him as he passes on or is pushed to the next exhibit. Your exhibit design must be broad-brush, simple.

Lettering. This should be as large as possible—for the main title, for titles on drawings, for picture captions, credits, and for the descriptive text. A simple test will show at what distances lettering may be clearly read. Although requirements vary from contest to contest (a point we shall return to later), main titles should be no smaller than 1 in./2.54 cm and may reach 1½ in./3.8 cm, if allowed.

Similarly, site and floor plans, elevations, sections, and product details should carry only the minimum quantities of identifying titles, and even these should seldom be smaller than 18 pt. type (or about ¼ in./.64 cm) high in capital letters. Numbers keyed to a legend is another option but, as noted in the section on submittal packages, it imposes on the viewer a series of irritating back-and-forth eye movements.

Drawings. These must be bold, with exaggerated pochéing of walls in plan and fat baselines and shadow indications on elevations. Ruthlessly exclude lines that will not help the viewer understand the drawing. Consider also the idea of gray tone or color to indicate different kinds of uses on a detail, floor plan, or site plan (see 3-18).

Photographs. These should be as large as possible. Aim for size over quantity. In some instances, a series of smaller photographs is needed to depict a sequence or pattern. In such cases, however, one or two images should be singled out for enlargement.

Descriptive statement. As the lettering for this needs to be as big as possible, writing it poses a major challenge to express the most information with a minimum of words. Here, as noted also in the next chapter, the text and picture captions of such tabloid newspapers as the New York *Daily News* offer an object lesson in simple clarity.

The descriptive statement is crucial, because it—along with the main title—is *the* key to unlocking the viewer's understanding of the project's intent. Unless there are strong reasons not to do this, the statement should be arranged in two parts—*problem* and *solution.* A good, active title—especially one written like a newspaper headline—along with a clear, simple text, will whet the viewer's interest so he will want to explore the rest of the panel to see how the solution was worked out. A dull, static title and long-winded, jargon-filled text will quickly propel

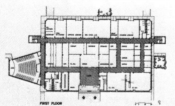

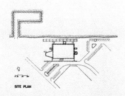

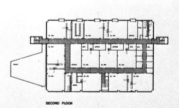

3-18 Floor plans on exhibit panels are easier to read if circulation space is set off from programmed space with tone or crosshatching.

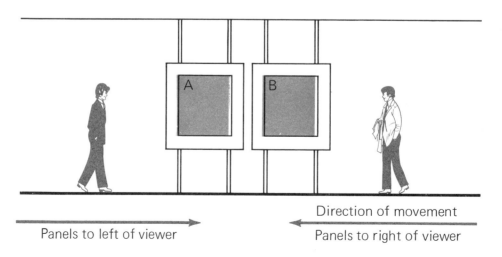

Direction of movement

Panels to left of viewer

Panels to right of viewer

3-19 Exhibit panel designer should realize that viewers may approach from two directions.

the viewer to your competitor's panels.

The example below is from an exhibit panel title. Note how the right-hand version has gained interest.

SUBURBAN HIGH SCHOOL   HIGH SCHOOL DIVIDES
4000-STUDENT
ENROLLMENT
INTO "HOUSES"

Credits. A key ingredient of panel design, the credit section is no place for false modesty. Credits should be clear at a glance and as large as contest requirements permit. There is little logic to making the sizable investment in labor and materials of submittal package and panel production, only to miss the viewer's attention by burying your firm's name in an obscure corner of the panel in tiny type.

Color. A useful tool for accent, color defeats its own purpose if used too liberally. Good targets for use of color are:

• One or two major photographs

• The main title

• Key portions of the text

• Picture captions

• Diagrams depicting a process

Special challenges

A special challenge in the planning of exhibit boards is to display the project that is not a building, plant, interior design, or industrial product, but rather a management *process* or *system of organization*. An example is the illustration of a successful community planning process showing the cooperation of government, private sector, neighborhood, and technical expert groups in seeing to fruition a playground, community clinic, or multi-purpose school house. Emphasis would be on process and organization, rather than on design and construction. To attract and hold the viewer, a special effort must be made to point up the process with the help of striking flow-chart graphics—activity "boxes," supplemented with shadows if necessary, colors, texture, tints and clear type. Photographs would be in order as support elements—such as well composed views of team members at work.

Focal point

All these elements are without rhyme or reason *unless they fit a concept, which, through written and graphic expression, forces your panels to stand out from your neighbors'.* Your project presumably has been chosen for display because of a certain unique quality of approach or execution. Seize on this—whether it is a design or cost-saving feature, energy conservation, access to the handicapped, site development, flexibility in use or expansion, a structural, mechanical, or electrical breakthrough, or a special esthetic quality—and focus on this as the central panel design concept. All elements should be subservient to this theme.

Final considerations

A final consideration is the reuse of panels. Since, as noted below, it costs money to produce them, it would help to know that they may be reused on another occasion. One drawback is that many sponsoring organizations put out mandated design requirements with little or no effort at coordination. One sponsor may set a limit of 1 in./2.54 cm lettering; another a maximum on the area of photographs; a third specifications on use of color; a fourth restrictions on the type of supporting information (area; costs; design statistics). The best approach is to develop basic panels for the exhibition that is most promising from a marketing standpoint, and to adapt a panel to other, later requirements.

A final creative marketing touch, if exhibit rules permit, is to display a model of the project next to the panels, and to hand out a simple fact sheet, which viewers may take away with them for more leisurely study.

Preparing the exhibit panel

These three steps should be followed when developing exhibit panels:

Step 1. Identifying a theme or motif. After determining the characteristics of the prospective viewing audience and the nature of the project, identify the theme or motif around which to organize the panel. Select illustrations, descriptive data, and any other required information.

For a start, review the materials of the original submittal package. Much of its contents should serve as a basis for the panel. Use its project statement, for example, as a starting point for composing the description that will appear on the panel. If site plan, floor plans, details, and other drawings were of presentation quality, they may be used for the panel; in most cases, only the titles may need to be simplified and/or enlarged. Re-examine the photographs, add others from your files, and make the final selections.

Step 2. Design and layout. Although the principles of graphic design are covered in Chapter 5, certain graphic aspects are especially important to the visual impact of an exhibit panel. One such aspect is the need for a focus of attention, to get the viewer "into" the panel. The focus may be the title or a very large photograph—some very effective designs use photographs that take up as much as 75% of the area of a panel.

Another concern is clarity and simplicity of organization. This may be controlled by a design grid (see Chapter 5) that allows the eye to move over the various elements of the panel in an organized manner.

The order in which the panels are to be viewed is a major unknown. If you are exhibiting a two-panel project, it helps to know if most viewers will be approaching the panels from the right or the left side. If from the right, they will see the second panel first; if from the the left, the first panel will come into view first (see 3-19). One solution is to design the panels so each is self-contained and the order of viewing does not matter, although this may reduce the effects possible through putting the panels together into a single super-unit. Whatever you do, do not forget to design the panels with a clear, strong "family resemblance," so viewers will take them in as a single design unit.

Begin design by developing thumbnail sketches. Gradually work these up to a larger and larger scale. Concurrently, develop and edit the descriptive state-

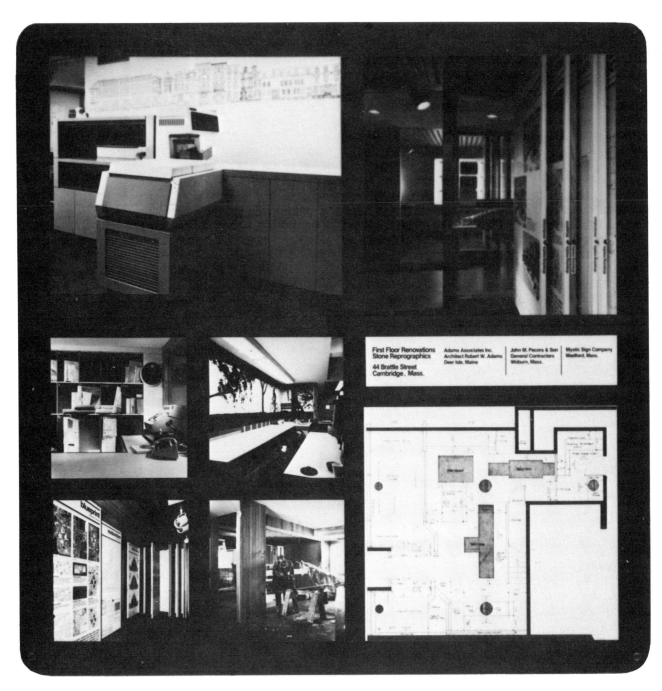

3-20 Surmounting halftone photographs individually on panel-sized sheet that contains line drawings and text brings sharper results than "single negative" method that averages out varying tones of several photographs.

ments, assemble credits, and see to any required adjustments to drawings, the main elements of which should have been prepared long before.

At this point, a marketing principal should review the materials. Especially important is his gut response to the text, credits, title, and the relative importance assigned to the various illustrative elements. After securing his approval, you are ready for production.

Step 3. Production. The various design components of a panel may either be photographed separately with the prints mounted directly on the panel or pre-assembled and a single photograph made of the resulting design. This single photograph is then developed and enlarged to wrap around the panel.

If the panel is to be adapted later to the requirements of other exhibitions, note that it is somewhat simpler to make substitutions with the first method. Also, the single-negative technique brings less satisfactory results: in order to find a happy-medium camera exposure, you forsake a large degree of quality in individual photographs used, especially if there is great disparity in tonal values between them. A common process is to imprint text and line drawings on a sheet that is wrapped around the panel, and "surmount" the sheet with individually printed photographs (see 3-20).

The task of mounting the panel, being tricky, is best entrusted to a professional. Most photographic laboratories offer this service; one or two in each city make a specialty of it.

To obtain the best service from the photographic house, furnish them with the individual elements of the panels—drawings, photographs, text—and indicate their relationship on a large-scale mock-up drawing. On the mock-up drawing, indicate desired size of elements, location, and color. The photographic house will take charge from this point on, photographing the elements, enlarging or reducing them to indicated sizes, and mounting them as instructed.

Many mounting options are open to you at this stage. The basic panel board may be tempered masonite, Fomecor, Duolux, Bainbridge board, homosote, or other materials that will not warp, are stiff, not brittle, and will accept the mounting adhesives. The mounting process may be wet or dry, with or without special backing. You also have a choice of mounting papers, and, if the panels are to be hung out-of-doors, a liquid vinyl may be sprayed on to protect the image from the weather. In addition, grommets may be punched in the corners for inserting hanging hooks or wires—however, some sponsors do not need grommets for hanging and do not like them.

Which of the many choices to opt for is best decided in a friendly discussion with the supplier of the service, especially as new products and processes keep coming on the market. If the panels are to be crated and stored in a possibly damp space in the convention hall basement and, later, in your office's own or rented warehouse space, then use the sturdiest of panels and the longest-lasting mounting method—wet mounting. For milder conditions, consider dry mounting (if permitted under the sponsor's rules) at considerable savings. Exhibit panels do not come cheap. A typical budget, which will vary with location and circumstances, is shown in 3-21.

Note that it will cost roughly $300 to prepare a pair of

	Cost per panel
Mounting	$35–40
Photoenlargements (line)	54
Photographic surmounts (estimated at 50% of panel area)	20
Weatherproofing	18
Accessories: Grommets (4)	2
Rounded corners	20
Total	$149–154

3-21 Typical exhibit panel production budget for 40" x 40" x ¼" thick Duolox, assuming negatives for photographic processes are supplied by the customer.

exhibit panels. This does not include your firm's labor. Nor does it take in crating and shipping to (and return from) the convention hall. It also excludes the exhibit fee, which, as noted, may reach $150 for a pair of panels. Additional expense may go for screens and other special photographic effects.

Thus, by the time the expenses are added up, and considering the relatively limited reuse potential of the panels (they may be hung in your office waiting area or conference room), it is clear that the resolve to exhibit must be made all the way back at the initial decision to submit the preliminary judgment package.

The consequences of success are costly, but, given the right viewing audience, the exhibit panel is a powerful communications device for bringing your firm's name before relatively large groups of client-viewers.

REACHING OUT BY DIRECT MAIL

The likelihood of eased ethical standards in matters of contacting client-prospects who are personally unknown to any member of your firm opens up broad new channels for your communications effort. One of these is direct mail marketing—the unsolicited mailing of brochures or other promotional materials.

Assembling lists

The principal task is to identify and assemble these lists of individual prospects. Such lists may be built up in several ways:

Society membership lists. Professional organizations to which prospective clients belong, such as school or hospital administrators, architects (as seen by their engineering consultants), apartment developers, and so on, maintain membership lists. Usually only members receive them, but many organizations offer associate memberships to interested outsiders that usually make them eligible for most benefits, including access to the membership lists.

Developed lists. Encourage staff members to submit to you names of prospects noted down at conventions and from business magazines, newspaper stories, and other sources.

Brokered lists. Mailing list brokers will prepare a list for you in any degree of specialization, from commercial developers in southwest Wisconsin to left-handed junior high school principals in Deaf Smith County, Texas. The list rental cost ranges from $25 to as high as $150 per thousand names, depending on the quality of the list. Quality is measured by evidence of past response to direct mail. Brokers are paid like travel agents, in that the owner of the list (an organization of higher education facility planners, for instance) pays the broker a commission each time he "rents" the list to customers.

Market development consulting firms. Over the years, these firms develop lists of prospects in your market area and will usually rent them to you for a fee.

Registration lists. Lists of people and organizations attending conferences and conventions may sometimes be obtained from the (sponsoring) group.

Lists are usually rented, not bought outright. This means that your rental fee allows you to send out a single mailing over the list. If you want to use the list again, you pay a second time.

What to expect

Do not expect miracles through direct mail. Given a sharply written sales piece accompanied by one or two choice items from your portfolio system, you should consider a 2 to 3% return good and a 6% return excellent. Remember, these are not clients but merely contacts whom you must then follow up to determine their short and long-term needs and preferences. The level of effort is easily matched to your budget. Typical costs are $25 per hundred names. This includes first class postage, production, and list rental.

Direct mail marketing is a novelty for most professional firms, but it is a potentially lucrative one if used with care and good judgment.

ADVERTISING, OR NOT

Advertising is a basic weapon in every manufacturing firm's marketing arsenal. Whether or not it is proper for professionals to use is a topic of heated debate. How effective advertising would be for individual offices cannot yet be determined, as it has only been tried on a professional-society-wide basis to date.

The options are many. At a modest scale, there is the tombstone approach—small, business-card-sized ads enclosed in a black box and listing your firm name, services, address, and telephone number. These find their way into convention programs of client organizations and, until recently, of political fund-raising gatherings.

At a grander level, unhappily out of reach for most firms, advertising space may be bought in specialized publications read by potential clients, in general business journals, such as *Forbes* or *Business Week*, newspapers like the *Wall Street Journal*, or the big city dailies. Space there may be bought for anything from $3500 for one-eighth of a page in the *Wall Street Journal*'s national edition; $28,000 for a full page in that paper; or $12,000 for a full page in *Business Week*.

But space that says *what*? "John Smith Associates are the greatest?" A picture of JSA's recent prizewinning water purification plant with a modest credit line? A statement on benefits of engaging mechanical engineers (or industrial designers or architects or planners), along with JSA's name, services, and location?

And at what cost/benefit? The $12,000 spent on buying a page in *Business Week* could well be applied to starting up a client newsletter, adding color to your portfolio/brochure and raising by 50% the amount allocated to travel in your marketing staff budget.

The other issues involved in advertising are whether the client and public will be taken in by unjustified claims of expertise, and whether, the richer the firm, the more publicity it can buy. These issues are really moot, because some firms will always, by choice or due to financial plenty, invest larger sums in self-promotion than others; with advertising off-limits, such firms merely find those other outlets for promoting their services. And no client worth his salt will select a designer based on an advertisement, anymore than he will pick one after reviewing only his portfolio.

Advertising can be an important promotional tool, but it must be seen realistically in the context of your overall promotional program.

If you wish to advertise, select those publications you feel are read by prospective clients in your key marketing fields (hospital administrators, hospital trustees, commercial developers, residential developers, and so on). Obtain or borrow the latest issue of the Standard Rate and Data Services (SRDS) *Business Publication Rates and Data Book*, and locate the entry for each such publication. It will tell you these four things:

1. The cost of the ad. This varies with size, frequency, extra color, bleed, and regional or national edition.

2. Detailed breakdown of readership—if the publication is a school journal, then how much of the readership is schoolboard members, school superintendents, school business officials, principals by grade level, teachers, and/or suppliers.

3. Name and telephone of the local space salesman or "advertising sales representative."

4. Closing dates for reserving space and for submitting final artwork, along with mechanical requirements.

You are now in a position to develop a budget, tie it in to your overall office promotional budget, and make a decision based on your priorities.

Successful advertising design is a complex blend of graphic and writing talent, motivational research, and good fortune. Its practitioners are at the center of a 30-billion dollar industry. It is a topic to which one cannot do justice in the limited space of a book chapter. Interested readers will find a first rate introduction in David Ogilvie's *Confessions of an Advertising Man.*

Advertising has been on the proscribed list of most professional societies for so long that even its sanction is unlikely to set off a flood. On the other hand, those firms who want to avail themselves of it will do well to examine its features and its great potential for supplementing traditional marketing methods.

4

Writing for impact

The point of writing for impact is to be clear and brief and to limit jargon to a level the reader can understand without a dictionary. All the rules of grammar and usage must bend to this basic intent in the end. If impact means splitting an infinitive or ending a sentence with a preposition, that's the sacrifice grammar must make before the altar of clarity.

GOALS: BE CLEAR, SIMPLE, BRIEF

Before proceeding to principles, it is important to dispel a pair of myths about the use of language when communicating with clients, the media or the general public. The first of these myths is that nothing beats a good, one or two-syllable Anglo-Saxon word for strength and clarity. Thus, *talk to* is better than *address; admonish* is not as good as *blame.*

Another, contrary, myth says that to capture the proper nuances of meaning, you must rely on words of French and Latin origin that came into the English language since the Norman Conquest through long-time use as the official tongue of law and the Church. Take the verbs *to perform, to institute, to implement, to accomplish* and *to achieve.* The distinctions, while subtle, are nonetheless important enough (says this myth) to apply them in place of the obviously shorter but broader verb *to do.*

Both myths miss the point. The purpose of language is to enlighten, and the means used depends on who will read what is written and the real importance, in each case, of shaded meanings. Thus, a formal research proposal to a government agency (but not necessarily the letter of transmittal and still less any preliminary letter of interest) should be closely concerned with fine meanings. This, for better or for worse, is best done by means of multi-syllable words with very specific meanings.

A typical example of this is the list of tasks a profes-

sional firm may be asked to take on as part of a proposal to develop, for instance, a building system for a network of ambulatory care facilities. This means that user needs must be defined, converted into performance requirements, and, sooner or later, expressed as a performance specification on which interested manufacturer-bidders can bid. The tasks—and their subtasks—have to be differentiated from each other so the agency's review panel knows exactly what the candidate plans to do. This has given rise to a special brand of English known as "proposalese," especially in the use of verbs, of which some especially uncouth samples are shown in 4-1.

No matter how clumsy such language, there is a strong argument in its favor: the words have precise, definitive meanings to the review board. What is more, by using words like *to document* and *to demonstrate* and *to implement,* you are, in effect, telling the board that you speak their language, a useful marketing ploy.

In other words, you are writing to influence a specific audience. Yet using long but very focused words does not excuse obscure style.

Density is suspect

Having assaulted the myth that long words and specialized phrasing are *always* wrong, it is still true that, in almost all cases, to obtain clarity you must be succinct. The message to be conveyed—whether it is a firm's printed credentials, such as the portfolio/brochure; a news release heralding a new appointment, job, honor, or promotion; a letter of interest to a client-prospect; or an article for a magazine—need seldom be so technical as to pass up short words and simple sentences. The motto should always be that the firm's printed message is to influence not peers and colleagues but the client, the media, or the public, as the case may be. And those groups will consider professional jargon and other dense forms of style not only puzzling, but, what is worse, suspect.

STYLE AND HOW TO MASTER IT

Chapter 3 took up the unique requirements of the different kinds of products or messages a professional firm is likely to put out. Good style is a prerequisite of them all.

What is style? It is, as one wit put it, a constant effort to "eschew obfuscation." Better still, style is the arrangement of words in context to bring the reader around to your point of view. How is this best done?

The following guidelines are a solid starting point. They consist of eleven reminders.

Analyze	Define	Identify
Assemble	Demonstrate	Implement
Classify	Design	Perform
Compare	Determine	Rank
Conduct	Develop	Review
Consider	Document	Search
Construct	Evaluate	Select
Consult	Finalize	Sort

4-1 Proposal writers and readers have created a special language—proposalese.

Reminder 1: Write as you would talk

The day is past when writing was done in a style different from speaking. People often tend to freeze when writing, and perfectly simple thoughts and ideas take on a rigid cast akin to the pronouncements of nineteenth-century German philosophers. The example below is from a letter of interest to a client-prospect (original version at left; improved version at right):

The nation is experiencing a major surplus of educational facilities.	We have more schools than we need.

Reminder 2: Keep sentences short

Styles of writing change. Some of the greatest works of seventeenth and eighteenth-century English literature contain swinging sentences of half a page or longer. But to do this well is hard; nor do we have the patience and time of our literary forebears. Even James Joyce's stream-of-consciousness style was less to convey information than to create atmosphere. To be on the safe side, fit no more than an idea or two into one sentence. The example following is from a client-oriented report:

In this day of changing building user requirements, inflated construction costs and swiftly evolving trends in education, health care, housing, leisure and business, it is crucial for those charged with planning these facilities to base their decisions on the true needs of their institutions.	The building user's needs are changing. Building costs keep going up. Trends in education, health care, living and business are altering all the time. Because of this, those who use such facilities must plan them with an eye to their own true needs.

This doesn't mean that all sentences must be equally simple and short. They may vary in length and certainly in structure; but the longer they run, the more work they are for the reader. The greater ease of understanding shorter sentences is backed by research findings. In *The Art of Plain Talk*, the linguist and grammarian Rudolf Flesch uses these findings as a basis for a table that relates sentence length to understanding:

Average length of sentence in words:

Very Easy	8 or less
Easy	11
Fairly Easy	14
Standard	17
Fairly Difficult	21
Difficult	25
Very Difficult	29 or more

Any word sequence separated by a semi-colon, a colon, or a period counts as a sentence. These, and other numerical grading systems reviewed later in this chapter, are a simple but useful check on verboseness.

Reminder 3: Handle professional jargon with care

This applies especially to letters and reports that go to clients who do not build very often, such as most school boards and hospital trustees. These clients rarely retain full-time staff professionals to translate jargon into plain language. The example below is from a brochure:

The firm has always concerned itself with the *plastic quality* of its structures, in the belief that the interior program requirements *generate spaces* and these should be *expressed honestly* on the exterior.

Several words or phrases are the culprits here: *plastic quality, generate spaces*, and *expressed honestly*. Unless the client reads the professional journals, he may suspect a very specialized meaning here but will remain in doubt. This kind of doubt is not the way to good rapport. The solution is to avoid this language or to define the doubtful words.

Do not confuse jargon with technical terms. Terms such as *program, elevation, addenda*, or *decibels* cannot be avoided. Define them when they first come up if there's any doubt as to their being understood. Words such as *program* are unusually perilous—what the professional thinks of as a written statement of facility goals, space needs, and relationships, the client may mistake for a computer program. It is not enough to rely on context for meaning.

On the other hand, if the client is known to have design professionals on his staff, do not insult them by talking down to them. Bear in mind, however, that these staff architects and engineers have nonprofessional colleagues and superiors whom they must keep informed. You can make this easier for them if you keep proposals, brochures, and reports clear and simple.

Reminder 4: Use no more words than you need to make the point

It is amazing how often a text can be pared, saving the reader time and the writer printing costs. This example is from a follow-up letter to a prospect:

We are writing to ask you whether the information on our firm, which we mailed to you recently, has arrived. If there are additional facts you would like to have from us, please do not hesitate to communicate with us.	We hope you received the information we sent you. If you need more, please let us know.

or the now classical—

In terms of our availability, we can begin to implement our agreement at any date that suits your schedule.	Availability? Say "frog." We'll jump. [Courtesy W.W. Caudill]

Special offenders are compound phrases (such as *with regard to, over the course of*, or *as a result of*). These do nothing but dilute the message and slow the reader down. They can just as well be replaced by *about, in*, and *due to*. This example is from a letter of interest:

| We are writing to you *with regard to* your plan to erect a new elementary school building, the need for which has arisen *as a result of* the anticipated enrollment increase *in the course of* the next five years. | We are writing about your plan to erect a new elementary school, needed due to the expected enrollment increase in the next five years. |

Other culprits are, among others:

In order to	to
In the event that	if
Inasmuch as	because
For the purpose of	to

Similarly, omit filler words and phrases that serve only to pad the text. Fillers, such as *basically, to our way of thinking*, for heating and cooling *purposes, this is a time which*, slow down reading and make the message harder to understand.

Especially bad are the words *hopefully* and *capability*. The example below is from a news release:

| The promotion of Richard Ramsbottom to partner *hopefully* will increase the firm's *capability* to plan and design materials handling systems. | The promotion of Richard Ramsbottom to partner will strengthen the firm in the field of materials handling systems. |

Reminder 5: Be concrete

A good strong word is worth any number of abstract phrases. The examples below are from a letter to a client:

| The self-contained *instructional space*—a splendid *teaching medium* for a specific objective—is simply inadequate for other tasks. | The classroom with walls, a splendid teaching tool for a specific job, simply won't do for other tasks. |

or

| Reluctance to engage expert consultants is often considered in management circles as an inefficient utilization of resources. | If you have a dog, why bark? |

Shun *interesting*. It is a word some writers fall back on when they cannot think of a more concrete, precise term.

Reminder 6: Eschew the pompous; aim for simplicity

Example from a planning report:

| Implementation of the construction program should be expected as soon as feasibility is established. | Construction should start as soon as the Board decides the project is feasible. |

Other words that should be on everybody's list of pompous no-no's are *finalize*, for finish; *utilize*, for use; *effectuate a resumption*, for resume; *aspirations*, for hopes; a *majority of*, for most of; *maximum*, for most; and *optimum*, for best.

Reminder 7: Be consistent

Agree to use *won't* or *will not; Federal* or *federal; July 26, 1977* or *26 July 1977; siteplan, site plan*, or *site-plan*. At about the time the Swedes moved traffic from the left to the right side of the road, a wag pointed out that the issue was not so much which side was best but that the drivers use the same side. In the same way, it usually matters less which form of punctuation or spelling is correct than it does to be consistent. Many dictionaries and style books, some of which are listed in References, exist to point the way to good usage. As for spelling, being a slave to Webster has always seemed less important than clarity and consistency.

Reminder 8: Organize statements logically

This is simpler than it sounds. The seventeenth-century French philosopher Nicolas Boileau wrote, "What is clearly understood is clearly expressed." From this the reader of a letter, proposal, or planning report is apt to conclude that what is *not* clearly expressed is obviously not clearly understood by the writer—and he will draw his own conclusions. The example below is from a planning report:

| The plan uses two general descriptive terms to specify the kind and quality of open space on campus. One is soft space being described as having more trees and landscape ground coverage as typified by the space north of the Science Building along Jackson Avenue. The other type would be hard space having more paving for movement of people and more intense outdoor activities such as the space east of the existing University Center. | The plan divides campus open space into "soft" and "hard." "Soft space" has many trees and other landscaping, as in the area north of the Science Building along Jackson Ave. "Hard space" is paved, for heavy movement of people, such as east of the present University Center. |

To change the old version to the new, the thoughts are simply rearranged as a logical chain and the words hung upon it (cutting the number of words by 34%).

Reminder 9: Use active, not passive, sentence forms

Active sentences are a much stronger way to keep the reader's attention. This example is from a proposal:

| It is intended that the project be undertaken by the engineer in association with a local firm approved by the owner. | We propose to associate on the project with an approved local firm. |

Reminder 10: Inject people into the content

Injecting people may be too much to ask in a technical proposal to a Federal agency, but no article, news release, client newsletter, brochure, or letter of interest should be without it. Clients and editors will identify more with the message if it is couched in terms of *people* doing something rather than as an impersonal, cold event. The example below is from a firm's client newsletter:

The site was flat and there was a serious problem as to how interest could be created through landscaping. In the end, earth berms and plantings were installed to create a better setting for the building.	Our in-house landscape architect had a real challenge because the company's site was completely flat. So they placed earth berms and plantings to create a lively setting for the building.

Reminder 11: Use words that evoke good vibes

Some words are better turn-on tools than others. If the point of writing is to cause favorable action or reaction, better be positive than conditional, personal than impersonal, colorful (within the realm of tact) than dull, you than I-oriented, specific rather than vague. The next example is from a proposal letter—the one on the right is longer but better:

This office has a long background of experience in the planning of university science buildings, and this would be utilized if the firm is retained for this project.	We have planned and designed six university science buildings in the past four years. All six projects were completed ahead of schedule and at an average cost of 2.3% below budget.

PREPARING COPY FOR PUBLICATION

Writing and *editing* copy calls for entirely different approaches. The *writer* of a report, letter, or of the descriptive text for an exhibit panel draws data from personal experience and from others and integrates all this into a piece of text.

The *editor* takes someone else's text, whether or not written to the editor's specifications, and transposes it as needed into a form the selected audience will be most influenced by. The better the writer, or the more conscious he or she is as to the target, the less the editor has to do.

This section takes up some sound editing principles and methods for carrying them through, along with yardsticks for evaluating the result. Anyone—the marketing partner in the 6-person firm, the senior partner's executive assistant, the manager of the 50-person firm's planning division, or its chief of market development—will profit by recognizing faulty texts in good time and applying those editing principles.

Preparing a text for typesetting or final typing entails three stages—initial review, detailed editing, and final review.

Initial review

In your first sweep through the text, look for a "feel" whether or not the message is going to enthuse the intended reader. For this, the text must be read fast—in fact, at about the speed of the eventual reader.

In this initial review, avoid the temptation to be slowed down by obvious errors of fact, phrasing, spelling, or punctuation. At best, limit the reaction to a simple pencil mark through the offending part or in the margin and keep on reading.

You will encounter very quickly one of three conditions:

1. The text is of high quality and geared to its audience. It will require a little editing that should not water down its flow and impact. In that case, go on to the detailed editing and final review stages, but with great restraint.

2. The text is obviously off the mark. Decide whether this is due to the level of technicality of the language, the slant of its contents, its organization—or all three. Record this in as much detail as possible and return the text to the author with the advice to begin again.

3. The text is adequate, but is too wordy, lacks spark, some of its parts seem out of place, the division of its sections lacks logic, or the paragraphs are too long—or all of these. Move on to the detailed editing step.

Detailed editing

Begin by rearranging any blocks of text that would work better in a different order—for better build-up, a more dramatic lead, or wind-up. Remove (or make a note to have removed) passages that slow down the flow. Do not waste time editing for style passages that will fall by the wayside.

After completing this broad-brush editing, apply the eleven principles of good usage spelled out earlier in this chapter. Try especially to do the following: condense by eliminating words and phrases; and replace abstract or pseudoscholarly words with concrete, evocative words. Example:

Inefficient use of financial resources	Wasting money

Check for consistency and, definitely, conformity to office policy in the matter of spelling and punctuation. Avoid:

Smith, Smith and Bragg (1st paragraph)

Smith, Smith, Bragg (2nd paragraph)

Smith, Smith & Bragg (3rd paragraph)

SS&B (4th paragraph).

Use active rather than passive phrasing:

The pedestrian preferences of the East Campus students were explored.	We asked East Campus students where they liked to walk.

Eliminate hackneyed phrases:

The campus grew, like Topsy.	The campus grew without plan or order.

Once the text is tight, active, and concrete, look again at its beginning and end. Whether it is a letter of interest, a news release, or the opening of a planning or research report, chances are the lead and closing paragraphs will need that extra polish that will get the reader into the piece and leave him with an urge to interview or hire your firm. For examples of good lead-ins and conclusions, see 4-2 and Chapter 3, *News release.*

As the last step of this phase, add or revise titles, subtitles, decks, and scans for accuracy, impact, and brevity. These aids to reading are covered later in this chapter.

Final review

Back off at this stage, and then look at the text one final time before adding instructions for typesetting or final typing. Here is your chance—like Rubens adding that final bit of white paint to the brow of the goddess—to give the text its final sharpness by changing a word here, a phrase there, replacing a head, or amending a subtitle.

This step is not laborious. It should not take longer than the first reading. But do not pass it up.

Some final cautions

It is a rare editor who is not tempted to overedit. Overediting means two things. First, not just the flab but the very muscle is cut from the text. The result is either totally anemic or so cryptic it reads like a table of contents. This does not mean there is never a place for a severely condensed text; but there must be overriding reason for it, such as space shortage or the nature of the material—for example, brief descriptions accompanying a listing of tasks in a proposal.

The other kind of overediting is far more insidious. It happens when the editor sets out to impose his or her personality or style on the writer. Unless the original text is bland to the point of being a nonentity, restyling is difficult, offensive, and pointless. The editor's task is to bring out the contents so they serve their purpose of influencing an audience. If the muse is upon him, he should write the piece in the first place. If not, let the writer write and the editor edit.

Sexist language

Sexist language is the name given to a written style that stereotypes males and females according to gender. Since both men and women design, draft, project manage, and write specifications, it is held discriminatory to refer to designers, project managers, specification writers, and those who draft as *he* or as draft*smen*.

A number of professional societies and commercial publishers have written or unwritten guidelines prescribing the use of sexist language in their publications. Techniques used to obviate the problem include:

1. Avoid using terms that include the word *man* or *men*.

Draftsman	Drafting personnel
Mankind	Humanity, the human race
Chairman	Chairperson
Man-made	Manufactured

2. Avoid turns of phrase that require use of *he*, *his*, or *him*.

The client said he might need to add to his building within ten years.	The client foresaw a need for expanding the building within ten years.

3. Adjust a sentence from singular to plural.

The designer took his cue from the steep slope of the site.	The designers took their cue . . .

Fire in tall buildings

Lead-in

Not long ago, smoke caused by a conflagration of burning papers sent large numbers of workers out of a prestige Park Avenue office building into the street while firemen forced their way up to a high floor to put out the fire. There were no casualties.

The month before last, in Atlanta, they weren't so lucky. A fire that began in a suite of law offices on the 20th floor of a modern skyscraper on Peachtree Street spread, and four people died before the fire was brought under control. The killer was not the fire, but the smoke.

It is mere luck that fires and fatalities in tall buildings have not been worse than they have. . .

Conclusion

. . . We have been lucky to date with a low rate of human and material losses in tall buildings. The luck won't last forever.

4-2 Good lead-ins capture the reader's attention and a strong conclusion also helps.

1. Generic types	
Who	Professor shows the way
What	Urethanes are useful
When	Current research shows possibilities
Where	Structural system developed at MIT
Why	Why some joints fail
How	How one office uses computers
Question	How about urethanes?
Title label	Urethanes
Quotation	New formula works, says professor
Label with headline	Urethanes: how they work
Alliteration	Urethanes are useful

2. Grammatical types	
Two complete sentences	Space frame tops school; tests show great strength-weight ratio
No verb	Brick vs. block
	Sealants and coatings
	Flying saucers: serious business
	Things to come
With active verb	Plastics perform well under stress
With passive verb	Urethanes used for cavity walls
"To be"	New tests to be made on vinyls

4-3 Writing headlines: formulas for all occasions.

Use masculine terms (he, mankind, draftsman) but indicate in the text that you are doing this for brevity, and that the terms are meant to cover both genders.

A strict and severe policy can lead to a style of incredible intricacy and ugliness. Terms like *chairperson* or *draftsperson* would make Shakespeare blanch. Carried to extremes, it can breed unconscious humor: late in 1976, a New York State supreme court judge denied a Ms. Cooperman a change of name to *Cooperperson*, arguing that on similar grounds someone called *Jackson* would change her name to *Jackchild, Manning* to *Peopling*, and *Carmen* to *Carperson.*

Each firm must set its own policy in this regard. A firm submitting a proposal for interior design services to a bank whose chief executive officer and half the trustees are women, would be foolish to disregard the sexist language problem. Other firms may see discrimination as a problem but feel that forcing language into a new mold without looking at hiring and promotion practices dwells on the sizzle at the expense of the steak.

Meanwhile, whether nonsexist language spreads or dwindles is something each firm can observe and, indeed, influence, according to its convictions.

AIDS FOR THE READER

The client-prospect or magazine or newspaper editor does not read by text alone. He must be helped along by devices that allow him to pick up rapidly the gist of any proposal, newsletter, brochure, or news release that comes across the desk.

There are several of these devices. Most helpful are *titles, subtitles, decks,* and *scans.* They are well known to editors and graphic designers, who use them judiciously as they prepare news items or articles for publication for their readers.

When you write an article or review a book for a newspaper or magazine, chances are that the editor will take care of providing these aids for his readers.

But in the case of the portfolio, or planning report—and even a long letter proposal made up of many parts—these helpful devices are up to you. Lured by these aids, the reader will read. Faced by columns of unrelieved text, he will read with ill will, file for reading later, or not read at all.

What are these devices and how should you compose and use them?

Titles

These should give the reader an idea, at a glance, of what the piece is about. For example, a study report on the feasibility of two alternative large sites for erection of an auditorium building across the river from an existing campus is bound to be read by many people: administrators, trustees, faculty, bankers, possibly students, and townspeople. The title of the report and of its main chapters accordingly should be not dry but active, lively, evocative—see the example below:

SITE FEASIBILITY STUDY AND ANALYSIS FOR ERECTION OF PROPOSED AUDITORIUM

HOLTON OR JARVIS? Two auditorium sites compared

The point, one which applies not only to reports but also to its sections or chapters and to articles, is to select a title that is catchy, active, and short. If more needs to be said, use a secondary title or line, as in the above example. See 4-3 for formulas for catchy title and headline writing.

Subtitles

These not only help orient the reader who wades through a long text but also work as a visual device that rests the reader's eye, as noted in Chapter 5. They should not be longer than one line, include an active verb if possible, and tell the reader enough about the piece of text that follows so he can skip it if he wants to.
Example, from a proposal (dull version at left):

Definition of problem	Your problem as we see it
Scope of work	What you need
Approaches and methods	How we would work with you
Qualification of proposer	Who we are
Time schedule	Milestones
Compensation	Your cost to hire us

For a bright and original variant of this formula, see 4-4.

Other examples of subtitles (editors who use them to break up long article texts or news stories also call them "break heads" or just "subheads") may be found by the dozen in any competently edited journal or newspaper. Watch for them in your paper or professional magazine. Especially well-done are the titles and subtitles in the weekly *Engineering News Record.*

Another useful model for getting the most impact mileage with the least verbal means is your basic city tabloid newspaper, such as the New York *Daily News* or the Chicago *Sun-Times.* I do not suggest that you emulate their brashness, but there are no finer examples of how meaning can be compressed into a few words. Below are examples of heads, the first from a daily newspaper and the second from an office portfolio case study:

CITY POLICE CAPTURE TWO SUSPECTS WHILE CROWD OF 300 LOOKS ON	COPS NAB TWO AS 300 WATCH
COMPLETION OF HOSPITAL ACHIEVED IN 28 MONTHS THROUGH USE OF PHASED CONSTRUCTION	FAST TRACK MANAGEMENT COMPLETES HOSPITAL IN 28 MONTHS
	or, better still
	PATIENTS, STAFF MOVE INTO FAST TRACKED HOSPITAL IN ONLY 28 MONTHS

The second variation, while longer, is better than the first because it is couched in terms of the client.

Decks and scans

These are additional devices to help strengthen the message to the reader. Decks are one-sentence, not-over-35-word statements that run under the headline and tell the reader in more detail what he is about to read (see 4-5).

Scans are statements in larger type that good editors like to place in mid-article to identify, in a capsule way, the gist of the article *at that point.* They usually are placed one to a page, either in a separate space at the top of the page or between thick rules in the middle of a column of text (see 4-6).

Like titles and subtitles, decks and scans are merely devices to be adapted to almost any product developed by your firm, such as project or services fact sheets or planning reports.

Unlike titles and subtitles, they are not essential but are a useful aid that will help make it easier for the client-prospect or media editor to "see" your copy and make it stand out from the competition.

Paragraphing

Much has been said about the art of paragraphing. It really comes down to the intent of the text. A series of short, rapid-fire paragraphs can make for easy reading (see 4-4) but can make a page look visually choppy. Long paragraphs (especially those that measure a full column) are the darlings of many graphic designers, but anathema to readers who must plod through an unrelieved forest of words.

A good rule is to make the paragraph only as long as needed to express a single idea. Most editors have a style rule setting 12 to 15 lines of type in a column as their limit. This encourages tight writing without visual disintegration of the page. Legibility of the type itself is covered in the next chapter in the section on typography.

HOW TO MEASURE QUALITY

The ultimate measure of the editorial quality of your message is the client or media editor, and if they do not get the message, it is too late. One individual in each firm—no matter what its size—must be given the charge of monitoring the quality of its printed materials.

One ingredient of this monitoring is the written or printed word. Over the years, various objective (and some judgmental) methods have been developed for assessing the readability of a piece of writing. Most of them consist of taking a representative passage or passages and—after applying various kinds of arithmetical measures—coming out with a simple number or index.

This index is usually tied to the presumed level of understanding of the reader (for example, 4 years of schooling, 8 years, 12 years, and so on) or linked to descriptions, such as easy, fairly difficult, difficult, very difficult. By judicious editing, an index rating can be improved to match the reading level of the audience. Two of the common indices are the *Fog Index* and the *Difficulty Score* (see 4-7).

CONCLUSION

Indices such as these measure only three aspects of writing quality: word length, sentence length, and personal interest. They are not much use when it comes to assessing flow, organization, turn-on/turn-off features, and appropriateness of a piece of writing. On the other hand, as early indications of how well any given text can be understood, such measuring devices have their place. They

JACK, I've done my homework:

A. WHAT YOU HAVE:

1. The Board of Public Instruction of Howard County, Florida is operating on the advanced edge of primary and secondary education - individualized instruction, team teaching, and ITV being the major educational methods used.

2. Recently constructed elementary and middle schools most vividly show in no uncertain terms manifestation of the team concept which appears to be synonymous with the "open plan" idea.

3. Howard County schoolhouses make up a 3-D history of education in this country, ranging from the 40+ year old two-story mission-type schools through the self-contained finger plan multi-lateral lighted schools, to the compacted open plan EFL-inspired plant. Howard busted the box.

4. There are not enough schools to go around, even by busing. Double sessions are inevitable unless drastic management and technological changes are made to deliver schools at a faster rate.

5. The new schools are going up too slowly to take care of rapidly increasing enrollment, and, in some cases, rather wastefully -- overhangs that protect neither people nor windows, unnecessary geometry for small auditoriums, false structural expressions, and mansard "roofs" that are not roofs. Unfortunately, too, the new schools lack the amenities -- those human values which the 1926 Northside Elementary School possesses.

6. The old schools need both air-conditioning and functional conversion. For example, the self-contained classroom -- a splendid teaching tool for a specific job -- simply will not do for another task (team teaching), like a cotton-picking machine is no good for threshing wheat.

B. WHAT YOU SHOULD HAVE:

1. For one thing you need better schoolhouses to match your fine curriculum. The school -- the most important and expensive machine for learning -- either helps the teacher teach or gets in his way. The old schools deter. Howard County's commitment to high-quality education is a commitment to high quality facilities.

2. You need faster ways to plan and construct schools, such as fast track, critical path and system building.

3. You need more economical ways to beat rising construction costs and inflation, making use of techniques mentioned above (2), plus sophisticated programming that

4-4 Proposal letter with spark and impact—the recipient was a county superintendent of schools. This is an actual letter; only names and places have been changed.

separates "wants" from "needs," pares the "fat," and sets up early computerized cost controls. You need to work fast with effective teams of many specialists.

4. You need to supplement local talent/experience with outside expertise that can help the school board, the superintendent and his staff initiate these new ways -- better, quicker, and more economical -- to provide those urgently needed high-quality facilities.

5. Overriding any one of the methods suggested is the need for a high level centralized team to motivate and manage the school planning/construction program that brings into full play the coordinated efforts of users, designers, manufacturers and builders. Such a management team must be systems oriented, must have the sensitivity to human values as related to the physical environment, and at all decisionmaking times must have empathy for the child and his teachers.

C. HOW YOU CAN HAVE WHAT YOU SHOULD HAVE:

1. You need outside talent/experience -- a team of experts whose members are highly competent in both system building and management of planning/construction programs.

2. You asked if the ABC team is qualified and available. We are on both counts.

3. Availability? Say "frog." We'll jump.

4. Qualified? We are 24 years old, a team of highly competent specialists. Baltimore (public schools), Minneapolis (public schools), Hartford (public schools), New York (higher education); each can vouch for high professional performance of the ABC team concerning the aspects of management. Texas (mental health), Merrick, Long Island and SCSD (development) substantiate ABC's experience in system building.

5. People? Consider these members of the ABC team: (There follows a listing of seven individuals with expertise in the areas of school building systems development, school design, project management, research, "fast-track" construction, building technology).

If you want to take quick action (you need to), pick up the phone anytime and call (713) 621-0000. Talk with either me or my secretary, Jan Smith, and be assured we will schedule two or three key men (specialists in management and system building) to fly in immediately (on us) to discuss ABC services -- scope and cost -- with you, your staff and your board.

You wanted action. You got it.

CLOSING THE INTUITION GAP

How new tools and processes will help provide the architect with a factual back-up for his design decision making.

Today's architect, in trying to make integrated designs out of a fast-growing mass of design data, has reached a point where he can no longer know the full impact of all his design decisions. As buildings become more complex, with a continuing flow of new products and techniques, more demanding and informed clients and more stringent liability requirements, it has become glaringly clear that help is needed.

Over the past few years some progress has been made. This has involved a close look at the architect's design process, so as to better understand its make up and then to be able to identify those areas which can best be assisted by automation.

The history of machines has led from an extension of man's physical abilities to increasing his sensory powers. It is then only a natural next step for man to develop machines to extend his cognitive

while working on a relatively simple design problem—the re-design of a residential bathroom. This verbal behavior plus sketches and notes taken by the experimenter are then analyzed in an effort to determine what information the designer used, in what sequence, and what operations he applied at each stage of development to produce the best.

The greatest insight gained thus far from these studies, Eastman says, has been the significance of representational languages to problem solving ability, since information processing often depends in the end on some means for representating it. The human problem solver is able to use many 'representations'—words, numbers, flow diagrams, plans, perspectives and sections—to compare and manipulate information.

"Most methodologies" Eastman goes on, "are in fact new representations that allow comparison of data that could not be related before. Like other representational languages, they augment intuitive design, not replace it. In this sense, engineering possibly differs from architecture

4-5 Decks help the reader decide whether he would rather read on or switch.

'We must give to communities something that is of value professionally and technically, rather than just do-gooding.'

longtime director, Augustus Baxter. Although Baxter's training has been in social work, he conceives of the workshop's mission as being first and foremost that of providing architectural and planning services. "What made CDCs so valuable," he says, "is that for the first time they made architectural services available to people who couldn't otherwise afford them and that's what they should continue concentrating on. We must give to communities something that is of value professionally and technically, rather than just do-gooding." The workshop is involved in numerous community planning projects, feasibility studies and creation of alternative plans to city and state proposals.

During its more than 10 years of operations, the Pratt Institute Center for Community and Environmental Development has kept the bulldozers from the doors of scores of New York residents. Recently, it saved the predominantly Eastern European northside neighborhood in Brooklyn from destruction. Earlier, the Center was involved in the establishment of the Bedford Stuyvesant Restoration Corporation, in which Robert Kennedy had been active. Although director Ron Schiffman has a staff of only eight, he has at his disposal 30 to 40 Pratt students each year, as well as Pratt faculty members. On one thing he is adamant: "We don't ever use the community as a laboratory for students. Our

velopment Center operates with two full-time professionals, five VISTA volunteers and approximately 35 UYAs. This CDC and North Carolina's Community Development Group are the only U.S. design centers whose work is mainly confined to rural areas.

When asked "what is the main problem of your center?" almost all CDC directors answer "getting funds."

The most viable types of community design centers have been those that have ties with a university and/or are affiliated with and utilize local publicly funded programs for prime support, programs such as the Community Action Program, Neigh-

labor-health, education and welfare by Charles H. Kahn, AIA, chairman of the Institute's community development committee: "Unfortunately, there is no alternative to federal funding. Revenue-sharing is not a satisfactory source for community design center operating funds for several important reasons. Because design centers operate in widely different geographic areas and not necessarily within one municipality or city, there is often a conflict of interest between projects undertaken by a center in more than one local governmental jurisdiction and projects funded through revenue-sharing in only one jurisdiction. In Los Angeles, for example

---

n is that be done, erhead to ago the lity, now personnel y plants. hen cus- and are l get it." to be the printing

eps crop- ion—Na- Iagazine. int to it t it is a hat hap- demands pay for

like Na-

with. One out of every five four-color ads, he says, does not meet the standards of the publication it is being run in.

Most printers agree that as agencies switch ads from process to process they cause a gigantic quality problem.

"The problem is that they're not standardizing quality—they're just standardizing."

"Agencies want to save money, so they provide offset material to gravure, or gravure to letter-press, or letterpress to offset. Creating new engravings or positives is expensive, but they

standards president Graw-Hil improven materials fications 1972.

"I magazine that don usually in where th more ink run," he erally try problems off spec be done."

Ur lishers d they have the wron Salesmen an adver

4-6 Scans make the reader's task easier. They restate pithy excerpts from the text, either in a wide top margin (top) or (above) in mid-text.

Before Editing

Events of recent months have added credibility to fears and warnings that continued reliance on fossil fuel energy sources involves serious short- and long-term problems. With non-polluting fossil fuel energy sources in short supply, a need exists for exhaustive studies of possible alternative energy sources. Such studies must involve technological, sociological, environmental, and economic aspects.

One possible alternative energy source is that of solar energy; specifically in terms of the use of this energy source for the heating and cooling of buildings. At the present time there are a small number of physical structures actually using solar energy for space conditioning.

After Editing

Americans will run into serious short- and long-term problems if they continue to rely on fossil-fuel energy, recent events have shown. Because non-polluting fossil fuels are scarce, man must study alternative sources of energy. Such studies must look at the technical, social, environmental, and economic sides of possible sources.

One such source is solar energy, especially when used to heat and cool buildings. A few physical structures today actually use solar energy for space conditioning.

4-7 Two common indexes for measuring readability were developed by Robert Gunning and Rudolf Flesch. Gunning's Fog Index puts a premium on short words and short sentences. Flesch's Difficulty Score measures sentence length, affixes (prefixes and suffixes), and personal references—the shorter the average sentence length, the fewer the affixes, and the more the personal references, the better the score.

COMPUTING THE FOG INDEX

1. Select a 100-word passage.

2. Count the number of words of 3 syllables or more.

3. Count the average number of words per sentence.

4. Add 2 + 3, and multiply by 0.4

5. That is your Fog Index.

The Fog Index corresponds to the years of schooling to which a text is geared. A Fog Index over 17 presumes over 17 years of schooling; an Index of 13 is geared to those with 13 years of schooling, etc.

   According to Gunning, the following average Fog Indexes are typical of:

The Atlantic Monthly	12
Time Magazine	10
Reader's Digest	8

COMPUTING THE DIFFICULTY SCORE

1. Take the average length of sentences and multiply by 0.1338.
2. Take the number of affixes per 100 words and multiply by 0.0645.
3. Take the number of personal references in 100 words and multiply by 0.0659.
4. Add 1 + 2, subtract 3, then subtract 0.75.

According to Flesch, a score of:

	Ranks as
Up to 1	Very Easy
1 to 2	Easy
2 to 3	Fairly Easy
3 to 4	Standard
4 to 5	Fairly Difficult
5 to 6	Difficult
Above 6	Very Difficult

SCORES

Before editing

101 words

Words of 3 syllables or more:	24
Average number of words per sentence:	20

Fog Index: 18

After editing

74 words

Words of 3 syllables or more:	16
Average number of words per sentence:	15

Fog Index: 12

SCORES

Before editing

101 words

Average number of words per sentence:	20
Affixes:	42
Personal references:	0

Difficulty Score: 4.6

After editing

74 words

Average number of words per sentence:	15
Affixes:	19
Personal references:	3

Difficulty Score: 2.7

EVALUATION FORM

Subject	Editorial (grade +3 to –3)	Graphics (grade +3 to –3)
1. Planning and structure of publication	+2	+1
2. Clarity and reader orientation	+2	0
3. Style	0	—
4. Illustrations	—	–1
5. Covers (if any)	+2	+1
6. Production quality	—	+3
7. "Pacing"	+1	+2
8. Sparkle	+1	+1
Average:	+1.3	+1.0

Rating	Description
+3	Excellent
+2	Superior
+1	Good
0	No strong impression
–1	Needs work
–2	Poor
–3	Start over

JUDGMENT CRITERIA

1. Planning and structure of publication

Are contents logically organized?

Is there a clear graphic expression of contents?

2. Clarity and reader orientation

Are charts, graphs, matrices, tables easily comprehended by the layman?

Are titles/headlines clearly worded?

Are visual devices (decks, scans, subheads) used as aids to the reader?

Is there a table of contents?

Are illustrations clearly captioned?

Is the "white space" around text and artwork organized cleanly?

Is color used efficiently?

Are paragraphs limited to a comfortable reading length (15-20 lines)?

If typewritten, is typewriter type used with graphic skill?

Are display (headline) typefaces appropriate to topic?

Are text typefaces appropriate? easy to read?

3. Style

Are words short? sentences short?

Is there consistency in spelling, punctuation, abbreviations?

Is material expressed in simple language appropriate to topic and reader?

4. Illustrations

Are photographs of good quality?

Are photographs cropped to focus on main subject matter?

Are line drawings sharp?

Are plan titles legible even though reduced?

Are illustrations logically related on a page according to scale and subject matter?

5. Covers (if any)

Is all required information included and easy to read?

Is there an appropriate use of the logotype?

6. Production quality

Are paper stock and cover stock appropriate to the purposes of the report?

Is there a pleasant combination of ink and paper color?

Is printing quality good?

Is binding appropriate to the purposes of the report?

7. Pacing

Is the front-to-back movement of the contents a pleasing experience for the reader?

8. Sparkle

Is the overall impact of the publication fresh and lively?

4-8 Evaluating the quality of a typical printed report. One or more judges grade publication for editorial and graphics according to an 8-point yardstick.

are simple to use and are good for a rapid before-and-after assessment of the text.

There are other methods that do measure total impact, but they require judgment and are necessarily subjective. They measure not only text but graphics. Most commonly, a set of criteria is established and a jury chosen to apply them to the product being judged. The criteria vary with the product. For example, a planning report for a client may be judged for:

1. Planning and structure of the publication

2. Clarity and reader orientation

3. Style

4. Illustrations

5. Covers (if any)

6. Production or quality

7. Pacing

8. Sparkle

These eight elements must clearly be broken down farther, as is shown in 4-8, which has been adapted from a judging framework developed for the American Institute of Architects by the author in collaboration with Evagene Bond and Ivan Chermayeff.

A scoring method of –3 to +3 is used for judging both editorial content and graphics. The two columns are totaled and averaged and an overall editorial and graphic score given each judged item.

Clearly, measuring yardsticks will vary somewhat from item to item—from brochure to report, from letter of interest to house organ. Some design firms have included publications as part of their overall project quality control program.

Every design office should have such a program, not only to judge results but to make principals and staff conscious that quality is no less important for communications than it is for the firm's professional projects.

5

Graphic format: choice and execution

It is not the aim of this chapter to make the reader into the complete graphic designer. Graphic design is a unique professional discipline requiring training and experience, much of it far beyond what is taught in most schools of architecture, engineering, planning, and industrial design.

The smaller and medium-sized (up to 50-person) office is unlikely to have a volume of communications that justifies a full-time graphic designer. Yet, like the larger firm, it needs to be able to tap the knowhow reflected in a flow of new developments in typesetting, engraving, printing, and binding, and gain access to the graphic design talent that brings it all together. Such a firm should, without letting go of the reins of management, be able to benefit from this talent and these developments at a cost it can afford. This chapter shows you how—

• By identifying sources of help (such as graphic consultants, typesetters, printers) and how to evaluate and select them.

• By introducing the vocabulary of graphics so you can discuss problems intelligently with those sources.

• By highlighting basic graphic design and production procedures to make you familiar with graphic designers' methods.

• By pointing out some cost considerations, however unstable and inflation prone.

• By listing (in the references at the end of the book) printed sources to consult for more detailed information.

• By offering ideas you can develop yourself.

The purpose, therefore, is not to *teach* graphic design, but to show you how to *obtain* the kind of graphics that work.

PRINCIPLES OF GRAPHIC COMMUNICATION

Every firm should become familiar with a handful of principles to help guide its graphics efforts. These are, in no particular order of merit: *appropriateness, image, consistency, reproducibility*, and *cost/benefit*.

Appropriateness

It is easy to declare, after the fact, that this piece of graphics is "right," or that is "wrong." But what we are really saying is that it is right *for this purpose*, or wrong *for that purpose*. For example, it is clearly inappropriate, to take an extreme case, to machine-typeset a news release and print it on heavy paper with an embossed letterhead. It is just as unsuitable to put out a planning report that is cheaply printed on poor paper with an ephemeral binding if it will be widely seen by senior corporate or public officials.

Thomas F. McCormick, Public Printer of the United States, told a 1976 seminar for graphic designers that "... even some top-grade newsprint looks 'cheap and dirty'—but it's still the most cost effective paper there is for publishing daily news. But to put the *National Geographic* on the same paper would ruin it."

Similarly, it is hardly fitting to clothe a proposal, the goal of which is to provide services at presumably minimum cost to a community client, in an armor of elaborate binding, glossy overlays, embellished with all colors of the rainbow.

But appropriateness is more than a *general* impression created on the client by your report, brochure, news release, or newsletter. Appropriateness is also a matter of detail. Take typefaces. (Typography is taken up in more detail below, but it is a useful example of the appropriateness principle.) A typewriter face is good for a news release, a proposal, or whenever you want to convey an impression of controlled economy. An elegant, old-line serif typeface may work well for a formal report dealing with restoration of a major national landmark. A more playful typeface would be proper for an exhibit panel showing the prize-winning design of an amusement park. (Playfulness may also be achieved by the way typeface is used.)

A community planning report that was to be made into a book for commercial sale ran into difficulties because the jacket—which was otherwise handsome and in excellent graphic taste—had the title set so small that it was illegible to bookstore browsers. On another occasion, a monthly journal put out by the state chapter of an architectural society retained the services of an otherwise gifted and original graphic designer, only to find that the pages, which looked beautiful in their arrangement of solid type next to handsome photographs, were impossible to read because of the unbroken denseness of the type. Again, appropriateness was the issue.

The same goes for page sizes. There is little value in abandoning without good reason the standard 8½ x 11 or 8 x 10½ format for proposal correspondence or brochures. Chances are they will be filed, and odd page sizes will thwart that effort. On the other hand, news releases are read, used, and discarded, so it is often good to issue them on 8½ x 14 paper in order to fit more meat on the first page. Other products—large reports, for example, especially those with maps—may be larger, on the assumption that they may well be filed on a shelf or other flat

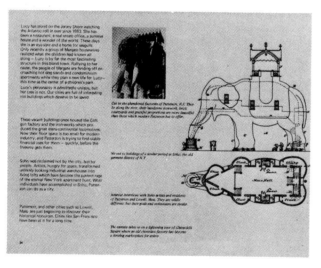

5-1 Two kinds of images expressed through type, layout, paper size, and stock. Dignified image (above) contrasts with informal image, below.

surface rather than in a conventional file cabinet.

A case is made from time to time for designing off-size reports and brochures as a kind of irritant that will force attention. This is risky unless the odd size has a specific function, is part of an overall kit or publication series, or has to conform to European standards.

As for the suitability of drawings versus photographs to express a feeling in a report or exhibit display—photographs tend to create a heavier, more solid impression on the page and convey a greater sense of reality. Drawings, especially when done freehand, are lighter, and have the big additional asset of showing exactly what you want—no less and no more. Even though you can deftly retouch photographs to play down or eliminate unwanted portions, drawings are more versatile.

Image

Unlike appropriateness, which applies to the project, image expresses the firm. Graphic image is a key component of the firm's overall communications image as discussed in the first chapter. As argued there, each firm needs to determine—discover is, perhaps, a better way of describing the process—*what the firm is* and *how* to express it. Do you want to convey an informal, friendly, even convivial image, or one of formality, sobriety, and restraint? Is the impression you want to come across one of tradition and concern for historic values, or are you after up-to-the-minute trendiness? Does your concern lean chiefly toward the client's schedule and pocketbook, or toward a strong esthetic expression that will contribute design monuments to history? Do you want to stress youth and innovation or longevity, wisdom, and experience? Do you like to market gently, or do you favor the hard sell?

All of these kinds of images are valid. Yet they pose difficult—even awkward—questions, and your firm's answers to them will necessarily help form the image your client has of you. If you seek to project stability and experience, you may want, graphically, to think in terms of elegant serif typography, dignified page design, heavy, off-white, watermarked rag bond paper, bulk, formal language, and precisely delineated drawings.

If you care less about tradition than about innovation and seek a quick impact, then some contemporary graphic techniques from the world of advertising may be more in your line. That means strong, bold type; a highly pictorial approach and open arrangement of type; free use of color; and unconventional paper sizes and shapes (see 5-1).

In between these extreme profiles are many intermediate niches. But each firm must search its soul and "position" itself (as they say in advertising) at a point on the scale that reflects and satisfies its leanings.

Consistency

Consistency of graphics, one outward expression of image, is so easy to achieve yet so simple to neglect. Consistency does not have to mean coming up with and following the rigid kinds of graphic guidelines that in recent years have been developed for many manufacturing businesses and certain public agencies, such as the U.S. Department of Labor. These guidelines—which control

	LOGO	TYPEFACE	TYPEWRITER FACE	PAGE SIZE	DESIGN LAYOUT	USE OF COLOR	PAPER STOCK	BINDING
● Consistency important ○ Some freedom appropriate								
Brochure/portfolio	●	●		○	○	●	○	○
Construction sign	●	○			○	○		
Design award submittal	●		●	●	○	●	○	○
Exhibit panel	●	○			○	○		
In-house communications (memos, time sheets)	●		●	●	●	●	●	○
News release	●		●	○	○	●	○	○
Newsletter (for client prospects)	●		●	○	○	●	○	○
Project communications (drawings)	●				○	○		
Project communications (specifications)	●		●	●	○	○	○	○
Proposal	●		●	●	○	●	○	○
Report for client (planning, etc.)	●	○	●	○	○	○	○	○
Stationery	●	●	●	●¹	●	●	●	○

[1] Some firms also use a two-thirds height sheet for short messages or simple forms

5-2 Matrix shows desirable areas for graphic consistency. Read *down*, seek consistency among items marked with solid circle.

everything from building signs and product packaging to stationery and publications—are often so detailed that they fill a thick binder.

The design firm needs no such elaborate manual. A good, workable range of consistency may be obtained by control over just a few graphic elements (see 5-2). The only way to assure consistency is to plan for it, formally, with principals and graphic designer present and involved. (How to achieve such control is discussed in Chapter 10.) Once a set of basic graphic products has been developed, it is much simpler to use it as a guide than to invent a new visual format for each occasion.

As indicated on 5-2, consistency among items does not necessarily equal absolute uniformity. For example, even though the firm may have a preferred typeface, there could be enough freedom, especially when designing reports or exhibit panels, to select a new face if it will make for greater impact. Elsewhere, however, such as in design of the logo, letterhead, choice of typewriter face, and even colors, a high degree of uniformity is appropriate.

Reproducibility

One concern of graphics is whether or not a design is simple to reproduce. A common example is the logo. If the enclosed spaces of a logo, such as those formed by the capital letter B, are made too small, they will very likely fill in with ink when printed at a reduced size. A similar danger will occur when the design consists of many curlicues or closely spaced lines. And, conversely, a device that is handsome when small may appear gross when enlarged to the size of a panel or a sign.

Another factor to consider is color. A logo or letterhead must always be devised so that it is equally strong whether printed in black, in a color, or even in two or three colors (see 5-3).

A third concern, discussed in detail later in this chapter, is the use of graphic aids such as screens, tints, sprays, press-on letters, and felt-tipped markers. These are familiar to students and designers, who use them skillfully for original, one-of-a-kind presentations, without regard to how they will reproduce in print. A rendering, for example, that is striking in its use of color, may look weak and dull when reproduced in black and white as part of a design award submittal. Similarly, titles made of press-on letters will look uneven and makeshift when enlarged or when placed next to type that has been machine set.

To forestall these dangers, be sure to know in advance which shades of gray colors will convert into (see 5-4). Also, invest in machine-set titles if the report is to be printed for widespread distribution.

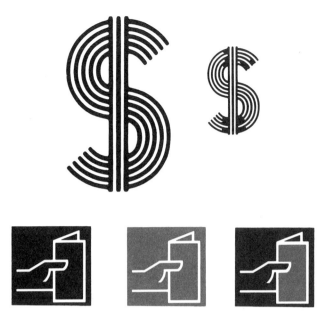

5-3 Marks, symbols, and logos should be reproducible at different scales and in different colors without impairing their impact.

Reproduction

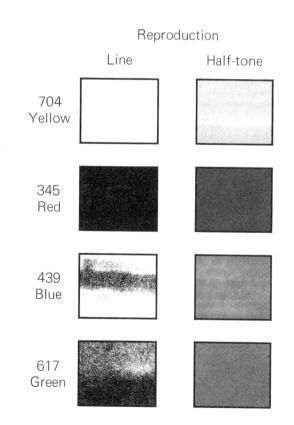

	Line	Half-tone
704 Yellow		
345 Red		
439 Blue		
617 Green		

5-4 Pretest the way certain colors will convert to shades of gray as halftones, or will keep or disappear as line cuts, by applying frequently used colors to blocks as shown. Then order inexpensive halftones and line cuts from the engraver.

Cost

Cost is, or should be, an ever-present watchdog over a graphic communications program. The principals are all too aware that funds spent on communications graphics are usually not immediately or directly income-producing. Every dollar spent on such graphics must therefore provide proven value. (Some of our greatest architectural, engineering, and product masterpieces were the outcome of healthy discipline imposed by a tight budget. Too much money can be as destructive of quality as too little.)

Accordingly, cost-consciousness in graphics will not only keep a rein on overhead but may improve quality. Some typical areas to look out for are:

Paper size. A squarish, 8½ x 7½ size for stationery and memoranda as an alternative to 8½ x 11 is not only handsome but saves paper costs for short messages. Folded once, it will fit the standard No. 10 envelope.

Using black plus one additional color. That is the way this book is designed—it will meet most needs for a color other than black without incurring the far greater costs of preparing 4-color overlay mechanicals, platemaking, and printing.

Using screens or bendays. A technique for printing portions of text or artwork at less than 100% intensity, this can often do away with the need for a second color. If used with a second color, it can provide countless variations at no additional printing cost.

Using typewriter type. An inventive graphic designer can produce a very strong impact with no more than an office typewriter and some graphic accents. Many proposals and client reports can be composed on the typewriter to avoid the cost of typesetting.

Restricting the number of typefaces. Most typography houses set a basic charge for each new face because of the extra labor involved each time they set up their machine. When you use computer-based photo (or cold) type, you can usually use a range of from 6 pt. type to 72 pt. type and sometimes go from light to bold within one family of type without an extra charge.

Selecting paper stock with an eye to cost. Papers (as discussed on page 104), vary widely in cost, and an experienced graphic designer will always be able to find papers that are good value for the money and meet the graphic purposes of the stationery, report, brochure fact sheet, or other communications product. The printer, too, should help in the selection. For example, he will tend to charge less for paper he has in stock.

A final aspect of graphic cost is one that no firm can afford to underestimate, namely, the *perceived* or *apparent cost* of its communications product. Is great richness (as shown up through lavish color, typefaces, paper, and binding) what you want to convey to present and future clients? Or do you want to convey austerity?

Bear in mind the following axioms: it may cost a lot of money to make your proposal look thrifty; an expensively produced brochure may look cheap; and a low-budget report can look crisp and elegant. It all depends on how you use the available means, which are discussed next.

THE ELEMENTS OF DESIGN

Text (including typography), artwork (including photographs, drawings, charts, and tables), and "white space" are the three elements of design. Like the 26 letters of the alphabet and the 12 notes of the musical octave, they can be put together in an infinite number of ways, and, like literature and music, the outcome will be either disagreeable or sublime depending on the skill and judgment of the designer.

This section reviews these elements from the viewpoint of the communications impact, first separately and later as parts of a final design.

Typography and text

Typography and text are totally dependent on each other—they are really two facets of the same subject.

Typography. That so much has been written about text, type, and typefaces is due in part to the endless fascination this ancient art has always had for experts and laymen alike. The language of type itself has romantic overtones that have come down to us through terms like *shoulder*, *beard*, *serif*, *justify*, *leading*, *nick*, *galley*, *ragged*, *furniture*, and *body*.

Typefaces. Typefaces come in serif and sans-serif (5-5), yet to know this is about as useful as to know that "into" is a preposition and "his" a pronoun. It is much more important to recognize the response that use of one or the other evokes. Serif type is, by and large, easier and less tiring to read in bulk than is sans-serif, and it has a more dignified feeling besides. Sans-serif type is of more recent vintage, conveys a contemporary feeling, and has over the past 50 years become the favorite of young American and European graphic designers. Especially when used in bold for titles and other nontext display purposes, such as subtitles for planning reports, key information on exhibit panels, and signs and letterheads, sans-serif type is excellent because it is simple, straightforward, and highly legible at a distance.

Why the serif makes for easier reading of text is an extremely large subject, but briefly its basis is the ability of the eye to rest subconsciously on the serif that completes the stroke of each letter, thereby producing a more relaxed act of reading. Some excellent solutions have been obtained by mixing the two families—using a serif face for large bodies of text and a sans-serif family for titles, captions, charts, and tables, where quick readability is important.

A face that has never been properly recognized is the one produced by the everyday typewriter. Of course, it is now possible to choose from a limitless selection of faces for the typewriter, but there is a basic face (5-6) that has come down to us from the machine's beginnings in the late nineteenth century and is still a model of clarity and legibility. What is more, it is cheap to produce since it bypasses the need for setting type. It evokes in the reader a feeling of immediacy and up-to-dateness and is therefore a fine medium for correspondence, news releases, proposals, and even for certain kinds of planning reports. There is nothing more inappropriate than to install in your office's standard typewriter a face that seeks to parody the more elaborate serif and sans-serif faces from the type book.

Most type houses will gladly give you a copy of their type book, which lists faces they offer. The inventory of some of the larger houses, such as Photo-Lettering, Inc., in New York City, will run to several volumes. The catalogs issued by manufacturers of press-on letters also make for fascinating study. A handful of good, inexpensive books about type are listed in the reference section at the end of the book.

Everyone should at some stage in his career spend a rainy Sunday with a book on type and a collection of typebooks. There is no better way to develop a feel for what is available and how a face looks and reads, small or large, bold, medium, or light, italicized or roman, in large blocks and small.

Caution: the inventory of typefaces is so rich that it is tempting to try them all, like a child faced with a large box of different shaped chocolates (see 5-7). The result, if applied to the elements of your brochure or exhibit panel, is visual indigestion. It is best avoided by rigidly limiting the faces you use to two or, at most, three.

Setting type. There are many kinds of machines for setting type, and the results you get and the bills you pay will depend to some extent on which you choose.

At one time, type was set by a machine that cast hot lead over a "matrix" of letters or "fonts." It had the drawback—aside from the heat and clumsiness of the equipment, the setup time, and the limited range of papers on which to proof the copy—of dictating the spacing of letters in a word or line, since each letter was a separate block and no overlap was possible. Thus, the creators of the type tried to allow for this by varying the space to either side of each letter (the "shoulder"), so a complete word would look well spaced (for example, by giving a generous shoulder to the left of a capital L but little to the right). But there was no way they could solve the optical spacing problem caused, for example, by setting the word VA in capital letters (see 5-8). The dilemma may clearly be solved by cutting up the letters as they come on the proofsheet and rearranging the spacing through notching to get the right optical effect, but this is an extra, time-consuming step.

The old metal type-setting machines have been largely superseded for most (but by no means all) uses by cold typesetting. One version is the phototypesetting machines which possess enormous flexibility. By selecting a basic face (like Helvetica, Univers, Baskerville, Times Roman, or Clarendon), you may, depending on the sophistication of the machine, obtain a wide variation of height, letter widths (from infra-condensed to ultra-expanded), slants (5-10), boldness, and tightness or looseness of letter and word spacing (see 5-11)—all from a single font or matrix.

Metal type (set on a linotype machine) still has its uses, especially for setting copy that will be corrected or revised, such as financial tables, programs, and timetables. Type is set in one-line slugs, and changes can be confined to the line without resetting an entire section of copy.

One great benefit of phototypesetting is the ability to overlap letters without cutting and pasting. A line of display type can be set by a trained typesetter so the spacing between letters *seems* optically equal. The typesetter does this by making the spacing *unequal*—by overlapping, for example, a capital V and A, or a lower-case w and e (see

5-5 Some common typefaces, with serif on the left, sans-serif on the right. Continuous type is usually easier to read in serif; headlines and other display type are stronger in sans-serif.

Feds apply fre
Spending less
demonstratio
School boards
Multipurpose a
study looks

5-6 The simple elegance of typewriter face is often neglected.

Will it be one of these????

WATCHING THE BUCK

Where they are planning to spend those
petro dollars.....Pg. 6

PLAY IT SAFE

OSHA Guidelines tell you how. Pg. 7

All YOU ever wanted to know about the
ENVIRONMENT--and more......Pg. 3

Many, many more from which to
choose inside.

5-7 It is tempting to overuse the infinite variety of available typefaces. (From a government circular.)

5-9). This is made possible because in the photographic process a letter image from the basic matrix registers on film or paper, and, by proper adjustment, the image of the next letter can be projected at any desired spacing.

The business equipment industry has in recent years developed many typesetting machines small enough to install in your office and cheap enough to buy or lease. While the quality and versatility of these machines is more limited than that of the large commercial equipment, they have their uses if you have a fairly large, evenly distributed volume of reports to produce. Most manufacturers will train your secretary at no extra charge. (Equipment is discussed in greater detail later in this chapter.)

Besides determining a typeface, you must also select an arrangement of type in terms of line *length*, line *separation*, and *justification*. This concerns design and is discussed in the next section in this chapter.

Legibility of type. This is a function of typeface, type size, line width, spacing and alignment, ink color, and printing surface. One of the great gurus of legibility of print, Miles Tinker, spent a lifetime of research on the topic. His findings, spelled out in *Legibility of Print*, provide some practical guidelines in this respect. Tinker finds a relationship between height of type, length of line, and the space between lines known as "leading" (see 5-12).

Legibility is an inexact science. Tinker's findings rely largely on tests of opinion, and people vary in sensitivity. Still, as a rule of thumb, a line of type should rarely exceed 30 picas (about 5 in./12.7 cm) in common text type (8 pt. to 12 pt.) unless you resort to exorbitant, paper-consuming line spacing. This is why the typical typewriter line, which measures around 40 picas, requires so much space between lines to be read with comfort. Other things equal, Tinker found that readers preferred a larger type "set solid" (that is, without leading) to a smaller type with leading.

Nor, on the other hand, should a line be set at any measure *less than* 14 picas. Ultra-short lines cause problems. One is the difficulty of getting whole words in, resulting either in an excess of hyphenation, which is irritating, or large gaps between words to fill out the line, a "flush right," which is unsightly. Another problem is irritation caused by too much line-to-line eye movement. That is one reason why the New York *Times* switched in late 1976 from an eight to a six-column page, expanding column width from 10 picas to 16.

Short paragraphs (12 to 15 lines) are easier on the eye than long ones, and the transition from one paragraph to the next should be marked by extra space or by indenting the first line. A new variation on paragraphing extends the first two or three letters of the first line *into the margin*.

Finally, there is the issue of alignment (or lack of it), of text along imaginary vertical lines to the left and/or right of the column. Whether a text is read easier when justified (flush left and right—see 5-13) or remains "ragged" (5-14) is moot. By and large, a ragged margin allows for an even, natural spacing of words. It also cuts down on the need for hyphenation.

Specifying type, or getting what you want. Specifying or "spec-ing" (pronounced "specking") is the act of telling

V A

we

5-8 Hot typesetting precludes overlap of letters, except by cutting and pasting proofs.

VA

we

5-9 Phototypesetting permits visual balance by overlapping letters.

HELVETICA MEDIUM

Typography

Condensed 24%

Typography

Condensed 16%

Typography

Condensed 8%

Typography

Expanded 24%

Typography

Expanded 16%

Typography

Expanded 8%

Typography

Oblique

5-10 Phototypesetting equipment is able to create many typeface variations from one basic film type font by using special lenses. It can expand, condense, backslant, or oblique almost any face from its normal setting up to a variation as high as 34%.

HELVETICA MEDIUM

Typography

Touching

Typography

Very Tight

Typography

Tight

Typography

Normal

Typography

TV Spacing

5-11 Phototypesetting can space letters in a range from very tight to very loose.

11. When my mother saw the marks of muddy shoes on the floor, and all over the nice clean beds, she was surprised to see how careful the children had been. 12. When the little boy next door had both of his legs broken by being run over by an automobile, we were afraid he might never be able to see again. 13.

Comparison I: 8 point, 16 picas, 2 point leading

11. Frank had been expecting a letter from his brother for several days; so as soon as he found it on the kitchen table he ate it as quickly as possible. 12. A certain doctor living in a city near here always has a very serious expression on his face. This is perhaps because in his work he meets only

Comparison II: 6 point, 14 picas, 2 point leading

11. Frank had been expecting a letter from his brother for several days; so as soon as he found it on the kitchen table he ate it as quickly as possible. 12. A certain doctor living in a city near here always has a very serious expression on his face. This is perhaps because in his work he meets only well people. 13.

5-12 This example shows three type sizes set in optimum line widths and leading.

JUSTIFIED

Fine typography is the result of nothing more than attitude. Its appeal comes from the understanding used in its planning; the designer must care. In contemporary advertising the perfect integration of design elements often demands unorthodox typography. It may require using wrong fonts, cutting hyphens in half, using smaller than normal punctuation marks; in fact, doing anything that is needed to improve appearance and impact. Stating specific principles or guides on the subject of typography is

5-13 Justified text is flush at the left and right.

the typesetter what you want. You should become familiar with a clear method of conveying your intent.

There are seven elements that you must point out to the typesetter. These are listed in 5-15. To see how a piece of text is typically spec-ed out for typesetting, see 5-16.

If you use a standard combination of typefaces and line arrangement for regular items, such as additions to the office brochure system, it pays to order rubber stamps indicating your requirements.

The selection of typefaces nowadays is well-nigh infinite. Yet a typeface either is or is not compatible with the other design elements on the page spread, with the end purpose of the publication, or with your office style. Good judgment—yours and your designer's—becomes the deciding factor.

Typography by typewriter. Often overlooked in the rush to set type is the beauty, simplicity, and sense of immediacy of the common typewriter. Typewriter type is especially apt for such purposes as proposals, newsletters, and many research and planning reports.

To distinguish it from typing everyday correspondence, this concept can be called the "enhanced typewriting" approach. The additional creative factor may be obtained by a combination of means that exploit the versatility of the keyboard and add some inexpensive, simple hand-applied devices, such as circles, squares, or other symbols to mark the beginning or end of a key passage or to emphasize (see 5-17). Note the varying degrees of emphasis possible by:

- Underscoring
- Capitalization
- Underscoring plus capitalization
- Headline inset as part of first paragraph
- Headline set on its own line
- A symbol indicating start of an article
- A symbol indicating the end of an article
- A symbol indicating special emphasis
- A symbol indicating the end of the issue or publication

But that is not all. Pieces of typewritten text may be used as elements in composing the page, as shown in 5-18. Note how an imaginary grid divides the page into two unequal blocks, with the wider block used for the message and the narrower block for heads and titles.

The same example also shows how, by the simple process of enlarging the type photographically combined with a skillful use of rules, you can draw the reader's eye to a major headline. A simple color block offers still another way of enhancing a typewriter face.

Clearly, then, good graphic effects are open to you without exorbitant outlays for typography.

Text. From a visual viewpoint, text must strike a happy balance between *legibility* (as defined in the previous section) and *compatibility* with the graphic design. When determining typeface and arrangement for your copy, follow these suggestions:

Legibility comes first. Avoid column-high paragraphs of text. If sans-serif type is used for text, select the width of line and spacing between lines with utmost care. Where a sans-serif type face is too light or the lines too long or too densely packed, reading even a single column can be an exasperating experience.

Give the reader visual relief. Columns of unrelieved text, even if type is well-sized and spaced, can be made easier to read by inserting subheads, subtitles, scans, and appropriate breaks (see 5-19). A typewritten document, such as a long proposal letter or typewritten report, should also be interspersed with such breaks, appropriately underscored, and even set off with bullets (see 5-20). Also, seize the transitions from paragraph to paragraph as an opportunity for adding a line of space or indenting the next line of text.

Designing with text. On occasions, especially where there is little other artwork, complete or partial columns of type may be used to liven up a spread. By a careful play of text and white space using short columns of type broken at logical places, an exciting and lively design is possible—you can, for instance, "hang" type of various lengths from an imaginary line or build type up from an imaginary base (see 5-21). Or, place text that is not essential to the flow of the main message in boxes or side bars. In some cases you could convert such information into a graph, chart, or table.

Artwork

Think of artwork as everything printed that is not text. This includes linework (drawings) and half-tone work (photographs). It also includes titles and headlines, as these are important graphic elements that shape the liveliness of a page. Charts, tables, and maps also must be used for their graphic impact.

Artwork of whatever type—drawings, tables, process or organization charts, matrices, or maps—should be approached with great vigilance, for few clients are trained to understand them. *Far from a picture being worth a thousand words, a picture may sometimes require a thousand words to explain.* Therefore, if the nature of the client or the intricacy of the chart raises any doubt, be sure to include "how to use" directions.

Drawings. Aim for a reduction of up to 40% in a drawing to be printed—and remember it is sharper when reduced.

Photographs. Photographs complement drawings and other artwork and should show what is already shown elsewhere. Their strength is in presenting items in context—a group of buildings in a landscape, a sign against a building, a new building next to an older neighbor, people and furniture in a room, staff members at work, students using the school's library (see 5-22).

When using photographs, insist on sharpness, clarity, and contrast. For design reasons it is possible to make a sharp image fuzzy, to reduce or eliminate detail, and to bring down contrast. It is very difficult, and usually impossible, to work the other way. Sometimes a gray print can be saved by subtle retouching, by printing it on high contrast paper, or by ordering a so-called line conversion print that does away with all gradations of tone. Obtain the negative whenever possible and have the photolab work from that. Other than that, a good-quality print made from a well-exposed and well-composed subject is a must.

UNJUSTIFIED: WITHOUT HYPHENATIONS

Fine typography is the result of nothing more than attitude. Its appeal comes from the understanding used in its planning; the designer must care. In contemporary advertising the perfect integration of design elements often demands unorthodox typography. It may require using wrong fonts, cutting hyphens in half, using smaller than normal punctuation marks; in fact, doing anything that is

UNJUSTIFIED: WITH HYPHENATIONS

Fine typography is the result of nothing more than attitude. Its appeal comes from the understanding used in its planning; the designer must care. In contemporary advertising the perfect integration of design elements often demands unorthodox typography. It may require using wrong fonts, cutting hyphens in half, using smaller than normal punctuation marks; in fact, doing anything that is needed to

5-14 Other variations are flush at the left and ragged at right, or the other way around. A further subtlety (top) allows you to eliminate hyphens.

---

1. Type face

Identifying name and/or number (for example, Clarendon #2)

Size (in points)

Weight (light, medium, bold)

Slant (roman, italic)

Case (upper, lower, small caps)

2. Leading between lines (in points)

3. Line width (in picas)

4. Word spacing (normal, tight, loose)

5. Type alignment (justified, flush left, flush right, ragged left, ragged right, in desired combination)

Since clearly no consistent line width can be specified for type set ragged, the practice is to call for a *maximum* and *minimum* width. This way, in a given piece of text, no line will exceed the maximum in width nor fall short of the minimum.

6. Proofs and paper

Indicate how many proofs and whether they should be on paper or film, transparent or opaque, with or without a gummed or adhesive backing.

7. Any special instructions

Special positioning or effects

5-15 A checklist for specifying type. Type size and leading are indicated together; thus, 8/9 means 8-pt. type with 1 pt. of leading; 12/14 means 12-pt. type with 2 pts. of leading.

Set, except where noted:
10/12 Century, caps + l. case, Roman
Flush left, rag. right,
20 picas max, 18 picas min.
Tight word spacing. Hyphens OK.

HOUSING
CHARACTERISTICS

[18/20 Helv. Med. CAPS]

Four ingredients of housing are discussed in this report. They are: siting, design, construction methods,
and materials.

SITING

[14 Helv. Med. CAPS, 6pts above, 4pts below]

With the relatively primitive wind risk maps, little
regard has been given to the placement of houses in
relation to danger. Good site location or orientation
linked to local terrain and natural cover can be, but
usually has not been, determined from historical wind
data. This data provides the frequency, velocity and
direction of the prevailing winds, especially in their
extreme form. Hence, windstorm damage can be reduced
a great deal by placing buildings so they are protected
by hills, stands of trees and other natural elements.

DESIGN

[14 Helv. Med. CAPS, 6pts above, 4pts below]

Windstorm resistance can be notably improved by various
simple measures. These include horizontal bracing of
certain types of roofs over houses made of adobe mason-
ry and other small unit construction; a more rational
disposition of openings in bearing walls; reinforcement
of critical areas of a building subject to being over-
stressed; and the strengthening of connections at
joints.

[Indent all but 1st ¶]

All this may not be enough. Special studies on how
turbulence in a storm is distributed are required. It is

5-16 Example of specified or "speced out" type.

Depending upon the overall design, consider these points when using photographs:

Cropping. Most photographs must be cropped to properly focus on the subject and to fit the proportions set down in the page design. Many shots are ruined because of extraneous material. Seas of asphalt, acres of lawns, and firmaments of skies should be brutally cut away if they do not add to the picture. Nor is there a need, when showing personnel pictures in a brochure or newsletter, to leave in collars, ties, and double chins; after all, the client is interested in the facial expression, not the haberdashery. Most people-pictures are too small anyway; why waste valuable space by keeping in extraneous detail? Crop in order to focus the eye on what is important.

Scaling photos to fit layout space. A photographic original will seldom be of the right size or proportion to fit its assigned space in a layout. The picture may need to be scaled up or down or cropped along its long or short side. The procedure is simple. On a transparent overlay, determine which part of the image you want to preserve for its content. Draw a rectangle around the desired area. Next, place over it a rectangle the exact size and shape of the assigned space in the layout. Draw a diagonal through it, and extend this until it meets a side of the original rectangle. This determines the amount of area that must be cropped (see 5-23). Apply the same procedure to drawings and other artwork that is larger (or smaller) than its assigned space on the page.

In another method, the correct proportions may also be computed by proportional disk or calculator, using the formula $A = \frac{BD}{C}$, where C and D are the sides of the assigned space, B, the fixed side of the photograph, and A, the variable side.

Bleeding. This is not a sixteenth-century physician's last resort, but a handy tool for gaining extra area for a photograph on a page. A bleed photograph extends beyond the established margins of a page, to one, two, three, or even four edges (5-24). This can make for some very striking effects, but should be used sparingly to avoid diluting its impact.

Half-tones. A half-tone is a reproduction of your photograph converted for printing by means of dots of varying size to simulate the different tones. The denser the dots, the finer the image.

The degree of density is determined by the spacing of the special lines on the screen used to convert the photograph to dots and is measured by the number of lines per inch. These can range from a coarse 85-line screen used in newspapers printed by letterpress, and 100 to 133-line screens for newspapers printed offset (usually on smoother paper stock), up to 150-line screens for magazines and high-quality offset lithography. Screens as fine as 200 to 300 lines are possible but require great control and fine-quality paper. See 5-25 for some examples of effects obtained by different-sized screens.

A glossy finish makes for sharper reproduction than a matte finish. Note that printing platemakers prefer to work from mounted prints or transparencies.

Moiré. The moiré effect (see 5-26) is the irregular pattern created by two superimposed screens not in register to

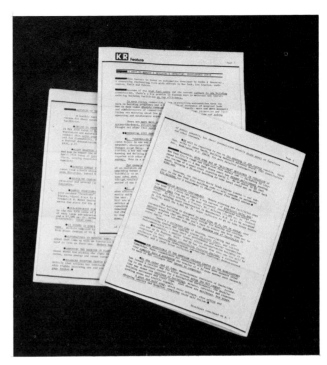

5-17 When using typewriter face, note the varying degrees of emphasis produced by underscoring, capitalization, underscoring plus capitalization, headlines set in as part of paragraph, and symbols indicating the beginning and end of the article for special emphasis.

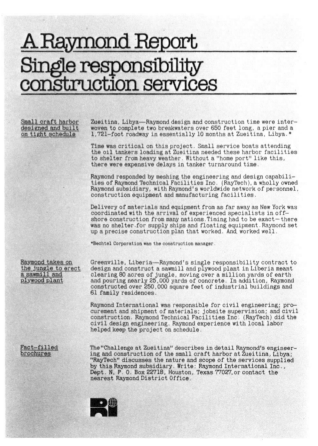

5-18 Skillful use of typewriter face for design.

Intermediate	To achieve a more continuing integration of man-built environmental education subject matter into scholastic curricula, in primary and secondary schools, and to provide specific methods for using the materials. Course content in colleges of education will be integrated similarly to include environmental education content, with a special emphasis on the man-built environment.
Long Range	To achieve a more concerned, better informed citizenry, more deeply sensitive about the quality of its man-built environment. Few know that our physical surroundings influence us consciously or subconsciously, for better or for worse. Studies by such behavioral scientists as Edward Hall, Robert Sommer and others, (conducted in such environments as schools, hospitals, mental institutions, and correctional institutions), point out the direct relationship between the physical environment and man, both as an individual and in groups.

H. J. Heinz Co., are listed for failing to comply with schedules previously agreed to for the construction of sewage treatment facilities. Neither facility was convicted in court for its failure to meet control deadlines.

Del Monte contested EPA's authority to promulgate the list, but in a decision issued on Nov. 8, a U.S. district court judge in Puerto Rico upheld the environmental agency.

Del Monte vice president for public affairs, Michael P. Roudnev, says the company is contemplating an appeal of the decision and adds, "It would be far better if EPA would let court actions proceed and find out if alleged discharge violations occurred before coming out with their blacklist. We've been found guilty before our day in court."

Not a new trick. The blacklisting of recalcitrant polluters was authorized in 1970 under the Clean Air Act and in 1972 under the Water Pollution Control Act. Former President Richard M. Nixon ordered the program into effect in 1973. And EPA set up administrative procedures to implement the program in

must meet pollution control requirements before being removed from the list.

Jawboning. But, rather than going through all the official procedures, says Hanmer, the threat of being placed on the list, or even knowing that it exists, has been an effective coercive tool for regional enforcement officials. Even if a company does no business with the federal government, its customers and stockholders don't like the stigma of being on the black list, she contends.

While the two facilities now on the list got there through actions of the regional office in New York City, Midwest enforcement officers are also pursuing polluters.

The Chicago office of EPA says it has begun actions against three facilities and has sent notices to 45 firms that present potential compliance problems. "We're very serious about going ahead with this. It lets us speak in dollars and cents, something that businesses understand," says David Ullrich, an attorney.

The three facilities, Inland Steel's East Chicago complex, a Campbell, Ohio, mill owned by Youngstown Sheet & Tube Co. and Cleveland Municipal Electric Co.,

5-19 Subtitles serve as aids to the reader. They may be set in the margin (top) or set into the text, in bold type (above).

Immediate	● A significant increase in the number of elementary and secondary school teachers and administrators (particularly curriculum specialists) who are aware of, sensitive to, and actively planning and teaching about the total environment in which we all live. ● Development of a greatly expanded awareness and concern amongst these same individuals for the less obvious problems and processes of the man-built environment as an integral part of the total environment. This would be measured by an increase in actual teacher use of the wide variety of excellent environmental education teaching and learning resources currently available.
Intermediate	● Widespread and permanent curriculum modification in all elementary and secondary school levels -- modification which is integrated with rather than added to the full breadth of existing curricula and which will allow the infusion of man-built and natural environmental elements and concerns. ● Creation of a well-developed, evaluated and tested presentation and workshop format, with appropriate written materials, as described in this proposal, which will be fully replicable by scores of interested educational and related organizations, societies and individuals.

5-20 Bullets help set off key passages.

each other. Therefore, if you find an important photograph in a newspaper or a journal, make every effort to track down the original print.

Movement. A sense of movement or change over time is often useful when seeking to portray a sequence of architectural spaces. An effective way to show this is to use strips from a 35mm black and white contact sheet, the frames of which were taken at properly spaced intervals. The method is also helpful for showing scenes of office personnel at work or in conference.

Special effects. Photo laboratories and printing platemakers offer special techniques that use photographs as a basis for an out-of-the-ordinary impact on the printed page. Some of the more valuable are:

● Drop-out half-tones. The platemaker removes some dots from the plate to make for greater contrast. This is also known as highlighting.

● Aging. Special screens are introduced into the platemaking process. These supply an overall artificial texture that can imitate the feel of an old etching or of brush-strokes.

● Retouching. Using an airbrush, a professional retoucher works on the original print to play up, play down, add, change, or eliminate selected features. A skilled retoucher can remove people, cars, or unwanted signs from buildings, sharpen up details, and in other ways adapt a photograph to your needs. The greater his skill, the more natural the outcome.

● High-contrast line conversion. This means dropping out all grays and converting the photograph into a total black and white image. You gain in drama what you lose in detail.

● Duo-tone. If you have a second color, you can obtain great richness in reproducing a black and white photograph by calling for a duo-tone. The platemaker makes two plates from your original—one in black, one in the second color. The printed combination of the black and colored dots yields the rich effect.

If you wish to explore photographic printing effects further, consult one of several fine publications issued by the major paper manufacturers. For a cross section of these, see the reference section at the end of this book.

Charts and tables. Tables of facts and figures can add order to a page or turn it into a chaotic jumble, as can a free-floating graph. It helps to arrange tabular information in clear-cut columns, aligned along an imaginary vertical line to the left or right (see 5-27). Avoid grouping more than 8 to 10 lines of tabular material without a "relief" separation. For separation, an extra space or a thin (1 to 2 pt.) line or rule running the width of the table helps clarity. To title key subcategories within a table, use the same typeface a degree or two bolder, or else use a second color if possible.

When setting up a table on the typewriter, rely on subtleties of spacing for legibility. For example, *single* space the main tabular material (with a *double* space or a typed full-length line every 8 to 10 lines of type), and *triple*

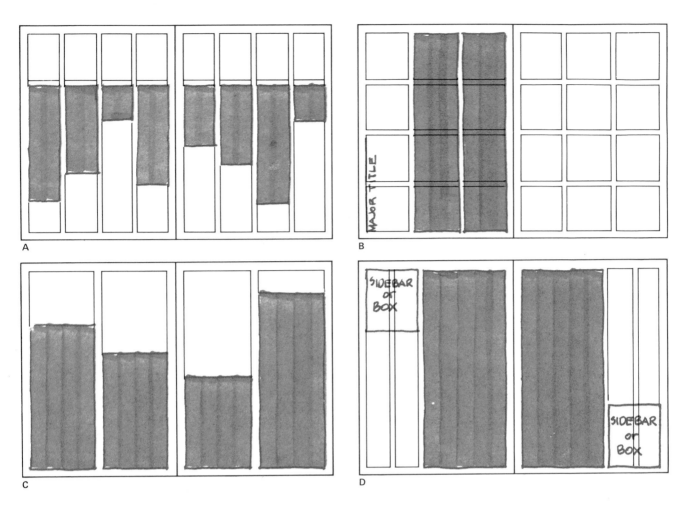

5-21 Text is a versatile building block for page design.

5-22 The strength of the photograph is in its ability to show people and objects in context—buildings in a landscape, a new building next to an older neighbor, staff members in each other's company, and students using a schoolroom.

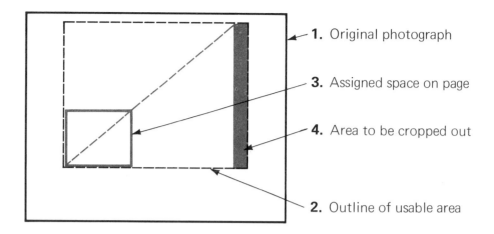

1. Original photograph

3. Assigned space on page

4. Area to be cropped out

2. Outline of usable area

or

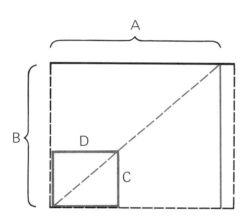

$$A = \frac{BD}{C}$$

5-23 Photos may be scaled to size geometrically in four steps (above) or arithmetically (left).

space major breaks. Remember that in setting up tables and charts, too much blank space can be as confusing as too little.

No matter how lucidly the table or graph is set up, the overall impact on a page will be spotty. To avoid this, there are three options. *First*, consider a fine dot pattern, or screen, over the material to provide a well-defined edge. *Second*, create a negative, or reverse, image of the table, with white type and a black or dark-colored background. Note, though, that white type on a dark background is tiring to read in large amounts—limit this technique, therefore, to tables, charts, and boxes or side bars, and avoid reversing whole pages of running text. *Third*, thicken key lines in a graph or, if possible, print these lines in a second color. This will focus attention to it and detract somewhat from the ragged nature of most graphs (see 5-28 and 5-29).

Information can often be organized for logical clarity and visual impact in the form of a matrix chart. (A typical example of such a chart is 5-2.) For instance, a research report may require relating different building types to applicable building codes, standards, and regulations. By listing and arranging the building types in a column and the various regulations horizontally across the top of a squared grid, it is simple to indicate, with a bullet or other symbol, the type and degree of interaction wherever a horizontal and vertical line intersect (see 5-30).

Another way of compressing information for graphic benefit is visual representation of a process or of an organization as a flow chart. In lieu of merely connecting the usual plain, labeled rectangles with lines, consider these four alternative techniques:

1. Reverse the text in the boxes. For a low budget report, this may be done simply by typing the words on to stick-on labels, affixing the labels to black or dark paper in the desired arrangement, applying appropriate connecting lines, and ordering a negative photostat, which then becomes the original.

2. Use shadow lines to create a three-dimensional effect of the boxes.

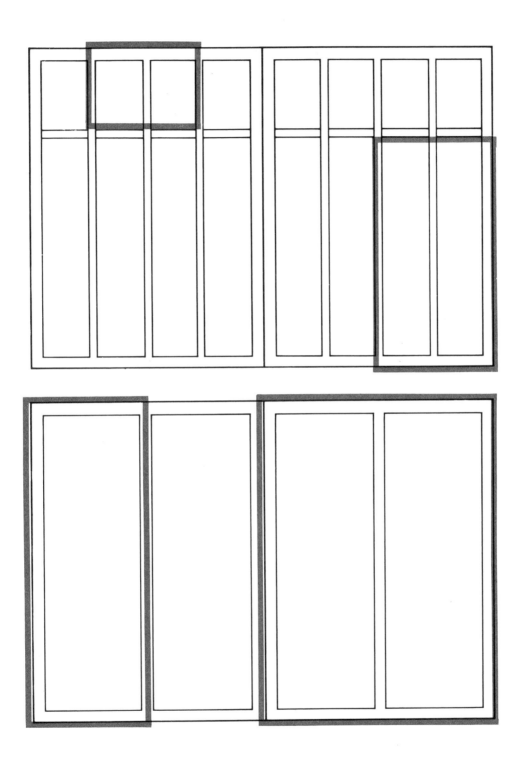

5-24 Bleeds can make for a strong visual effect on a page or spread, but should be used sparingly for greatest impact.

5-25 Choice of screen determines the effect of graininess of image. The 55-line screen (right) is coarse compared to the 133 line screen (opposite page).

5-26 A moiré or double-screen effect is caused by using a halftone as the basis for making a new halftone.

3. Use not only rectangles but also squares, circles, diamonds, and other shapes whenever there is more than one category of titles. Most stationery stores carry a wide selection of label shapes suitable for typing.

4. To show relationships, consider wider lines, which can be printed in a light screen—in color, if available (see 5-31).

Maps. Maps are a challenge because of their size and the variety of detail they must often represent. If you need to show maps in a brochure fact sheet or planning report, much depends on the budget. At the simplest level, principal areas, streets, buildings, and special features are drawn on a base sheet and identified with a compatible series of textured screens and typefaces. If a phased sequence of development must be shown, order photostats of the base sheet—one for each phase—and use screens and typefaces as before to record the progressive development phases. You can often obtain a black and white base map from a bought ordinance or from other maps in color—the maps are just converted by a special process (now offered by most reproduction houses) that screens out unwanted color and allows you to impose your own information.

Color simplifies the task of identifying map areas and development sequences, but for a price—in in-house preparation time and printing production. Use an overlay sheet for each additional color up to a maximum of four (including black), being sure to register each sheet with the one below using special marks (see 5-32). If the colored areas do not touch but are free floating, they can all be on the same base map and merely coded for color.

You may obtain more than four colors (including black) by combining any two, three, or four to create a new color. Any printer will furnish a color chart showing how his inks may be mixed to form new colors. In practice, it is more realistic and certainly less costly to try to cover all possibilities with four colors (including black) especially since many additional shadings are possible by using varying screens (for example, 75%, 50%, and 30%) of the same color. The most expensive option is to print the transparent overlays along with the base map, usually on acetate, and bind them into the report. In any event, do not attempt to carry out effects of this complexity without professional graphic advice.

As to map size, you can print a large map to fold out for a modest surcharge. In practice, the repeated opening and refolding of a large map into a small pack is both irritating for the user and bad for the map's joints. If a fold-out is not possible and the original must be reduced photographically to fit the page size, be sure to pick the type sizes carefully so they will be legible when scaled down.

White space

White space is the third element of design, and the most neglected. Yet it is a key element in making pages more attractive and readable. Select a typical cross section of letters, proposals, portfolio fact sheets, and exhibit panels, and take a close look at how white space is used around the text and artwork (see 5-33). Note in many cases how unorganized it is—instead of simple shapes, it

Exhibit III
Life cycle characteristics of five retail institutions

Institution	Approximate date of innovation	Approximate date of maximum market share	Approximate number of years required to reach maturity	Estimated maximum market share	Estimated 1975 market share
Downtown department store	1860	1940	80	8.5% of total retail sales	1.1%
Variety store	1910	1955	45	16.5% of general merchandise sales	9.5%
Supermarket	1930	1965	35	70.0% of grocery store sales	64.5%
Discount department store	1950	1970	20	6.5% of total retail sales	5.7%
Home improvement center	1965	1980 (estimate)	15	35.0% of hardware and building material sales	25.3%

Sources: National Bureau of Economic Research, U.S. Department of Commerce, *Progressive Grocer, Discount Merchandiser,* National Retail Hardware Association, and Management Horizons, Inc.

5-27 Tabular material is easier to absorb when arranged in clear columns aligned along imaginary vertical lines. Horizontal rules also help.

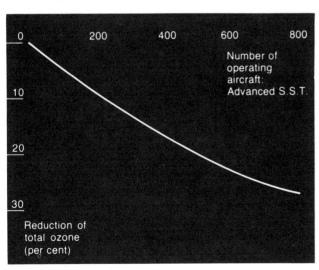

Table 1			
	Increased return required (versus current year) if income is received in:		
Interest rate increase (percentage points)	3 years (percentage points)	5 years (percentage points)	7 years (percentage points)
+1	3	5	7
+3	9	15	22
+5	15	27	41
+7	22	40	60
+10	33	61	95

Number of operating aircraft: Advanced S.S.T.

Reduction of total ozone (per cent)

5-28 A graph or table "dropped out" in white against a dark background makes for a less ragged appearance on the page.

5-29 Thickened lines (right) or use of a second color (above right) will bring out the clarity of a graph.

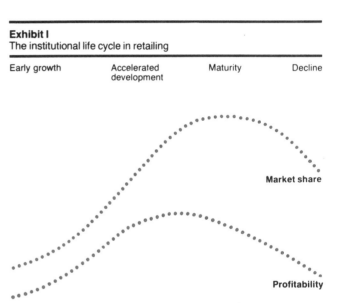

Exhibit I
The institutional life cycle in retailing

Early growth   Accelerated development   Maturity   Decline

Market share

Profitability

Note: The duration of the stages (horizontal scale) is variable, depending on many circumstances. The four stages are portrayed equally on the time scale for schematic purposes only.

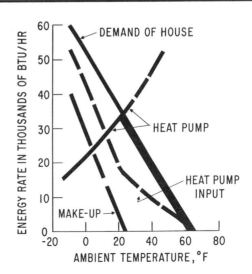

5-30 A matrix was used to good advantage to relate building types and applicable building codes.

TYPICAL BUILDING TYPES	P.L. 90-480 as Amended; Federal Property Regulations	Federal GSA Construction Standards	Locally applicable building code**	Zoning ordinance	Health Code (State & Local)	Housing Code (1–2 family dwellings)	Housing Code (Multiple dwellings)	Fire-safety Code	Plumbing Code	Electrical Code	State Housing Construction Corp.	State Educational Construction Authority	Regional Hospital Planning Council	FEPM (HEW) Construction regulations	Veterans Administration Construction Standards	Subdivision regulations	FHA Property Standards	OSHA regulations	Regulations of private food, service, hotel, retail, theater, service station chains	Insurance companies
Federal Buildings	X	X		X														X		
Other Public Buildings	X*		X	X	X			X	X	X								X		
Hospitals	X*		X	X	X		X	X	X	X			X		X	X		X		X
Schools	X*		X	X	X			X	X	X		X						X		X
Colleges	X*		X	X	X			X	X	X		X						X		X
Churches			X	X	X			X	X	X								X		X
Housing	X*		X	X	X	X	X	X	X	X	X					X	X	X		X
Theaters	X*		X	X	X			X	X	X								X	X	X
Industrial Plants			X	X	X			X	X	X								X		X
Shopping Centers and Other Commercial Buildings			X	X	X			X	X	X								X	X	X

* Where Federally financed
** May incorporate State architectural barrier legislation

snakes in and out of the printed matter in confusing, intricate configurations.

Look also for the ratio of white space to the rest of the page. Too little white space will tire the reader by throwing at him too strong and continuous a mix of words and pictures. Too much of it not only is a waste of paper but will quickly convey to the reader a feeling of lack of substance.

Logos and letterheads. Some designers distinguish between a *logotype*, which is derived from letters; *a symbol*, a simplified image with recognizable parts such as a flower, star, or castle; and *a mark*, an abstract device. For convenience we will use the term logotype, or logo.

A logotype, or logo, should come out of need and not fashion. It is a device made from letters or symbols (or both) to capture a reader's or viewer's attention with enough force so he will recall it and associate it with a company, product, publication, or event.

Why, then, would a professional design firm, in addition to spelling out its full name on the letterhead, brochure cover, report, or exhibit panel, also require a logo?

The reasons for a good logo are several:

1. On a table full of proposals and brochures, it will provide a distinctive focus.

2. On the letterhead and related paperware, the logo has potential value as the graphic link between all communications coming out of your office.

3. On your gate or front door, it will make you feel good.

4. On an exhibit panel, a logo can have the same impact that it does on a brochure or a proposal cover—a mnemonic device that will help connect your firm with the project shown on the exhibit panel.

Graphic designers will develop a logo as one of their services. Several of the press-on letter manufacturers will produce a logo to your designs in different sizes and colors suitable for use on report covers and other documents. Contact them for delivery time and minimum orders. A successful logo has the following features:

Distinctiveness. It should look like no other. This is becoming harder and harder, as a major broadcasting network discovered in 1976 when it chose a logo identical to that developed by a small midwestern studio, but paid one thousand times as much for it.

Logic. There must be a reasonable tie-in to the company's name or services. Some ingenious effects are possible with the first letters of the partners' last names. Bricks, compasses, scaffolding, rolled steel sections, plant

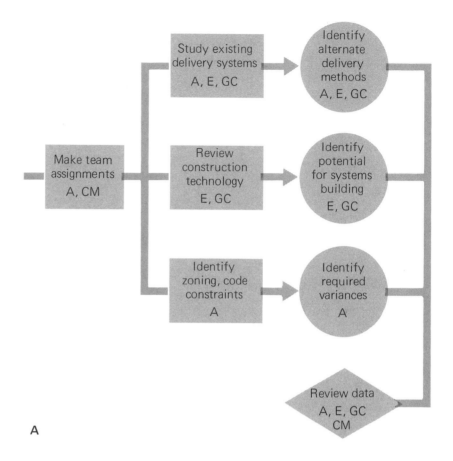

A

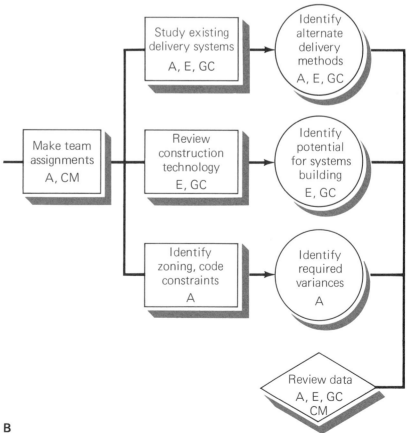

5-31 Two approaches to showing linkages between events on a flow-chart. The same concepts may be used when showing relationships on an organization chart.

B

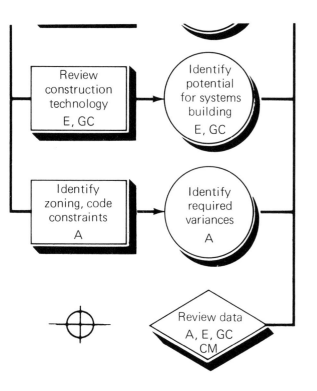

5-32 Register marks help engravers and printers align overlays when more than one color is used.

stalks, chairs, and tables have sometimes been used in stylized form to create logos, with mixed results.

Simplicity. A logo is no place to bring in involved combinations of wispy shapes, chiefly due to the following requirement.

Versatility. A logo must meet many needs. Its parts must be simple enough so it can be reduced in scale without loss of clarity. It should look as natural on your business cards as it does etched very large in the glass of your entrance lobby. It should work well solid or in outline, in black as well as in color, on a light background or dropped out in white against a dark background, or embossed (see 5-34).

The use and abuse of aids

The task of preparing copy for the typesetter and layouts for the printer is made easier by making use of a number of aids and devices that either are on the market or can be made simply in-house. Some typical aids are described.

The publication-at-a-glance. Whether you are planning a 96-page planning report, a brochure system, or a four-page client newsletter, it helps to have an overview of the entire piece. To develop such a thumbnail picture, draw a series of pairs of pages in the intended format (see 5-35). Each pair need not be very high—you should be able to fit up to fifteen pairs of thumbnail pages on an 8½ x 11 sheet. Duplicate these sheets and use as many as you need to test preliminary layouts for good front-to-back flow of subject matter. Do not try to use them for detailed layouts.

Manuscripts typing sheets. These sheets are especially helpful for repetitive items, such as additions to your brochure system, planning reports, and, for the large firm, the client newsletter. The sheet can be as simple or detailed as you need to make it. It can contain: numbered horizontal lines, spaced to conform to double-spacing on your typewriter; and vertical lines marking the beginning and end of your average line width. For example, if a column of type on the brochure fact sheet measures 44 letters, or characters, then the vertical lines on the typing sheet should be spaced 44 characters apart. This system allows you to convert the number of typed lines of copy into actual typeset lines of the final piece at a glance. Please note that you will need two right-hand vertical lines—one for *elite* type and another, slightly to the right of it, for the larger *pica* type. Avoid using a typewriter with proportional spacing for typing manuscript copy (see 5-36).

Dummies. A dummy is a worksheet the size of your publication. It is used for loosely positioning the various parts of the layout. Dummies of all the pages are sometimes assembled to create a realistic mock-up of the final report.

Grids and grid sheets. The grid is designed by the graphic designer to give himself and those who will prepare camera-ready mechanicals a tool for layout. It is usually prepared only if there is a multiple of similar pages, such as a report or the components of a portfolio/ brochure system. The grid helps establish a column layout and reference points for alignment. Transparent grids provide options for design and layout (5-37). A set of grids may provide for the following:

- A two-column format (text only)
- A three-column format (text only)
- A format for laying out artwork and related captions
- A mixed format (text and artwork)
- Special pages (table of contents, lists)

Grids serve as a discipline for the orderly and controlled layout of a publication, whether it is a four-page project fact sheet or a 72-page feasibility report. They allow you to be flexible in positioning titles, charts, photographs, captions, and text.

A good grid offers the chance to design layouts that are symmetrical or asymmetrical, dense or loose, and "weighted" to the top or the bottom of the paper.

A rigid grid allows for few or no exceptions, and the resulting publication may therefore be very repetitious. A grid that has too many layout options built into it usually fails to help make the publication unified.

Grids may be preprinted on grid sheets in nonreproducible blue ink and are used for positioning the final camera-ready art (or mechanicals). An extra ⅛ in./.32cm is left all around to allow for inaccuracy in trimming after printing and before binding. Grid sheets can come as left-hand and right-hand pages, and the two differ only in such details as location of page numbers and width of vertical margins. Some graphic designers prefer to work with grid sheets printed up as pairs of pages.

Screens. These help superimpose visual order when printed over irregular or untidy material, such as charts and graphs, floor plans, and sections. Screens are patterns of dots (or lines) the size (or the thickness) and density of which determines whether the overall tone appears to be black or a shade of gray. Density is measured as a percentage, and the screens are usually sold in 10% increments from 5% to 95%. A 70% screen is very dark; a 10% screen very light (see 5-38). To select a screen to overprint a table or drawing, the percentage should be light enough to contrast with the lines of the drawing (20 to 30% is a good upper limit), or dark enough to allow for a white line "drop out" of the chart or graph.

Although art supply stores sell screens in adhesive-backed sheets in a wide variety of shades, you will obtain better results by merely outlining the desired screened shape on an overlay, and letting the printer put in the screen.

Press-on type. The lure as well as the bane of our graphic vocabulary, press-on type is in great demand. One manufacturer's catalog alone lists 211 different typefaces, serif and sans-serif, each with up to a dozen size variations, not to mention a plethora of rules, stripes, patterns, and symbols. There are also tapes of diverse widths, colors and configurations.

Notwithstanding this horn of plenty and its dangers, press-on type is a simple and effective way of producing titles for proposals, exhibit panels, and other one-of-a-kind items. Similarly the various bullets, squares, triangles, north arrows (solid or hollow), and rules and bars, are a straightforward way of adding accent to dull material. To avoid giving in to uninhibited fun, it is im-

Project:	Public School 55
Architect:	Richard G. Stein and Associates
Location:	Koch Blvd., Osborne Ave., Arden Road, Staten Island
Owner:	Board of Education City of New York
Consultants:	
Structural:	Fraioli Blum Yesselman
Mechanical:	S. A. Bogen
Landscape:	Peter Rolland
Estimating:	McKee Berger Mansueto, Inc.
Acoustics:	Michael J. Kodoras, Inc.
Graphics:	Chermayeff & Geismar Associates
Specifications:	Leon Langner
Artist:	Costantino Nivola
Capacity:	980 Pupils
Building area:	78,270 S.F.
Bid Date:	March 1964
Construction Cost:	$1,999,895—25.50/SF
Cost per pupil:	$2,040.00

Description:	The school was designed to provide elementary education for 980 children in a rapidly growing semi-suburban area of Staten Island.
Site:	The site slopes sharply with a difference of twenty-two feet between streets that are less than 200 ft. apart. This allowed the building to be kept low in scale with all the classrooms on two levels and the lower level containing the cafeteria and service facilities to be kept out of the ground.
	The areas outside the allowable building area become kindergarten playground, school gardens, terraces and sitting areas. Immediately adjacent to the school property is a playground jointly operated by the Parks Department and the Board of Education.
Building:	Starting with a typical Board of Education program several new features resulted from a complete restudy of all the components of an elementary public school.
	The plan is a pinwheel with the classrooms located around an interior gymnasium and auditorium.
	The typical classroom was given a new type of window wall treatment. A low series of horizontal windows provide glarefree light and outlook for the pupils. At the front of the classroom a projecting vertical window brings a glow of light onto the area of the chalkboard and teacher's desk while shielding the students from the direct brightness. It has a low concrete platform suitable for potted plants and growing flowers. From the outside, the projecting windows reestablish the scale and variety that are often lost in large public buildings.

In addition, provisions were made for experimental team teaching. On each teaching floor two classrooms can be combined for larger demonstrations and another classroom can be subdivided for individual instruction. The auditorium can be used for still larger teaching purposes.

The school is built of simple natural materials that are immediately understandable to children. The structure is a reinforced concrete frame. Exterior walls are composed of brick cavity infill walls and aluminum windows. Interior materials are exposed concrete, ribbed ceilings, plaster and block walls and applied finishes as required for education and maintenance purposes.

Intense colors were used throughout the interior as well as in the asphalt paving outside.

---

istration formulated wage-price "guidelines" as an official index of productivity to which labor leaders were supposed to tailor their wage demands. Later, the so-called "jaw-boning" tactic was employed to use public pressure, via Presidential statements, to keep wages and prices from spiraling higher. The present Administration's program has enjoyed some success in placing a limit on wage increases, but the effect does not seem to bear heavily upon the inflationary process, perhaps because wage ceilings were applied too late. In any event, controls are administratively hard to enforce and can be evaded in many ways.

The fact remains that actual living standards cannot be increased more rapidly than the actual output of goods. When the total disposable income rises more rapidly than the output of goods and services, inflation is the result.

Taxation

In general, higher tax rates combined with wage and price controls would be expected to slow inflation simply by reducing spendable income. This, in turn, helps to reduce the scramble for goods. If the consumer demand is allowed to continue unabated, supported by growing disposable income, prices could break through controls and rationing could be required.

Anti-inflation Measures

Quite obviously, the inflationary spiral in the United States has reached alarming proportions. There are a number of measures that can be taken to arrest the inflationary process caused by excess aggregate demand:

1. **Reducing government purchases**—if prices are stable, but investment has increased, it is only necessary to reduce the level of government purchases by an amount equal to the expected increase in investment. However, if the resources released as a result of lower government purchases cannot be used for business investment, then prices may continue to rise and additional measures are called for. While the Administration ·has attempted to reduce Federal spending in a number of areas, the Congress has not modified its posture toward spending. Federal money continues to be pumped into an overheated economy.

2. **Reducing consumption**—it would be difficult, indeed, to induce the consumer to curb his con-

sumption. In fact, not too long ago the consumer was urged to pump his disposable income back onto the economy as though it were a patriotic duty!

Consumption can be slowed by increasing the proportional tax rate or raising the lump-sum tax. Obviously an increase in the tax rate is not totally sufficient in itself, and must be coupled with other anti-inflation measures.

3. **Wage and price guidelines**—if wage and price ceilings are imposed uniformly, they can serve a useful purpose. The problem, as we have seen, is that such measures have been irregularly and sporadically instituted.[3] Politically, wage freezes are an explosive issue. It might, in fact, be seriously questioned what effect falling wages and prices might have upon the contemporary American psyche. The fear of a boom-bust cycle is deeply ingrained. If wages and prices were to decline significantly during a short period of time after the alarming rise, the effect might be a serious deflation "rebound."

Retail Pharmacy and Inflation

Retail pharmacy, like any segment of American business, is affected by inflation in a number of ways. Perhaps the most observable effect is the increase in cost of most of the usual business expenses, particularly the rising cost of labor. Recent increases in the prime interest rate, at this writing 9%, and other indications of "tighter" money in the immediate future, point to restrictions in the supply of money for expansion and other purposes in the immediate future. Finally, tax increases, while unpopular, may well be in the offing if the current Administration's anti-inflation program is unsuccessful.

Pharmacists like consumers, are watching the present economic cycles with a mixture of feelings—those of caution, skepticism, concern and reserved optimism. It remains to be seen what long-term effect Phases IV and V will have upon the economy. One thing seems certain—both wages and prices will be considerably different from those of the 1960's.

[1] Samuelson, Paul A., **Economics, An Introductory Analysis,** Seventh Edition, McGraw-Hill Book Company, New York, 1967, pp. 260 ff.

[2] Heilbroner, Robert L., **The Economic Problem,** Third Edition, Prentice-Hall, Inc., Englewood Cliffs, New Jersey, 1972, p. 376 ff.

[3] Keiser, Norman F., **Macroeconomics,** Random House, New York, 1971, pp. 225 ff.

5-33 Clean organization of white space makes the difference between clarity (top) and confusion (above).

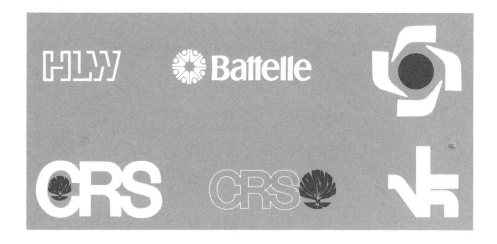

5-34 The well-designed logo looks good solid and in outline, on a light background, or dropped out, in black and in color.

5-35 Thumbnail layout sheets are used to obtain an overall view of a planned publication.

portant to have a consistent plan in the use of these aids, from the beginning of the planning report or proposal to the very end. Select a coherent "vocabulary" of title faces and accents, and adhere to them without fail.

The quality of text or longer titles prepared in press-on type is never equal to that of machine typesetting. Moreover, especially if used liberally, it is wasteful of sometimes highly paid in-house labor—like most hand operations. Therefore, when the type is to be used over and over (such as for the logo on a brochure project factsheet), where there is a great quantity required (such as in titles for divisions of a planning report), or where top quality counts (such as in the titles and text of an exhibit panel), it is false economy to use press-on type. A commercial typesetter will do a superior, faster job at a cost little or no higher than type pressed-on by hand in-house.

The log sheet. A management rather than a graphic aid, the log sheet is an invaluable tool for keeping track of the status of a printed project. The larger or more complex the project, the greater its use. The log sheet is best arranged by columns, using the first column to identify the page and the other columns to trace its progress (see 5-39). The log sheet is ideal for monitoring long, printed reports and the development of a brochure system, where many elements often progress at different speeds.

Color

Color is a useful additive to good graphics but a dangerous substitute for unimaginative design. When you add color, you are expanding the scope of your effort in terms of in-house labor and outside costs, and the benefits must justify this.

Color is best used in six kinds of situations: to help provide instant visual *continuity* throughout the pages of a report or brochure system; to provide instant *contrast* between covers or dividers and the inside pages of a report; to provide instant *recognition of key elements* on a page (such as a headline, title, letterhead, or logo); to provide instant *legibility* of complex charts, tables, or drawings by enhancing the contrast between the parts; to provide instant *pleasure* at seeing a building or a product shown in its real colors; and to provide an instant *feel of quality*.

The key word is *instant*. Color has the quality of attracting the eye far more directly than pure black. Used judiciously, it can replace a great deal of otherwise elaborate design effort in black and white to make a desired impact on the reader. Even one extra color will provide a great deal of flexibility, as its use in the design of this book shows. Color used sparingly is more effective than in a 50:50 ratio with black. Color should either dominate clearly, or be used for accent only.

E 1/13   P 1/13   E 1/20   P 1/20 E 2/13

1 HOUSING

2 CHARACTERISTICS

3 Four ingredients of housing are discussed in this re-

4 port. They are: siting, design, construction methods,

5 and materials.

6 SITING

7 With the relatively primitive wind risk maps, little

8 regard has been given to the placement of houses in

9 relation to danger. Good site location or orientation

10 linked to local terrain and natural cover can be, but

11 usually has not been, determined from historical wind

12 data. This data provides the frequency, velocity and

13 direction of the prevailing winds, especially in their

14 extreme form. Hence, windstorm damage can be reduced

15 a great deal by placing buildings so they are protected

16 by hills, stands of trees and other natural elements.

17 DESIGN

18 Windstorm resistance can be notably improved by various

19 simple measures. These include horizontal bracing of

20 certain types of roofs over houses made of adobe mason-

21 ry and other small unit construction; a more rational

22 disposition of openings in bearing walls; reinforcement

23 of critical areas of a building subject to being over-

24 stressed; and the strengthening of connections at

25 joints.

26 All this may not be enough. Special studies on how

27 turbulence in a storm is distributed are required. It is

E = elite typewriter

P = pica typewriter

5-36 Frequently used formats are best translated to preprinted typing sheets. ''E'' denotes elite type; ''P'' pica. Numbers indicate typeset width of column in picas, a printer's measure equal to about 1/6''.

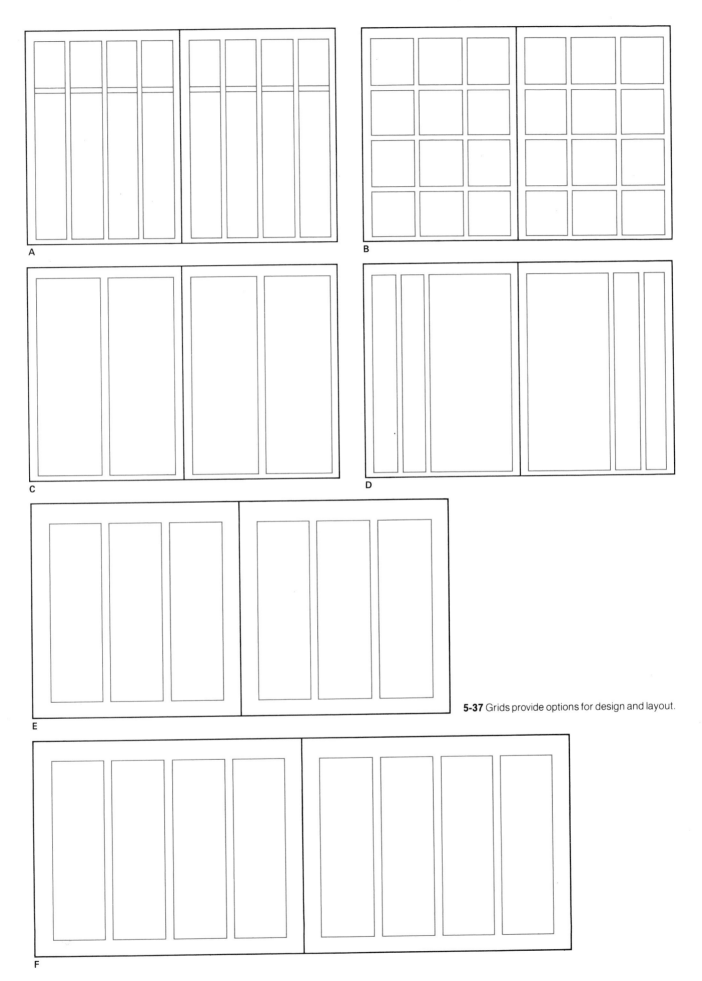

5-37 Grids provide options for design and layout.

A

B

C

D

E

F

Using color. Color can be used in three ways—by adding it to elements, such as dividers, letterheads, logos, titles, captions, key lines on drawings, and key positions of texts; by using the colors as found in the original art (colored photoprint, transparency, or rendering); and by using colored paper stock.

The first and last routes are the simplest and least costly. A decision to employ color for emphasis should be carefully planned and coordinated so it is applied consistently to the same elements—not to main titles on one page, subtitles on the next, dividers on the third.

Colored paper stock used with a small, two-color printing press is a simple way to obtain color without much additional press work. A good solid light shade of brown, for example, blends handsomely with basic black, along with accents of red. By using more than one shade of paper stock, you can differentiate the parts of a longer report or proposal (see 5-40).

To specify color, obtain a swatchbook of Pantone Matching System (PMS) colors from your printer. Each color corresponds to a printing ink. Most are identified by a three-digit number, but some are identified by a name, such as Super Warm Red or Rubine Red. Swatches come on matte and glossy paper stock and should be selected according to the paper stock to be used.

Working with a full-color photograph, transparency, or rendering is a far more elaborate and costly process. The print, transparency, or rendering must be broken down or separated by the printer into its component (so-called process) colors of yellow, cyan, magenta (roughly, yellow, blue, and red), and black by means of an expensive separation procedure. He then makes a separate printing plate for each color.

Four-color process requires a great deal of hand labor to prepare and a corresponding amount of additional time in the press room. As an example of cost, a full-page black and white half-tone engraving may cost $25. The price of a set of four-color separation plates may exceed $400.

Converting from color to black and white. An important sidelight in the use of color is the need to be conscious of how key colors reproduce in black and white. Two situations in particular can give rise to problems—the conversion of a four-color slide or photograph to black and white, and the translation of colored felt-tipped and magic marker work into black and white.

As to the first problem, the best thing to do is not to submit the four-color original directly to the engraver,

but rather to first test the result at moderate cost by requesting a photographic laboratory to use its screening and filtering resources to prepare an internegative, a black and white negative, and then a positive print. By submitting three or four candidate shots to the lab, you will quickly see which (if any) lend themselves to true reproduction in black and white.

As for renderings, experienced professional renderers expect their work to be reproduced in black and white as well as in color, and will select pigments with that in mind.

The second problem—translating colored felt-tipped and magic marker work into black and white—may be solved by selecting the two dozen or so magic marker hues in most frequent use in your office and placing a 2″ / 5.1 cm strip of each color on a sheet of plain white paper, while recording next to each strip its identifying number. Order from an engraver a half-tone reproduction and a line (or ungraded tone) reproduction. Using the identifying numbers as a guide, place a dab of the original color next to each now gray or black strip. This will serve as a guide to your staff using magic markers to prepare a drawing or rendering for printing reproduction (see 5-4).

In sum, color should be used as part of an overall graphic plan for your publication, and not inserted arbitrarily on a random, page-by-page basis. Because of its unusual optical impact when used next to black material, use color sparingly—a little of it goes a very long way.

Paper

The paper you or your graphic designer specify is a relatively small part of the printing budget, and its impact on the reader, except in cases of blatant incongruity, is largely subliminal. Yet the choices of paper type, weight, and finish are so many, and the pleasure of a well-chosen paper so great, that a close concern for paper can be very rewarding.

Papers come *uncoated* and *coated*. The former offer glare-free reading, the latter a feeling of greater quality and a strong, even brilliant, image.

The two categories in turn come in many grades. *Grade* refers not only to its size, weight, and grain but to its intended use (see 5-41).

Before selecting a paper, ask for swatches usually furnished to printers by paper manufacturers. Check for opacity and grain. Do not just look at swatches, though. Relate the paper to its use, to the proposed ink colors, and to the compatibility of the cover and "run-of-the-

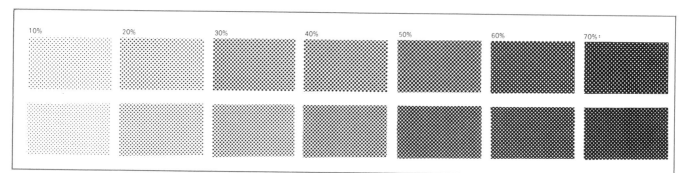

5-38 Screens help to impose visual order on a busy page—a range from 10% to 70% is shown.

ITEM: Planning report for Greggsville Medical Center

DUE DATE: 24 MAY 1977

PAGE	Type ordered	Artwork complete	Type in	Proofread	Layout complete	Review	Mechanicals out	Page proofs in	Page proofs out	Press proofs in	Press proofs out	Delivery at office
COVERS Front Back	4/2	4/10	4/9	4/12	4/17	4/22	5/1	5/7	5/11	5/18	5/18	5/22
DIVIDERS A B C	4/2	4/12	4/9	4/12	4/17	4/22	5/1	5/6	5/10	5/18	5/18	5/22
PAGES 1 2 3 4 5 6 7	4/2	4/16	4/9	4/16	4/19	4/22	4/30	5/9	5/14	5/19	5/20	5/22
8 9 10 11 12 &c.	4/2	4/16	4/11	4/17	4/21	4/22	5/1	5/11	5/16	5/19	5/20	5/22

5-39 The log is a helpful management aid for keeping track of progress on multipage publications.

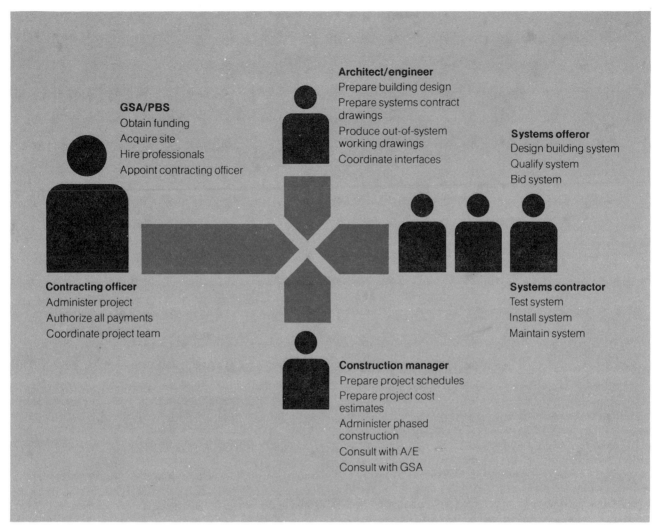

GSA/PBS
Obtain funding
Acquire site
Hire professionals
Appoint contracting officer

Architect/engineer
Prepare building design
Prepare systems contract
drawings
Produce out-of-system
working drawings
Coordinate interfaces

Systems offeror
Design building system
Qualify system
Bid system

Contracting officer
Administer project
Authorize all payments
Coordinate project team

Systems contractor
Test system
Install system
Maintain system

Construction manager
Prepare project schedules
Prepare project cost
estimates
Administer phased
construction
Consult with A/E
Consult with GSA

5-40 Versatile effects are possible by using a combination of black, one other color, and tinted paper stock. In this example, the background paper color was a light buff.

Grade	Use
Offset (Text)	Inside of brochures, reports, newsletters (printed offset).
Book	Inside of brochures, reports, newsletters (printed letterpress).
Bond	Correspondence, news releases. Similar to offset paper but has added erasing feature.
Cover	Covers. Has greater strength than above papers.
Index	Manuals and similar pieces subject to unusual wear.
Bristol	A stiffer paper suitable for die-cutting, embossing, scoring, and folding; hence may be used for brochure system folders, and formal announcements—such as promotions, relocations, and mergers.

5-41 Common paper grades and their uses.

book" stock. Then get a realistic impression by asking the printer or paper supplier to do a full-sized mock-up of the publication. Heft the mock-up, leaf through it, and obtain a feel for appropriateness. Papers may be used to convey substance or lightness, slickness or austerity, clumsiness or elegance.

To specify papers (and this is important as part of an overall specification on which to obtain printer's bids), you need to spell out *grade, finish, color,* and *weight.* A typical paper specification for a printed planning report might read:

Text: Coated matte, Starlight White, or equal, 60 lb.

Cover: Felt finished, Pearl Blue, or equal, 60 lb.

Even though the cover and text stocks in this example are both designated as 60 lb., this does not mean they are the same weight. Weights of paper are based on the weight of 500 sheets of that grade's basic size. Since the basic size of text stock is 25 x 38 in. / 63.5 x 96.52 cm and that of cover stock 20 x 26 in. / 50.8 x 66 cm (or 45% less area), cover stock of the same *designated* weight actually weighs almost twice (or is twice as thick as) a sheet of text stock of the same size. The table in 5-42 gives a synopsis of popular paper weights in the various grades.

The paper specification must also state the number of copies to be printed, the trim size or format (e.g., 10 x 10 in./25.4 x 25.4 cm), and the type of binding. You are more likely to obtain the desired paper by using a manufacturer's trade name and color based on your review of the swatch. The printer should then consult with you or your graphic designer if he wants to substitute another paper due to delivery or other problems.

Even though paper is a fairly small part of a printing budget, major economies are possible by designing a publication in a format that will not cause wastage when cut from the standard 25 x 38 in. / 63.5 x 96.52 cm text or 20 x 26 in. / 50.8 x 66 cm cover sheet size. A 25 x 38 in. / 63.5 x 96.52 cm text sheet, for example, will give eight 8½ x 11 in. / 21.59 x 27.94 cm sheets with minimum wastage. Many innovative styles are possible by further folding and/or binding of the 8½ x 11 in. / 21.59 x 27.94 cm sheet. The standard 17 x 22 in. / 43.18 x 55.9 cm bond sheet size also lends itself to many variations (see 5-43).

Special finishes are available to protect and give a feeling of depth to the cover. Covers can be varnished in a matte or glossy finish, or they can be plastic-coated, sheet laminated, or liquid laminated. Most printers and reproduction houses carry samples.

Paper is an important part of communications and should be selected as carefully for everyday correspondence as it is for the one-time, glossy report. Those interested in a more detailed study of paper should turn to the major paper manufacturers. Paper making is highly competitive; as a result, the producers offer a wealth of high-quality printed information on papers, manufacture, types, and use. (See the reference section.)

Binding

An otherwise strong report or proposal can be marred by neglecting the binding, the last of the ingredients of a successful publication. Before choosing a binding, review the main determinants. These may include:

1. The need for the publication to lie flat when open.

2. The need to print a title on the spine.

3. The need to convey an impression of permanence *or* of flexibility.

Bond	Book text	Cover	Vellum bristol	Index	Tag
		Basis weight (lbs.)			
17" X 22"	25" X 38"	20" X 26"	22½" X 28½"	25½" X 30½"	24" X 36"
16	40				
20	50				
28	70				
36	90	50	57		90
		60		90	100
		80	100		
		90		140	150

5-42 Synopsis of popular paper grades. Weight designations mean little in terms of actual weights. Equivalent weights are arranged horizontally. Note, for example, that a ream (500 sheets) of *90 lb* book or text stock weighs roughly the same as a ream of *50 lb* cover stock.

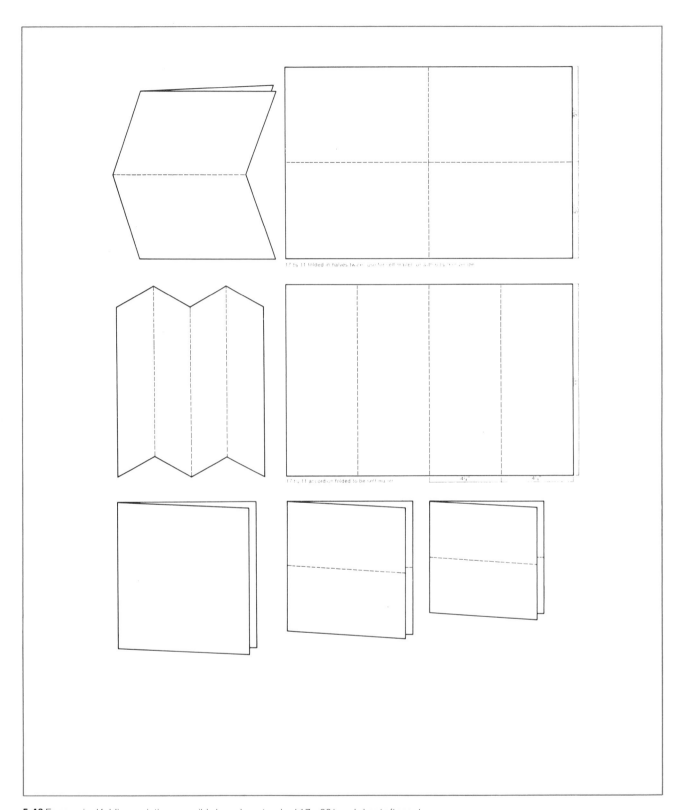

5-43 Economical folding variations possible based on standard 17 x 22 bond sheet after cutting into two 17 x 11 pieces.

4. The need for a sturdy cover *or* the need for the top regular sheet to serve as the cover (called self-covered).

5. The number of pages or thickness of the piece.

6. The need to replace, add, or remove pages in the future.

7. The need to fold the piece for mailing.

8. Budget.

The table of 5-44 identifies various kinds of bindings and their main applications.

GETTING IT ALL TOGETHER

There is an infinite number of ways in which text, artwork, and white space may be composed on a page or a spread. What makes one solution unacceptable, another adequate, a third one brilliant? Or, said another way, by what yardstick do you measure graphic success? If a building committee is impressed by one brochure but left cold by another or if a college board of trustees takes the trouble to study your planning report so it can intelligently discuss its recommendations, what was there about the graphic form to make it happen?

This is where we begin to use words like *flow, pacing*, and *clarity*. A publication is more than a sequence of pages—you can steadily build up an impression that can either turn the reader on in your favor or turn him off.

In order to accomplish the one and eschew the other, it will help greatly to follow a sequence of steps that apply, in a greater or smaller degree, to the development of any publication that leaves your office, from an occasional news release to a fully fledged brochure system.

The sequence may vary in its details, depending on such factors as the presence or absence of the various skills in-house, the size and specialization of the practice, and the size of the marketing and communications budget. Those features that are *unique* to each kind of communications product are described in Chapter 3. What they all have in *common* in terms of graphic design, layout, and production is described below.

The following steps apply to more complex projects, such as planning reports, brochures systems, and exhibit panels. They apply equally well, with appropriate streamlining, to simpler projects, such as news releases and newsletters.

Phase One: Preliminary planning

Step 1. Prepare a written statement of purpose. This should indicate the nature and character of the intended piece. It should ask and respond to such questions as: who will receive it? How long will it be in use (that is, what is its shelf-life)? Should it be hard sell or soft sell? To what level of technical understanding should it be geared? How is it commonly to be distributed (by hand, by mail)? In what quantities will it be required? Is it to be used as a working document to be marked up or a show piece for formal presentation? The answers to such questions will set the tone for the balance of the process.

Step 2. Prepare a preliminary budget. You will need to make some assumptions concerning format, quantities, paper stock, typesetting, printing, in-house labor, and consulting fees, if any. A typesetter will gladly provide a nonbinding estimate based on a simple specification that lists type sizes and length of copy. A printer will likewise work up an estimate, as will a photo reproduction house, for exhibit panels. Another possibility is to take cost figures from past projects and adjust for inflation. Update this budget continuously as you proceed, and the unknowns dwindle.

Step 3. Prepare a timetable. Based on past projects and opinions of the typesetter, printer, photo reproduction house (for panels), and the U.S. Postal Service or mailing house, work up a tentative total number of days needed to deliver the piece. Be sure to include days for in-house review and approvals, and contingency days in each phase to cover illness, delayed management approvals, and equipment breakdowns. Update the schedule as the project proceeds. If the delivery date is set by the client, the timetable will determine a starting date that, if unrealistic, will require infusion of additional resources to get the job done on time.

Step 4. Conduct your first planning meeting. This meeting may well be scheduled earlier in this phase, although it helps to prepare the statement of purpose, budget, and timetable first and to circulate these to the publication team members ahead of time for review.

The meeting should be attended by the concerned senior partner, the designated manager of the publication project, the writer/editor, the project planner/designer, and the graphic designer. In many offices several of these functions are combined under one hat. From this meeting should emerge a clear understanding of purpose, time milestones, and budgetary constraints.

Phase Two. Design

Step 5. Assemble available materials. Include text and artwork (drawings, renderings, photographs). Review; make a tentative list of additional needs, but carry out Step 6 before following up.

Step 6. Prepare preliminary design (thumbnail sketches). This is the time to develop alternative schemes and to begin to reconcile available materials with the statement of purpose. It is a sensitive phase, because the graphic designer is always reluctant to begin work until all the text and artwork are on hand.

As a rule, other factors resolve the dilemma. If a highly priced graphic designer has been retained, and especially if the design and layout are to be done in his shop and not yours, it is best to get the text and art into a completed state as soon as possible.

On the other hand, if you have an in-house graphic designer, or if you are merely following guidelines, you have somewhat greater flexibility. You may, for example, seek informal guidance from your in-house graphic designer in advance as to the arrangement of presentation-quality site and floor plans, the purchase of photographic prints (color, finish, dimensions, print stock), and how long to write the headlines or chapter titles given certain typefaces.

Thumbnail sketches should be done on a very small scale, using pairs of facing pages on a printed or mimeographed form such as in 5-35. This will allow you to begin to fit in the trees without losing sight of the forest; to get a firmer idea as to the number of pages you will need

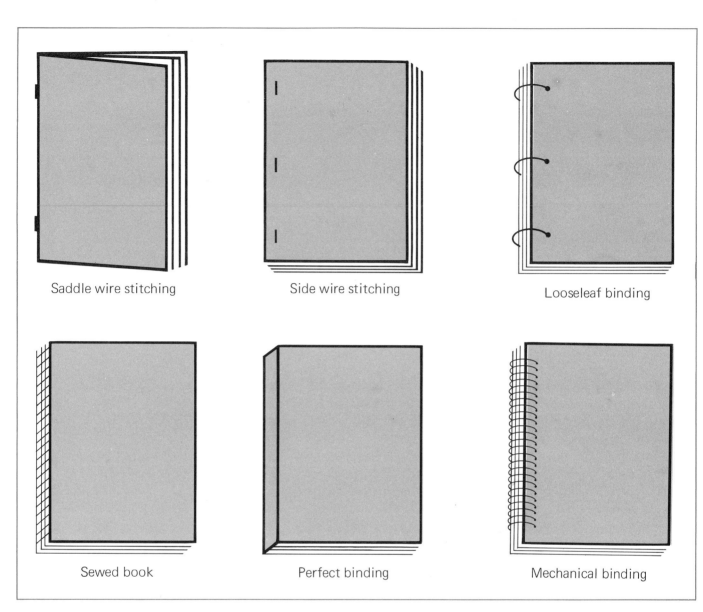

Saddle wire stitching

Side wire stitching

Looseleaf binding

Sewed book

Perfect binding

Mechanical binding

5-44 Common types of bindings and their uses.

Name	Uses	Remarks
Saddle wire stitching	Brochures, newsletters, reports	Look like staples through fold. Usually two to three are used. Good for 8 to 96 pages. Allows piece to lie open. Little flexibility for adding or substituting pages.
Side wire stitching	Brochures, newsletters, typed and printed reports, proposals	Staplelike wires are pressed through from front to back about ⅛"/.32 cm from edge. Good for 72 to 300 pages. Will not lie open—no flexibility. Needs cover to conceal wires.
Sewed book	Thick commercial books. Little application to professional communication program.	Folded sections are sewed, and the sections glued on the spine before cover is added. Long lasting.
"Perfect" binding	Brochures, reports	Pages are glued on the spine, with or without an added cover. If cover is added, title may be printed on spine. Opens flat, but is less durable than stitched or wired bindings. Good from 72 pages, with no limit. Inflexible.
Mechanical bindings	Proposals, reports, design award submittals, other one-of-a-kind pieces.	Pages are punches near binding edge, and metal or plastic round or spiral bands inserted. Allows for great flexibility of colors and use of thick, substantial covers. Lies open flat. Title printing on spine difficult or impossible. Allows for easy, last minute assembly of pages. May be done in-house on simple equipment.
Looseleaf and ring	Standard binders lie open flat and allow imprinting of title on spine. Variety of colors, textures.	Reports, design award submittals

for the contents; either to expand the pages or cut the contents if the discrepancy is too great; and, last but not least, to establish a character—pacing, flow, and emphasis. The character may be heavy on text and light on artwork, or vice versa; be loose, with ample white space, or tight and heavily concentrated; have many dividers, or few; have a pattern or sequence for colors; be based on segregation of text and artwork, or their integration. The statement of purpose should be your guide throughout this step.

Along with the thumbnail sketches, develop full-sized typical sample spreads to test the concept for fit in terms of type size, character count, size of photos and illustrations, and proportion of white space. Based on sample spreads, a grid is established showing column widths, horizontal and vertical alignment, and so on.

Frequent juxtaposition of art and text or charts/tables and text may call for a horizontal format. On the other hand, your office's graphic guidelines may specify a vertical 8½ x 11 format. This still would allow you to bind the piece on the shorter side—an option that costs a little more.

Typical grids used as vehicles for improving order and clarity on a page were shown on 5-37. A variety of ways in which you may exploit grids to obtain certain effects is shown in 5-45. This figure presents a number of methods for relating text, headlines, artwork, and white space in an exciting manner.

Whichever grid is selected, it is essential to stick to it throughout all the pages of the publication to present a consistent image. You should have a pretty good idea of a suitable layout grid before you complete the thumbnail design stage.

Step 7. Complete final text. Make sure style, spelling, punctuation, and so on are consistent, especially in case of more than one author. Compute length: if you have typed the copy on a manuscript typing sheet (5-36) that corresponds to the grid you will use, you need only add up the number of lines (N), determine how many lines will fit to the inch/centimeter for each type size and line spacing you plan to use (L), and obtain the length of text by dividing N by L.

If you are not using a manuscript typing sheet or if the number of characters per line (that is, letters plus spaces between words) is different on your typed sheet than it will be when set in type on the page, you must adjust the result of $N \div L$ either up or down. For example, if the number of lines is 400, and the chosen type size and line spacing provides 8 lines to the inch, you will have $400 \div 8 = 50$ inches of type to fit in. If, however, the typewritten manuscript has 60 characters per line, but the standard column width in the final publication only has 40, then the final length of text will be not 50 inches, but

$$50 \times 60/40 = 75 \text{ inches}$$

An alternative method for computing length of text is (after establishing a character count of the typeset line) to: count out the same number of characters on the first line of the typewritten manuscript, mark the spot, and draw a vertical line through the manuscript page. Now you have a rough number of lines on the left of the verti-cal line. Add up the leftovers to the right of the line, and figure how many additional lines this would make. Add the two and you have the total number of typeset lines the page converts into (see 5-46).

Step 8. Conduct a first review. Partners and others in your office who will have to use the final piece must have this chance to respond to the preliminary design.

Step 9. Incorporate revisions.

Step 10. Conduct a second review. Tack the proposed layout sheets to the wall, and obtain approval from the appropriate individuals who will use the piece. Recognize that from here on, *final* artwork and type will be prepared, so any changes will become increasingly costly in terms of labor and materials.

Phase Three: Layout and mechanicals

Step 11. Order type. Spec copy at this stage (see 5-16) and prepare camera-ready type either on an in-house typewriter or composing machine, or at a commercial typesetter. For larger jobs—15,000 words and up—obtain bids from three or four typesetters.

Step 12. Prepare a final printing specification. Include format and trim size; text and cover stock, weight and finish; anticipated number and area of linecuts and half-tones; use of color; print run (number of copies); binding; and expected delivery date. No printer should take more than two working days to compute his bid. After the bids come in, make your decision quickly so the selected printer can schedule the work and order paper if necessary.

Step 13. Prepare the final artwork. Order photographic prints in the appropriate size and finish. Size them and crop as needed to fit the layout (see 5-23). If drawings or renderings have been ordered, now is the time to complete them in final form—make sure that titles on floor plans, sections, and details are sized to reduce to a uniform specified size (or at least to a legible size). Any type size smaller than 4 pts. is impossible to read.

Step 14. Proof type and return for corrections (see 5-47). Type should be proofread three times by different persons. One should read for sense; a second for spelling and punctuation; a third (the graphic designer) for broken type, awkward hyphenation, uneven line spacing.

Step 15. Prepare camera-ready paste-up or mechanicals. These are done on the grid sheets and may be attached to boards for stability. Typesetters will provide self-adhering proofs if asked. Otherwise, use brush or spray applied rubber cement. Perfect alignment is essential. Work with a T-square and a triangle. Protect finished art work with tracing paper. Instead of doing mechanicals in-house, prepare a final layout using copies of original proofs and artwork. The printer will then prepare the final mechanicals from which the printing plates are made. If that is what you want, be sure to state it in the printing specification, as it will affect your costs.

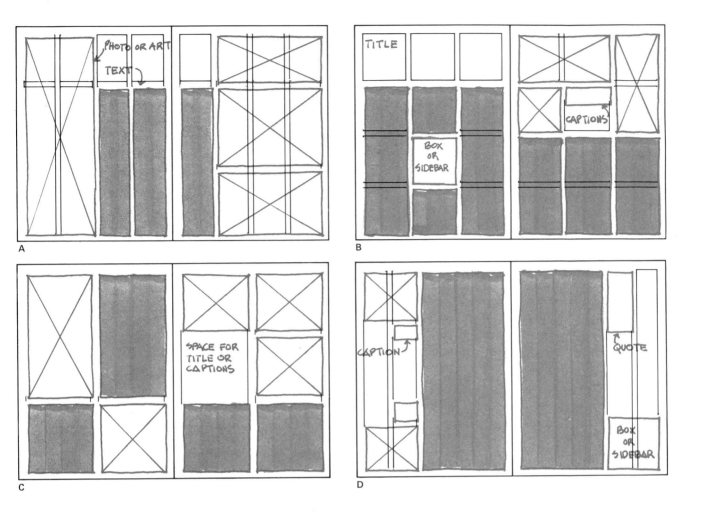

5-45 Grids may be exploited in various ways to obtain interesting effects.

Phase Four: Printing Production

Step 16. Review and approve page proofs. Page proofs are made from the same film negative that will be used to produce the printing plates. The proofs are known variously as silverprints, blue lines, brown lines, or salt-proofs, depending on the proofing method. This is your last chance to amend the publication, and every change is costly in the extreme. It is, however, better to pay to prevent a mistake than to pay for it a hundredfold later in errata slips and embarrassment. Look for: incorrect orientation of photos and other artwork, omission of lines of text or artwork, incorrect page numbers, "continued page" lines, continuity of text, and proper credits—all the items that should have been checked before the mechanicals were sent out but may have been overlooked. Also, at this point, look over the proofs for evidence of a dirty negative—this will show up as specks or streaks—and for art that has by mistake been misplaced by the printer and is missing on the proof.

Step 17. Review press proofs. These are proofs taken straight from the presses. This is usually done at the print shop on very important projects or on projects containing more elaborate graphics such as color work or sensitive half-tone or screen work. (There is obviously no way to check color work for tint and register by looking at silverprints.) For four-color work, the printer should provide you with progressive or "prog proofs" to allow you to check out tint and register. At this point, you are no longer looking to catch your own errors but to review the quality of the printer's work. If you are not satisfied and your objection is legitimate, the printer—usually with great reluctance, as he must stop the press—will make the adjustments on the plates or negatives. As noted in Step 16, it is better to delay to catch a slip in quality now, rather than to multiply the slip over 500 or 5000 copies.

Phase Five: Distribution

Step 18. Prepare for distribution. Large planning, research, and similar reports are often shipped in bulk to the client, except for presentation copies. Always order an additional 100–300 copies for reference and for promotional use. Since the client is commonly billed for the direct costs of producing the reports, additional copies will cost you next to nothing.

A brochure system, if based on *ad hoc* assembly and binding of components, is best stored unbound with the printer, except for a supply for day-to-day use.

Newsletters may either be mailed directly by the printer, to whom you furnish address labels, or mailed from the office, in which case the printer delivers the copies to you.

If the piece is an exhibit panel, the repro house will usually have facilities for crating and shipping panels to their destination. If your firm enters exhibits regularly, it is worth having shipping crates prepared. You can reuse them for other panels once the first set has been returned and discarded, put into storage, or hung on an office wall.

With experience, you will want to adjust these 18 steps, both in content and sequence, to meet your firm's particular circumstances. The steps reflect, however, a tried approach, and are an excellent starting point.

For convenience, the phases and steps are shown in diagram form as 5-48.

OTHER POINTS TO CONSIDER

You should consider whether to use an in-house or outside graphic designer and how to choose a typesetter and printer.

Using a graphics consultant

Whom you choose as a graphics designer can quite literally make or break the success of your communications program. Whether to appoint or use an in-house graphic designer if you have one, to retain a different consultant for each project, or to use one consultant for your entire program, what kind of background to look for, what types of agreements to make, and how to work with him or her—all these are matters to decide with great care.

In-house or outside. If your firm has a graphics department, chances are you will have little choice but to use it.

Retaining an in-house graphics department has several limitations, however. More often than not, the *raison d'être* of the department is profit oriented and geared to designing such items as building signage and product packaging. Communications graphics—unless it is a fee-paid planning report—is a cost, not a profit operation, and it is often difficult to obtain for the communications program the priority it deserves. As a result, a departmental graphic designer may not be available to meet with you until a week from Friday, or the delivery of the new brochure fact sheet's mechanicals may have to be put off by one week to accommodate work on the signage program for the new hospital. Nor, if you are a multi-branch office, will it help the Seattle and Atlanta branches if the graphics department is at headquarters in Minneapolis.

Another more insidious concern is the flow of fresh ideas from an in-house department. Some departments, because of the enthusiasm and inquiring mind of its chief, are the equal of any independent consultant. Others are in a rut, their work is derivative, and they will likely not give you the freshness you want.

The outside consultant, on the other hand, will have expertise and innovative ideas based on his work with many different kinds of clients and problems, and your firm will be the beneficiary of this experience. In addition, the outside consultant is more likely to fit his schedule to yours since you are, after all, his client.

The best of both worlds. In practice, a number of courses are open to you. If you are not satisfied with the in-house department, a good way to cause a change is to retain a prestigious consultant for a high-profile project, such as a crucial planning report, a new brochure system, or the logo and stationery. A few ruffled feathers will often be followed by a fresher outlook.

If you have no in-house graphics staff and you want to keep consultant help to a modest amount, you may retain the consultant to: develop the basic elements of the program; directly oversee the development of the first product in each area; set up a system of graphic guidelines. You may further ask him to be available on a retainer

HOUSING

CHARACTERISTICS

Four ingredients of housing are discussed in this report. They are: siting, design, construction methods,
and materials.

SITING

With the relatively primitive wind risk maps, little
regard has been given to the placement of houses in
relation to danger. Good site location or orientation
linked to local terrain and natural cover can be, but
usually has not been, determined from historical wind
data. This data provides the frequency, velocity and
direction of the prevailing winds, especially in their
extreme form. Hence, windstorm damage can be reduced
a great deal by placing buildings so they are protected
by hills, stands of trees and other natural elements.

DESIGN

Windstorm resistance can be notably improved by various
simple measures. These include horizontal bracing of
certain types of roofs over houses made of adobe mason-
ry and other small unit construction; a more rational
disposition of openings in bearing walls; reinforcement
of critical areas of a building subject to being over-
stressed; and the strengthening of connections at
joints.

All this may not be enough. Special studies on how
turbulence in a storm is distributed are required. It is

5-46 This alternative method for computing type length is described in the text on p. 112. There
are 279 leftover characters to the right of the line, enough for seven more 40-character typeset
lines.

Choose paper with imagination.	ℰ	take out
Choose paper with imagination.	⊂⊃	close up
Choose paper with imagination.	o/∧	insert letter
Choose paper with imagination.	#/∧	insert space
Choose paper with imagination.	h/∧	change letter
Choose paper with imagination.	STET	keep as is
Choose paper with imagination.	∿	reverse letters
Choose with paper imagination.	∿⊂⊃	transpose word
] Choose paper with imagination.	]	move in, align
[Choose paper with imagination.	[	move out, align
¶ Choose paper with imagination.	¶	start paragraph
Choose paper with imagination.	/l.c.	lower case
choose paper with imagination.	≡ u.c.	upper case
Choose paper with imagination.	ITAL	italicize
Choose paper with imagination.	≡	set in small capitals
Choose paper with imagination.	≣	set all in capitals
Choose paper with imagination.	∿∿∿	set all in bold
Choose paper with imagination.	⌐⌐	align, raise and lower
Choose paper ∧ with imagination.	⟨	use a ∧ to add a ,
Choose paper with imagination⊙	⊙	use a O to add a .
Choose paper with imagination⊙	⊙	use a O to add a ; or :
Choose paper with imagination!/	!/	use a / to add a ! or ?
Choose paper with imagination.	-/	use a / to add a -
Choose paper (with imagination.)	(/)	use a / to add ()
Choose paper [with imagination.]	[/]	use a / to add [ ]
Choose paper with imagination.	ⱽ	use a V to add ' and ""
□ Choose paper with imagination.	□	Em quad space or indent

5-47 Common proofreaders' marks for use in editing text or proofreading type galleries.

basis to resolve special problems; and, once or twice a year, critique the various products of you team's efforts.

For example, in the beginning, the graphics consultant may design the firm's stationery, logotype, brochure system, a typical report, a news release letterhead, and a pair of exhibit panels. He will document the effort for you by furnishing a set of guidelines or a graphics manual (see 5-49). Your office is now on its own, unless the consultant remains on retainer.

It is sad but important that guidelines, however clear and specific, do not insure excellence. There are always small scale decisions requiring the intuitive judgment of the professional designer when it comes to placement, sizing, typography, and format. Being aware of this may soften some disappointments.

Another option is to work with a single designer on those communications projects where firm-wide consistency matters most, such as letterhead, brochure, and proposal formats. Then, as a change of pace, retain different designers for special items, such as special planning reports and exhibit panels.

Choosing a consultant and what to look for. Most larger cities have graphic consultants in independent practice. Many other cities have local advertising agencies or local branches of the large national agencies. These agencies tend to have smart, bright designers and art directors who will usually be pleased to consult on a freelance basis. Printers are often a willing source of graphics advice, but such advice should be taken with caution and then only in matters dealing with the practical feasibility of a design concept.

Looking at each graphics consultant's record is, in any case, the first step. The work of graphic designers varies across a wide range. Some are exponents of the spare, dry, Swiss school of tight grids and Helvetica type. Others are more informal, choosing their type from a wide range of serif and sans-serif sources, and are given to a less stylized use of photographs, artwork, and layout. Some designers have a background of drawing and painting as commercial artists—this is reflected in a looser, softer, more informal approach to graphic design. Others are trained in architecture or industrial design and bring a more structured view to their work. Still others came up through journalism, thereby developing a special concern for the editorial and production niceties of communications.

There are also those (who should not be in the business) who will employ any device—introducing coy little sketches and random color, arbitrariness, and cuteness—to make an effect, without any overall consistency. Avoid them.

The work of the consultant you choose must, first and foremost, be sympathetic to your firm's image, as defined earlier in this book. After a close look at his portfolio, a "fit" or lack of it will immediately become apparent. If he passes this test, then consider these other criteria:

1. Familiarity with and recognition of the technical problems of publication production. He must know the range, availability, and costs of typography, paper, printing and binding, photography, and photo-engraving.

2. Attitude and personality. Avoid both the designer who is too domineering and the one who is too submissive.

The former will try to impose his ideas whether they fit the problem or not, and, like a horse with the bit in his teeth, will jump the fence into the highway when he should be walking calmly to the edge of the stream. The submissive fellow is, of the two, perhaps even less desirable, as he will agree to any ideas you have, and, instead of proposing an innovative scheme for discussion, will merely serve as a costly layout and production service.

3. Staff or access to staff. Graphic design entails access to many skills—drafting, photography, retouching, typesetting, layout and mechanical work, printing, and binding. When interviewing, be sure to question the designer as to the size and kinds of staff expertise, and the names and caliber of freelance resources he retains in the course of his work.

The fact that he has only one or two on permanent staff should not deter you from considering him. Chances are he has developed highly qualified networks of freelance specialists whom he can call upon and assemble to tackle a wide range of graphics projects. He often brings a fresh frame of mind that is sometimes missing in some of the larger, long-established graphics firms.

Agreements and compensation. Unlike architecture and engineering, there are no standard agreements between client and designer. The best course is to review the portfolio of the candidates, discuss your requirements informally (the interviews themselves will help sharpen your perception of your firm's needs), record these needs more formally in a brief written statement, and, based on that, ask the graphic firm or firms to prepare a simple proposal indicating scope of services, dates, and compensation (see below). The front runner's proposal letter, if accepted, is then signed by a principal of your firm and by the graphic designer and becomes a contractual agreement between the two. Your firm's legal counsel should look the agreement over before it is signed, since on occasion rather large sums are at issue in designer fees and production costs.

The designer's proposal should include the following information, as applicable:

1. Statement of understanding of your general needs.

2. Scope of services—an itemized listing of products to be developed, such as the brochure, three reports, newsletter, typing format, logo, and letterhead. This should include the nature or extent of the involvement—research, design concept, the design presentation to your key principals, the preparation of layouts and mechanicals, specification of type, bidding, printing supervision, preparation of a graphic design manual, continuing consultation after completion of initial products if desired.

A proposal may also be divided into phases, each with a fee attached. *Phase 1* may cover research, concept development, and presentation; *Phase 2*, the design of specific items; *Phase 3*, the execution of mechanicals; *Phase 4*, the guidelines or a manual. This way you have the choice to step in and stop the involvement after any phase.

3. Method of proceeding, assignment of responsibilities, and schedule. This should include the kick-off date and include dates and locations of milestone events. Usually, these consist of intensive fact-finding discussions involv-

5-48 Steps in developing a printed publication fall roughly into five phases.

Phase One Preliminary planning	Phase Two Design
1. Prepare written statement of purpose	**5.** Assemble materials
Define audience	Assemble text
Determine shelf life of piece	Assemble drawings, renderings
Determine method of distribution	Assemble photography
Will it be "hard" or "soft-sell"?	Identify additional needs
Will it be a "working" or "show piece"?	**6.** Prepare preliminary design
2. Prepare preliminary budget	Develop thumbnail scale sketches
Consider format, quantities, paper stock, typesetting (if any), printing, in-house manhours, consulting fees, photography, new artwork	Develop alternate full-size sample spreads (test for type size, line width, size of illustrations, proportion of white space to printed areas)
	Establish page size
3. Prepare timetable	Establish design grid (column width, column spacing, vertical/horizontal alignment)
Include time for planning, design, production, reviews and approvals, delivery, contingency factor	**7.** Complete final text
4. Conduct first planning meeting	Edit for meaning, style
Approve statement of purpose	Compute length
Approve schedule	**8.** Conduct first review
Approve budget	Review design
	Review text
	9. Incorporate revisions
	10. Conduct second review

Phase Three
Layout and mechanicals

11. Order type

Prepare camera-ready type (in-house) or ''spec'' type (for outside typesetting)

Obtain typesetting bids (large jobs only)

12. Prepare printing specification

Include paper stock; number and size of pages; number and area of line cuts and halftones; use of color; number of copies to be printed; binding; delivery date

13. Prepare final artwork

Order photographic prints

Scale and crop prints

Complete drawings and titles

Complete renderings

14. Proofread type

Proof for sense/meaning

Proof for spelling/punctuation

Proof for appearance of type

Return for corrections

15. Prepare mechanicals

Paste up text and art to grid sheets

Ensure perfect alignment

Protect finished paste-up with tracing paper

Deliver to printer

Phase Four
Printing production

16. Review, approve page proofs

Look for: incorrect orientation of artwork; missing or doubled up lines of text; missing artwork or parts of artwork; page numbers; credits; evidence of dirt

Return proofs to printer

Review progressive color proofs (3-4 color work)

17. Review on press and at bindery

Very costly—limit to special projects

Phase Five
Distribution

18. Prepare for distribution

Give printer distribution list (copies to client; in-house copies; other)

Alert mailing house (if used)

Arrange for shipping (if in bulk)

Prepare mailing labels

Furnish mailing envelopes, if needed

Advance postage money to mailing house

Stationery

Sizes (letter paper, envelopes, labels, business cards, memoranda, note cards, contract forms, project correspondence)

Paper stock

Typeface and placement of letterhead

Arrangement of typewritten message on paper

Use of color

Brochure/Portfolio Elements

Size

Paper (text and cover stock)

Typography—text and display (typical and special situations)

Layout (typical situations; special situations, such as charts, graphs and tables; artwork; photographs, captions)

Use of color

Binding

Client Report (Typewritten)

Size

Paper (text, divider, and cover stock)

Use of typewriter type (caps, underscoring, indentation, line width, line spacing)

Layout (inside). Typical situations; special situations, such as contents page; charts, graphs, and tables; footnotes; credits; artwork; photographs, captions.

Layout (covers and divider sheets)

Use of aids (bullets, rules)

Use of press-on or set type for headings

Binding

Client Report (Typeset)

Size

Paper (text, divider, and cover stock)

Typography—text and display (typical and special situations)

Layout (inside). Typical situations; special situations, such as charts, graphs, and tables; footnotes; credits; artwork; photographs, captions.

Layout (covers and dividers)

Use of color

Binding

5-49 Typical elements of a simple graphic manual to guide development of common communications items.

ing appropriate principals and staff of your firm; review of concept; review of detailed layouts; review of mechanicals; review of page proofs; and delivery.

4. Compensation. If the scope of the program is known precisely, you can ask the graphic designer to propose a fixed price or lump sum fee plus expenses. Expenses will usually include typesetting, photostating costs, messenger service, travel, and long distance telephone calls.

If the scope is imprecise, a good arrangement is to set a per diem fee plus expenses with an upper limit set both on fee and expenses.

Sometimes a third arrangement works best:

• A lump sum for initial research and concept.

• A lump sum for services leading to delivery of initial group of products, including the graphics guidelines.

• A per item lump sum for services leading to delivery of any additional products.

• A per diem fee or a monthly or annual retainer for general consultation over and beyond the foregoing.

• Expenses, with agreed-upon mark-up for administration.

Or pay by phase, as noted, on a lump sum basis.

The size of fees varies widely and is influenced by such factors as the firm's reputation, size (hence overhead), location, and backlog of work. Compare both the fees and the anticipated expenses proposed by the interviewed designers and do not hesitate to question them if there are apparent discrepancies in any of the items of service.

Working with typesetter and printer

Some of our best friends are printers and typographers. There is a fascination and even mystery about the process of delivering thoughts, words, and visual images to big machines so they can convert them into print. The men who work the machines have a special quality, handed down through a 500-year-old tradition, that still gives anyone who deals with those men—even in an age of sophisticated equipment and automated controls—the enjoyment of doing business with a dedicated craftsman.

Nevertheless, as in most things, there are good typesetters and bad typesetters, skilled printers and sloppy ones. How do you tell the difference, and how do you work with the ones you have selected?

Typesetters. Typesetting today has come a long way from the heavy, bulky machinery that sets hot type. Nowadays, anyone with a little capital can invest in photo (cold) typesetting equipment and go into business. Therein lies a danger. By opening up the range of variations in size and spacing of letters and words made possible by the photographic process, the need for judgment and a good visual sense on the part of the operator expands. You may specify "tight word spacing" or "tight letter spacing," but when it comes to converting these instructions to camera-ready type, you are in the operator's hands.

Therefore, when ordering type without the help of a graphic designer, screen the type houses with care. Some are affiliated with a printing operation; others are independent. Some, because of their equipment, can only set type within limits (for example, 18 pts.). Others will only position type in paragraphs free of charge up to a limit of 18 pts. For larger type, you must do this yourself; if the type house does it, there is a stiff stripping charge because it involves highly paid labor.

Display type is done either on a machine such as a Typositor up to a maximum height of ⅞″ / 2.2cm (capital letter height), or is set in linotype or linofilm and blown up photographically to the required size.

Even small, "store-front" typehouses carry composing equipment of considerable sophistication. Those that carry IBM Corporation's composing equipment offer a wide but traditional selection from the more common serif and sans-serif type fonts, in sizes from 6 to 12 pts. Since the spacing of words and letters is programmed and not determined by the operators, it is not possible to achieve some of the subtleties of the larger equipment. On the other hand, it is handy for day-to-day work and can shave as much as 50% off the cost of typesetting where a large publication is involved.

These IBM-type machines also have the advantage of various attachments, such as remote control transmission of text on tape using telephone lines. A magnetic tape feature allows a rough draft to be typed at high speed, and, after it is edited, it produces camera-ready type with minimal supervision from the operator. The machines allow for justification, centering, and the setting of charts and tables.

More sensitive (and, for its versatility, increasingly compact) equipment is continually being produced. Major manufacturers include Mergenthaler, VIP, Compugraphic Corp., Quadex Corp., Dymo Graphic Systems, Harris Intertype Corp., Varityper Division of Addressograph Multigraph Corp., and Alphatype. These machines offer great subtleties of word and character spacing for composition in most of the desired typefaces over a wide range of sizes.

Such computer-aided composing equipment works like this: your copy is typed on a special typewriter which converts the copy into tape or magnetic cards. The tape is then fed into a machine which can be programmed as to typeface, size, weight, leading, spacing, column width, ragged or justified edges, mixing of typefaces, rules, etc. It will set the copy to your specifications. If the specifications change in any way, your copy can be rerun at little cost.

The only expensive part about computer type is changes and corrections *in the copy* (as opposed to the specification), because these must be retyped on tape and re-programmed back into the old composition. The costs can easily double from the original estimate if you have extensive changes. That is, as noted earlier, why annual reports, financial tables, conference programs, or items subject to change or corrections are still composed in metal, line by line.

Long before a publication project gets under way, call your graphic designer or a friend at an advertising agency for the names of three or four reliable typehouses in your area. Summon a salesman, and discuss your general requirements without regard to any special project. Chances are he will leave a type book with you that shows the fonts he can offer.

An aggressive type house will be glad, when the time comes, to give you estimates on work, to provide pickup and delivery service, and to throw in additional repro proofs for easier working.

The final test is, of course, quality. What is the kind of quality you must expect from your typesetter? You should expect these things:

1. Proofs that have been adequately proofread. Reputable typesetters proofread text against your manuscript and make any corrections *before* delivering it.

2. Clean reproduction proofs. There should be no smudges or specks of dirt.

3. No broken letters. These were more common in the days of hot type cast in lead over a matrix, but it is still possible today for letters to be damaged or distorted during the composing or handling stages.

4. No unevenness. This may show up in the form of one end of a line of type being blacker than the other or the top part of a paragraph being darker than the bottom.

5. Consistent spacing between lines (see 5-50).

6. A final test is readiness of a type house to meet its scheduled commitments.

Costs of typesetting vary widely with the size of operation, location, work backlog, and the size of your job. Most houses have standard rates for setting display type (from 50 cents to as high as $4 per word). But for text type, prices vary widely. The cost of composing a page such as the one you are reading may be $15 or $25, depending on those various factors. So determine the costs by obtaining estimates, and, as the project gels, ask for bids.

Printers. As with typesetters, narrow the number of candidates by asking a graphic designer or adversiting agency for recommendations. Printers fall into two major categories: printing plants with large, so-called work presses (with letterpress, offset lithography, or gravure equipment), and smaller, so-called reprographic houses that use offset duplicators and copiers.

The idiosyncracies of the different machines are less important here than the need to know when to consider going to the large plant and when logically to fall back on the reprographic houses.

By and large, consider the large work-press printer under these circumstances:

1. Special concern for high quality (such as with a brochure system).

2. Work in more than one color.

3. Special paper stock requirements.

4. Need to exploit the economies of large-size printing sheets.

Offset duplicators can be entirely satisfactory for such tasks as letterheads, forms, newsletters, proposals, and planning or research reports that do not call for elaborate maps and other artwork. However, they have these limitations:

1. Since their printing surface usually does not exceed 11 x 17 in./27.94 x 43.18 cm, you lose the economies of using

Services include editorial,
writing and graphics consulting
to the publishing industry, agencies

of government, corporations,
professional firms and associations.

Services include editorial,
writing and graphics consulting
to the publishing industry, agencies
of government, corporations,
professional firms and associations.

5-50 Broken letters and inconsistent line spacing are signs you need to change typesetters.

a large sheet size, especially for multi-page publications.

2. Most duplicators have difficulty handling paper thicker than 110 lb. card stock or thinner than 16 lb. bond. This still admits most common paper stocks, but, especially in the finer quality text and cover stock, it requires precutting from the standard 25 x 38 in./63.5 x 96.52 cm or 20 x 26 in./50.8 x 66 cm sheet size to fit the equipment.

3. Most duplicators are geared to print a single color, although some will handle more than one color.

4. Detailed quality control (sharpness of imprint and evenness of inking) is more difficult with these machines than on a large work press.

Most large commercial printers with work presses also carry offset duplicators, and will be glad to recommend which type will furnish the quality you want at the least cost. As with the typesetter, so with the printer—quality in the product is measurable. Look for:

1. Even inking. No gray areas and, conversely, no overly black areas with filled-in letters and half-tones.

2. Absence of specks and smudges.

3. Correct reproduction of color work including registration—you should not see the red image printed slightly to the right of the black.

4. Consistency. The first brochure fact sheet should look as good as the 978th.

5. Accurate folding—contents set squarely and evenly on the page.

6. Good binding. Some printers will farm out this operation. Make sure the binding is square and the spine free of wrinkles. Trimming should be good and avoid uncut pages.

Printers are also useful because they can tell you the production implications of any design decisions. Typical concerns the printer can warn you against include: use of too light a screen (it will not reproduce well); the superimposition of two intense inks (say 100% black and 100% blue—they will smear); too narrow margins (they will magnify any errors in alignment); too dark a half-tone (some detail will be lost); and too rough a paper stock (evenness of impression will suffer).

Like typesetters, printers furnish early estimates to help you to budget and will make firm bids as needed. Whereas a graphic consultant will often pay for typesetting and bill it to you as an expense, sometimes with a small surcharge for administration, the printer's agreement is as a rule directly with you. The agreement should (over and above the details of the printing specification discussed earlier) spell out carefully such matters as turnaround times—the time needed for him to provide page proofs and for you to approve them; the number of proofs to be furnished; who prepares mechanicals; provision of pickup and delivery service; and access to the plant to approve pressproofs and binding.

After you have worked with a printer a few times, it is common to agree on some of these items verbally; but you do so at your own risk. Clearly, many of these steps and provisions, which are in order for a report or a brochure, are superfluous when applied to an order for letterheads or the printing of an in-house newsletter. In such cases, you would not go to the trouble of specifying turn-around times or checking on a pressproof.

Your relationship with the typesetter and printer is very like that of an architect or engineer with the prime building contractors or of an interior designer with suppliers and fabricators. Each has information and know-how useful to the other, and results are best when each is allowed to share this knowledge against the background of a good businesslike agreement.

6

Audiovisual presentation

The audiovisual (A/V) presentation has many uses—to help sell your professional services, to help your client sell your scheme to his constituency, to help your government disseminate technical information overseas based on your firm's work and that of fellow professionals. Chapter 7 takes up the use of A/V as part of an oral presentation. This chapter deals with the actual preparation of the materials.

A/V presentations come in at least four categories: the silent slide show with live narrative; the tape-actuated slide show with sound; the motion picture; and A/V for television. The last two are not often employed by the professional design firms, and the interested reader is therefore directed to longer resources on the subject as noted in the reference section.

DO YOU NEED AN A/V PRESENTATION?

Think of the A/V presentation as only one element in your overall marketing or communications plan. Decide beforehand whether such a show is in fact necessary, or whether the array of printed materials at hand—along with your own rhetorical skills at the microphone or client committee's interview table—will suffice. Such an assessment is important, because a good A/V presentation—and we do not mean a haphazard stringing together of your firm's latest picture-taking efforts—requires a sizable outlay of time and dollar resources.

Steps in developing the A/V presentation

The discussion that follows suggests typical steps to take once you have decided that the circumstances of the occasion call for audiovisual support. Chances are that for any but simple, single-screen presentations you will retain an A/V consultant. The entire process is nonetheless described below, so you may set objectives and coordinate the work of the A/V and other consultants.

Step 1. Draft a statement of objectives. The statement should cover such factors as allocated time (10 minutes, 20 minutes); time to complete (one week or three months); the type of audience (laymen, students, professionals); the purpose of the show (to sell, inform, entertain); the format options (self-narrated; two-screen; slide-sound package); the types of spaces in which it is to be shown and screening equipment available; the caliber of operator to be furnished; the possible need to tie the show in with development of a report or brochure. All these factors will shape the show's final form.

Step 2. Prepare a schedule and budget. Feed into the cost equation such items as *fees* (editorial, graphics, A/V consultants; illustrator; professional narrator, if used). To these costs add your in-house direct *labor manhours* to cover coordination and preparation of camera-ready artwork and special shooting; and *direct expenses* such as typesetting (for artwork), purchase and development of film and tapes, rental of projection and taping equipment where not provided by the client or sponsor; and rental of a studio for synchronizing visuals and sound, if applicable. (As noted later, many of the services provided by consultants may be safely carried out in-house for simpler projects.) Although all the costs are hard to identify at the start, due to the number of variables—such as the degree of fresh artwork required—some typical costs are noted later in the chapter.

Pinning down a time schedule faces a similar handicap, since by adding resources you can drastically reduce completion times. Record tentative times against each step, working backward from the date of the first showing. Very elaborate A/V sound shows have been developed in three weeks, whereas a simple, narrated 40-slide sequence for a school interview may take months when outdoor views are essential but the season, weather, or condition of the landscaping fail to cooperate.

Step 3. Prepare a preliminary script. The script is the skeleton on which hangs the entire flesh of the slide presentation. No matter whether the show is a multi-screen, multi-projector sound extravaganza, or a 35-slide segment with live commentary inserted at an interview or lecture, the script is the key ingredient for putting a show on track and keeping it there.

Develop a script the way you would a long letter or report. Begin with an outline, listing the main points to be covered. Suppose you have been asked by a major federal agency to prepare a 15-minute self-contained slide show, the aim of which is to demonstrate to potential professionals, builders, and product manufacturers the value of the agency's "systems approach" to the design and delivery of office buildings. To make a case, you may want to stress the following points:

- The program's goals

- Main concepts of the systems building approach

- Use of the performance specification as a basis for bidding

- Unique issues: technical; financial; administrative

- Participants and their roles

- Results of the program to date

- The future

Script Sheet

Page___of___Pages   Date:_____19___

Title:_____   Draft Number: 1 ● 2 ● Final

Visual Concepts	Script

Wollensak 3M

© THE 3M COMPANY, 1976

To order additional script sheets,
see order information at back of Guide (RM-MIP)

6-1 Script worksheets serve to record and relate narrative with visual concepts.

Remembering that the slide show builds its impact over a span of time like a movie, inject as much drama into the outline as possible. Now, the above outline covers the subject, but it lacks any kind of dramatic flow. A rearrangement of items could take care of that, and now is the time to do it. By recasting the outline into a series of typical sequences, you can attain that dramatic flow:

Sequence A. Introduction. The show would begin with some dramatic views of the systems concept as used in our society to date, perhaps including some striking shots of the old Crystal Palace, the U.S. Pavilion at the 1967 Montreal World's Fair, and even a shot of the Apollo space capsule.

Sequence B. Participants. Bring in the people. Show who is needed to make it all possible. The main participant groups are now introduced, and their special roles spelled out—the architect/engineer (design), the construction manager (management), the agency staff (overall administration), and the manufacturers (who develop the integrated system of building components).

Sequence C. Procurement. Having established the setting and the actors, a reasonable next step is to describe the office building procurement process. This consists of certain phases that may now be spelled out—qualification through technical proposals and management plans; selection of the design/owner team; design; bidding by the system component manufacturers; development of project bidding documents based on the winning manufacturer's component system; and construction.

Sequence D. The master document. The viewer has now seen how a project is developed. But that is not the whole story. The agency wants to get across the point that the office building was made to conform to a tight set of performance requirements as contained in a master document. This document is described in general terms—the next two sequences then take it up in more detail.

Sequence E. Requirements. In practical terms, this sequence of slides shows building module and bay sizes, typical (office) and nontypical (lobby, cafeteria) spaces, location of partitions on the space grid, ceiling heights, and the contents of the floor-ceiling "sandwich."

Sequence F. Seven subsystems. Expose the viewer next to the principal subsystems around which the office building is to be organized, their requirements, and how they come together.

Sequence G. Life cycle costs. Every innovative concept has some unique features and potential problems. This sequence and the next three take them up in detail. The meaning of the life cycle cost concept is brought out, as reflected in the *first* and *operating* costs of an office building, the costs of fuel, the costs of rearranging partitions, and of replacing light bulbs. Show a grading system used by the agency to evaluate and rank the bids by interested product manufacturers.

Sequence H. Quality control. Viewers learn about required testing, in the lab, on a prototype, and in the field.

Sequence I. Phased construction. Bring out the savings to be gained by overlapping the various design and construction phases.

Sequence J. Goals. Why bring in goals so late in the show? Because goals are hard to dramatize visually. In too many instances, whether audiovisual, a speech, or in a printed piece, goals are unthinkingly trotted out at the beginning without regard for the viewer's interest. By first showing the people and the process, the lead-in to goals can capitalize on a growing, latent curiosity.

Sequence K. Features. Now is the time to recapitulate. Bring out again the main features of the program in general, overall terms.

Sequence L. The evidence. Now also is a good time to show the viewer, who may have been asking himself what the agency's system program has produced to date. It is the place to present dramatic views of buildings completed or underway.

Sequence M. Conclusion. To wind up the presentation, restate the value of the program to building owners, users, and producers of systems components. End the show on a note of optimism about what it will bring in the future.

Now write a rough script or narrative to conform to this outline.

Step 4. The storyboard. While the script elements are being developed, you should also be thinking in terms of the visual images that will dovetail with the story. These images could include, in our example:

- Views of completed buildings

- Views of a job site

- Shots of historical structures where relevant

- Shots of covers and a typical page from key proposal or contract documents

- Simple computation of a bid evaluation formula

- A flow diagram showing the process

- A diagram showing organization relationships

- Views of people

- Views of a model

Record ideas on a thumbnail storyboard planning sheet (see 6-1). Most producers of audiovisual equipment and camera stores will supply preprinted scripts and storyboard worksheets, or you or your consultant may design your own.

Next, the visual concepts are developed in greater detail at the thumbnail scale, keeping in mind the lines of rough script that the visuals must match.

Carry this step through as many cycles as you need before freezing it at an acceptable level. Read the draft of the script out loud to obtain a preliminary time estimate and add 10 to 20% since some slides may be on view for short periods without narrative.

Step 5. Develop slides and artwork. This entails three kinds of effort:

1. Inventory. Identify existing photographs, slides, models, and drawings which could be used with little or no modification.

2. Schedule new photography on location.

3. Prepare special artwork. For a slide show organized around the theme of presenting recently completed projects, there is usually little special artwork to prepare besides title slides and adaptation of floor plans and other drawings to the slide format. Even so, you may need to devise a diagram slide or two, depicting how a job was organized. In the systems building example we have been discussing, special artwork is crucial to the impact of the entire show.

What are some of the guidelines for preparing such artwork so it will be not only understandable to the viewer but carry a dramatic impact too? Many of the same precepts that apply to printed graphics apply to slide artwork also, so take another look at Chapter 5. There is, however, a whole new set of viewing conditions that apply specifically to preparing artwork for A/V shows. For a list of these conditions and how to translate them into camera-ready artwork, see 6-2.

You may save a great deal of time and effort by getting extra graphic use out of charts and models. For instance, shoot the complete model, and then close in for details. When developing a flow diagram, prepare the artwork in phases and photograph the status after each phase before you complete the next (6-3). Also, why not employ the completed diagram twice—once at the start of the sequence to give the audience an overview, and again at the end? Use the same tactic when showing an organization chart or procurement tactics (6-4), the cross section of a building indicating the various subsystems (6-5), or a mathematical computation. This kind of "still animation," or buildup, adds suspense to what may otherwise be dull material.

The same principle of buildup operates for presentations based on an overhead or opaque projector, or when using a stack of hand-prepared flip charts.

Step 6. Prepare and record sound. A prerecorded narrative and/or background sounds and music make for a more controlled, tighter presentation than does a live narrative. If the same show is to be used several times over or concurrently in a number of locations, or if the presentor is not an important factor, your A/V consultant will suggest making a sound tape as the best plan. On the other hand, if you need the flexibility to change slides or their sequence from time to time, and if your intent is to have the spotlight on you or your firm, a live narrative is superior.

The sound track is prepared in one of two ways. In one case, it is not made until the artwork is completed and the slides are shot. The slides are then run through, and the team—script draft in hand—makes any adjustments in the order of the slides or in their exposure time on the screen. This is the time to add, ruthlessly subtract, or substitute slides. Adjust the script as necessary.

You are now ready for recording the narrative. This is always done in a recording studio with controlled acoustics and sophisticated equipment—rentals run to about $50 per hour. Engage a professional narrator (your consultant can recommend names); there is nothing more embarrassing than to have a high-quality slide show spoiled by an amateurish commentary.

This approach works best when sound is confined to a narrative. If you plan music or other sound effects (thunder, crowd noises, rushing water, or location interviews),

TYPE LEGIBILITY

It is a common fallacy to think that type for charts, diagrams, titles, and spacer slides (slides used to introduce a new sequence of slides) can be small because enlargement in the projection process will make the size come out all right. What really counts is the size of the detail *on the screen*. If that is too small to be read from the most remote seat, it does not matter how large or small it is. The following rules of thumb are helpful for determining size of lettering on artwork (all data courtesy Cambridge Seven Associates):

1. Ratio. The ratio you should use is:

$$\frac{\text{Maximum sheet dimension}}{\text{Minimum letter height}} = 70$$

Thus, if your artwork is being prepared on a 18 x 12 in./45.72 x 30.48 cm sheet, minimum letter height should be $\frac{18}{70} = .25$ in./.64 cm (or about 24 pt. type in capital letters).

On a 30 x 40 in./76.2 x 101.6 cm board, minimum letter size would be $\frac{40}{70} = .6$ in./1.55 cm (roughly), which is about 60 pt. type in capital letters.

2. Viewing distance. Given a maximum projected image dimension of D, the most remote seat should be no further than 6D to 8D. A better way to look at this is that if the distance of that most remote seat from the projection surface is E, then the projected image dimension must be at least $\frac{E}{8}$ to $\frac{E}{6}$. Thus, if the farthest seat is 40 ft./12.2 m, projected image size should be about 5 to 7 ft./1.5m to 2.2m (see opposite page top).

3. Typewriter type. By observing rules 1 and 2, pica caps will be legible if typed same size on to artwork done on a 5¾ x 8 in./14.6 x 20.32 cm sheet size. If larger sheets are to be used, the pica caps must be photostated up before being pasted down, in line with the 70:1 formula of rule 1.

ORIENTATION

1. Decide early to have all slides horizontal or all vertical. Then orient the artwork accordingly. This simplifies the process of photographing the artwork at a uniform focal length.

2. Maps and floor plans. In order to not confuse the viewer, orient a sequence of plans or maps so north always faces in the same direction (not necessarily "up"). Since a group of maps commonly has overlays to denote a development sequence or different land uses (or both), provide on the base drawing some recognizable form (coloring or shading of a key element, such as a building, park, or body of water) that the viewer can "remember" in the context of the various overlays of information.

COLOR

Slides that portray charts, diagrams, and other word-based matter may be made more lively by adding color. You may do this either *on the artwork*, by blocking out sections in zipatone or colored tissue paper, or *on the slide*, by means of a colored gel. Do not attempt the latter without technical help.

1. Color coding. Use color for coding—in our systems building example, you might always color the symbol for architect or engineer on an organization diagram *green*, the client *dark red*, the construction manager *orange*, and the manufacturers *light red*.

2. Reproducible colors. The following colors when used on artwork reproduce faithfully: *red, yellow, orange* (tends toward *brown* when Ektachrome is used), *black, yellow ochre, olive, green. Dark blue* and *dark purple*, on the other hand, translate almost into black in slide form.

SIZING

1. Proportion the artwork to conform to the proportions of the slide or other medium. These are approximately:

35mm (slides)	3:2
2¾ x 2¾ in./7 x 7 cm (slides)	1:1
16mm (motion picture)	4:3
TV (titles)	5:4

For preparing artwork, avoid selecting a basic sheet size so small as to make it hard to work with, or so large that lettering will need to be huge to be legible when reduced to slide size. By choosing a uniform sheet size for most of the artwork (say 8 x 12 in./20.32 x 30.48 cm), you can use uniformly sized typefaces knowing they will remain uniform when reduced.

2. Information area. Always extend the artwork a little beyond the dimensions of the area that will actually appear, to avoid showing the edges (see opposite page bottom).

SHOOTING AND EXPOSURE

When shooting for slides, make sure that several originals are shot of each piece of artwork. The exposures should be varied. You may then select the slide that has the effect you want (dark; light; hard; soft). Remember that if you use colors for coding, these will vary with different exposures—if you want these colors to reproduce uniformly, exposures too must remain uniform. Buy only film that corresponds to the lamps used with the camera. When ordering duplicates choose processing labs with care to avoid color variations.

Slide production kits are available commercially from the major film manufacturers, usually with a detailed booklet on how to make slides.

MOUNTING

Order slide mounts with rounded corners. They are less likely to jam in the projector.

6-2 Criteria for preparing artwork for slides.

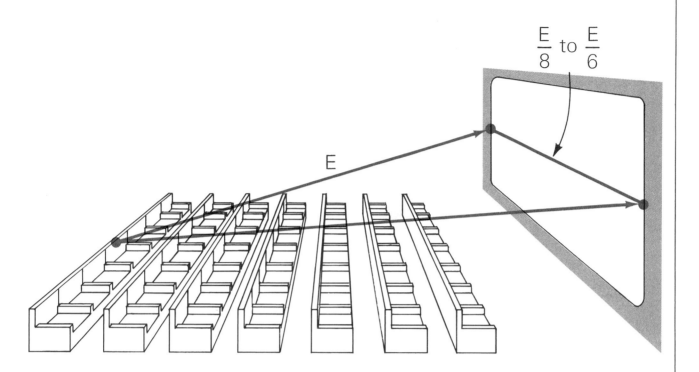

$$\frac{E}{8} \text{ to } \frac{E}{6}$$

E

The size of the image should be no less than one-eighth the distance to the most remote seat.

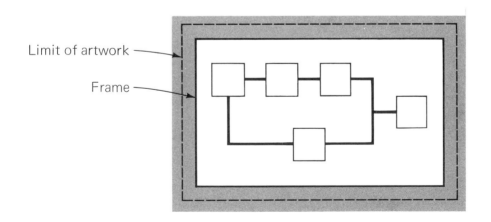

Limit of artwork

Frame

Extend artwork beyond the edges of the area that will appear on the slide to avoid showing the edges of the art.

6-3 Sequence B. Participants. Prepare artwork in phases, and photograph after each phase. This example shows the relationships of slides to the narrative. Note that the slide numbers preface the script.

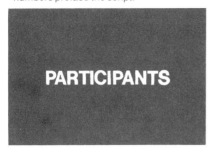

10 There are four participants in this program. Each has a unique role.

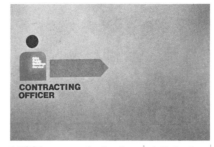

11 GSA arranges for funding and site for the project, selects the architect / engineer and the construction manager, and appoints a contracting officer to manage the project on behalf of GSA.

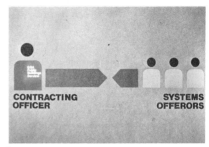

12 The system offerors develop building systems that respond to the performance specifications. The successful offeror becomes the systems contractor who installs and maintains it.

6-4 Sequence C. Procurement.

15 The process by which a building is procured under the program differs in many respects from traditional methods. It breaks down into five distinct phases or sequences:

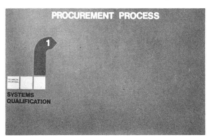

16 First, there is the *systems* qualification sequence. In this sequence, technical proposals and management plans are developed for the systems portions of office buildings. The purpose of this phase is to select a group of qualified systems whose offerors will later be asked to submit price bids on projects.

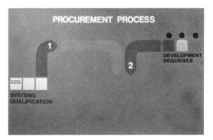

17 The second phase is the development sequence for an actual project. After funds become available and a site is selected, the architect / engineer and construction manager are chosen, and GSA's contracting officer is appointed. During this phase, system contract drawings are made and a price limit set.

6-5 Sequence F. Seven subsystems.

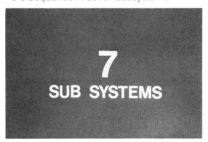

42 The systems portion of the building is made up of seven subsystems.

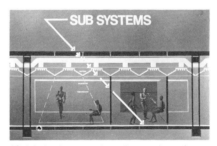

43 Jointly, these produce the user's environment of the typical office space, and they make up over one third of the total cost of construction of a project. The performance specification establishes the standards.

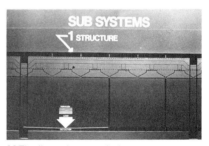

44 The first subsystem is the structure; performance limits are given for such characteristics as load capacity, deflection, vibration.

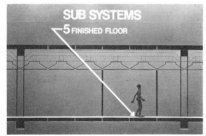

48 The fifth subsystem is the carpet and resilient flooring; levels of quality are spelled out, along with fire safety and other requirements.

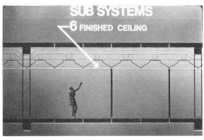

49 The sixth subsystem is the finished ceiling; among the criteria are strict acoustic standards.

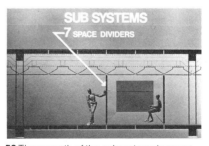

50 The seventh of the subsystems is space division. It includes partitions, screens, column enclosures, doors, and hardware.

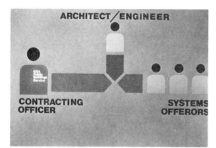

13 The architect/engineer designs the overall building, incorporating the systems portion into his design.

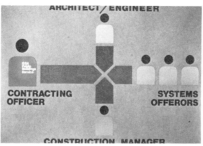

14 The construction manager is responsible for project schedules and cost estimates for the design, bidding, and erection of the building. He also administers the phased construction feature of the project.

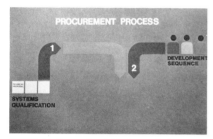

18 Third is the system bid phase, during which prequalified systems offerors submit price bids for the job at hand. One of them is then selected after submitting the lowest life-cycle cost bid, and becomes the systems contractor.

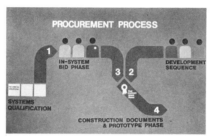

19 In the fourth phase—the post contract-award sequence—construction documents are prepared for the systems part. The contractor also submits lab and prototype test reports that certify that the building system complies with the performance specification.

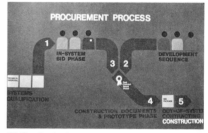

20 Finally, in the construction phase, the construction manager divides the out-of-system part of the job into appropriate bid packages; bids them, and goes on to coordinate the erection of in-system and out-of-system elements. Phased construction is used to expedite the work.

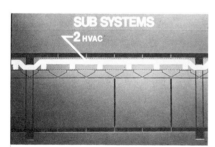

45 The second subsystem is heating, ventilating, and air-conditioning, or HVAC; the offeror is given a choice as to energy media—chilled or hot water, steam, or electricity.

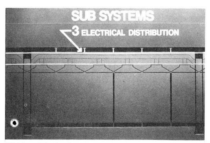

46 The third subsystem is electrical distribution; it includes office power, telephone and signal raceways, and floor outlets.

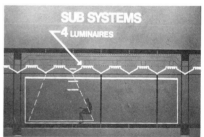

47 The fourth subsystem consists of the luminaries; illumination levels and photometric performance are specified for three categories of use—uniform, task-oriented, and background lighting.

Fees	
Editorial consultant and coordination	$2000
Audiovisual and graphics consultants—includes design, illustrations, artwork, mechanicals, and camera work	4000
Narrator	200
Expenses	
Studio rental—includes cost of tapes	500
Film purchase and processing—first set, no duplicate copies	200
Miscellaneous (typesetting)	100
	$7000

6-6 Typical budget for 15-minute slide show based on major outside editorial and graphic consultation.

the order is changed. Sounds are recorded first, the script refined as needed, and the narrative and the recorded sound mixed. Then the material is shot to coincide with the sound track. The developed slides are run through against the sound track, and the slides edited as needed. Then proceed to Step 7.

Step 7. Combine sound and visuals. After you have a sound track and a collection of good slides in the right order, return to the recording studio. There, technicians will insert impulses based on your consultant's directions on a spare track of the sound tape. These impulses will activate the slides and are "audible" only to the projector. Their time spacing is dictated by the script. The studio has the capacity to refine the sound track by extending or reducing the acoustic frequency range, shifting the range toward a higher or lower end of the scale, and even splicing in or cutting out sound or narrative. You may sometimes need to have this done if running time exceeds or falls short of the limit. Try to avoid it by carefully reading the script aloud early, allowing for periods of silence.

A word about pacing. A narrative can be delivered too slowly and slides can remain on the screen too long. How long is "too long" varies with the subject and must be determined by the creator of the show. Some slides need to be run through in a fast sequence for good effect. Although the pacing should be determined by the script, for most informational slide shows a good brisk pace is better than a thorough plod. A good standard is eight seconds per slide, averaged out over the length of the show. Thus, a 120-slide show would run to 16 minutes. The A/V consultant will tell you that a two-projector show will allow for greater speeds and variations than a single machine.

Step 8. Present the show. The live presentation of slides as part of an interview, speech, or lecture is taken up in more detail in Chapter 7. If the show comes with its own sound tape, carefully select the equipment to fit the need. A show that will do much traveling should not be tied to bulky equipment and elaborate stage arrangements. Some manufacturers now make very compact projector kits with a built-in screen, sound track, and speaker for less than $400. They require rerecording of the sound and impulse tracks on to a small cartridge (a simple operation) and usually have a running time of 15 minutes.

If there is more time to stage manage the show, it is better to go to a separate system of projectors; a dissolve control unit (which allows for instantaneous slide changes as well as for slow fades between slides); a tape playback unit; and loudspeakers. If the hall has any of these built-in, investigate them thoroughly beforehand to ensure a "fit" with your materials. For example, the impulses that move your slides forward are usually recorded at a frequency of 1000 cycles per second. If the hall's built-in tape playback equipment operates at 500 cps, you are in for serious problems.

COSTS

Costs can vary immensely. The variables include the running time of the show, the size and type of equipment, the required amount of new artwork and new photography, and the caliber of consulting help engaged to put the show on track. You may tell your client that it is possible, for example, to create a 15-minute self-contained slide show, for two projectors with dissolve control, one screen, tape playback unit, and two loudspeakers for about $7000, or over $450 per minute. Duplicate sets can run to $250 each. This is based on all artwork being prepared by other than your own staff, and includes fees to editorial, graphic, and audiovisual consultants, the illustrator, and the narrator, as well as expenses for film and processing, special typesetting, and studio rental. It does not include cost of renting or buying equipment.

Renting equipment is a negligible item—a tape playback unit can usually be rented for about $25 a day and a dissolve control unit for $25. *Purchase*, on the other hand, is costly. A good quality tape unit with built-in speakers costs close to $400; a dissolve unit, $400; a good basic slide projector, $250. For complex, multi-screen shows, a programming unit is needed at a cost of $1000 and more.

From this you can see that a full-fledged audiovisual show is not cheap. You may, however, cut costs in several ways. By writing your script and preparing artwork and mechanicals in-house, by not taping the script but reading it live, and by relying on skillful use of available materials, you may curtail outside costs dramatically—but at the price of increased in-house manhours. It all depends on the occasion and on the repetitive mileage you feel you can obtain from the show.

In-house or not?

Preparing an audiovisual show totally in-house is risky, since most design professionals receive only the most superficial formal training in that specialized field. As noted, A/V is different in many basic respects from conventional printed communications and has evolved its own cadre of consultants. If your budget only allows for minimal outside expenses, even a modest fee paid to such a consultant can save you many costly forays up a wrong path (see 6-6 for a typical budget).

7

The spoken word

Queen Victoria used to complain that when Prime Minister Gladstone came to brief her on affairs of state, he would address her "as though we were a public meeting." This lapse is one of many in the art of public speaking that makes the spoken word as different from the printed word as television is from newspapers. The rules that apply are different. What you say must be intelligible at once; if a listener has missed a word or a phrase, there is no way for him to go back the way a reader can. And you, in turn, cannot go back to "unsay" a wrong word, phrase, or thought. It must be right the first time.

Consequently, communicating by word of mouth has its own peculiar set of needs. Contents and delivery must be more direct; this is no place for recondite theory and convoluted phrasing. Shun statistics, except with visual backup. Sentences must be short. There must be restatement—the old rule about telling your audience what you are going to say, saying it, and then telling them what you said is one way to do this. Not repetition, but restatement. The Psalms, which were written to be sung and not read, are an early example. Read almost any verse and you will find it made up of two parts—the second part restates the first, as these examples show:

> Who shall ascend into the hill of the Lord:
> or who shall rise up in his holy place?
> —24th Psalm, Verse 3

> Thou shalt go upon the lion and the adder:
> the young lion and the dragon shalt thou
> tread under thy feet.
> —91st Psalm, Verse 13

When speaking to another person or a group, you face two additional challenges. Just as in printed communications, the graphic format can make or mar the impact—your words must work against a background of looks, gestures, how you look, and, indeed, the whole physical setting. The other challenge is the proven fact that most people find it a great deal harder to take in a message by listening to it than by reading it. If the listener really wants to retain what he hears, he takes notes or turns on a tape recorder. The former detracts from total absorption in the talk; the latter takes up time when he replays or transcribes it.

A final note concerning the two-way feature of the spoken word: the good speaker is closely attuned to instant responses from his audiences—boredom, exhilaration, interest—and swiftly adjusts his delivery to fit the case.

The design professional may have to talk on a number of occasions, some of which are reviewed below.

THE CLIENT INTERVIEW

Like virtually all speaking activity, the client interview is anything but a one-way show. If all the client-prospect wanted to know was what similar projects your firm did in the past and the experience of your principals, he could read it in your brochure. The point of the interview is to enable the client to see for himself what your firm may be like to work with, how its representatives handle themselves, and how skillfully they respond to still unresolved questions about the project's potential.

Interview marketing tactics

These tactics are better covered in books dealing with that aspect of the subject, but some key communications aspects of interviews are highlighted here.

Not a speech. An interview is not the occasion for a speech. It is a flexible occasion where your presentation, geared to an assumed time limit, may at any time be broken into by a query. Many skilled presenters use the event to ask the client's interviewing group questions themselves, such as the status or condition of the building site, the possible need for zoning changes, or how the client will be organized to oversee the project.

How many people to bring. Do not intimidate the client by bringing more of your staff to the interview then the number of members on the client's committee. Whoever comes should have a role to play. Two individuals are better than one. The two-way interchange that marks most interviews is more wearing than a speech, and an "over to you, Charlie" switch relieves the tension as well as providing a change of pace for the client.

You, slides, and other aids

Bring your own slide projector, including a spare lamp. For some reason, projectors provided by the hosts break down after the third slide. Call in advance about the room layout. If the interview is in the daytime, find out how daylight may be shut out. Ask about the distance from the projector to the nearest electrical outlet (bring an extension cord anyway); if a screen is to be provided; whether there will be an easel on which charts may be rested, a board to which charts may be attached, and a surface suitable for making diagrams.

Do not, however, rest your case on the use of too many mechanical aids. A breakdown can be lethal. The client is interested in you as a potential solver of his problem, not as a dramatic wizard. Try to control the slides yourself; incessant calls for "next slide, please" disrupt the show.

When using a stack of prepared charts on an easel, keep the top one covered until you are ready to use it. Try to concentrate audiovisuals into one period of the presentation, to avoid a continuing on-and-off of lights.

Questions

Respond to questions with an answer, not a speech. Be no more specific than you can afford to be, in view of the incomplete information about the project at your disposal.

Jargon

Use of jargon is even riskier in a verbal presentation than it is in writing. Chances are your listeners will be laymen. Avoid professional trade terms, such as "plastic qualities of a facade" and "integration of plan elements." Pay special attention to choice of visuals. Steer clear of complex diagrams showing how the boiler plant works at St. Mary's Hospital; or computer printouts and charts describing your prowess in estimating and in cost control. Most laymen are hard put to follow charts and diagrams: again, a couple of words are sometimes worth a thousand pictures.

THE CLIENT/PROJECT CONFERENCE

Many of the rules of the interview apply to client presentations made once a project is in design. The goal of such presentations is usally not to impress the client with your skills, but to update him on progess and to get a decision so you can go on to the next phase. Involve him in the making of the decision, not in merely responding to a fait accompli.

Many techniques have been developed to further this process, especially during the early, more analytical phases like programming. Analysis cards, 5 x 8 in./12.7 x 20.32 cm, each containing a single idea or concept, may be tacked to a board and reviewed with the client for instant feedback. The opaque projector is useful for conveying the content of these cards or other written or drawn information to a bigger audience. Large sheets of wrapping paper tacked to the wall are a good, informal working tool on which to orally develop and record options in programming or preliminary design situations. Similarly, replies to questionnaires previously sent out to members of the client team may now be jointly analyzed using cards, brown paper, and like aids.

Sometimes decision making between the client's team and the professional's team may be made more productive by means of gaming, a communications technique in which members of both teams act out the roles of key people or groups in an imaginary environment in line with a carefully planned scenario.

THE LECTURE/SPEECH

The requirements of the keynote speech to a conference of commercial developers, the evening lecture to an engineering school assembly, or a major address to a convention of state construction officials differ from the client interview or project conference mainly in degree. There is less verbal interchange—you are guaranteed a block of time in which you can organize your materials and delivery almost at will.

Pitfalls

The following common pitfalls sooner or later face most inexperienced speakers and, now and then, the practiced ones.

Stage fright. The Roman statesman and orator Cato reportedly said: "Hold to your matter and the words will come." The speaker in command of his materials should have no fear, so long as, in those bad few hours before delivery, he focuses on the subject matter and not on the idea of giving a good speech. Some stage fright is desirable—and indeed common—to most professional actors, who say their performance is the better for it.

Rapport with audience. A read speech is an insult to the audience. They could have read it themselves at home in half the time. Focus on one person, preferably nearer the back of the audience than the front, and talk as though you were speaking only to that person. From time to time, sweep your gaze to one side of the audience and then the other.

Breakneck speed. Seasoned speakers claim it is easy to speed up, but almost impossible to slow down, the rate of delivery. For the first few speaking assignments, practice passages on a tape recorder to gauge your speed. If speed is a problem for you, a good hint is to mark your notes at intervals with the word *slow down* in large red capitals.

Other bad habits of delivery. Playback on the tape recorder will also reveal such faults as saying "ah" before every sentence; not pausing regularly for a rest (mostly your listener's rest) before going from one major idea or theme to the next; dropping your voice at the end of sentences (instead of raising it); slurring, or bad articulation of individual words; and a lack of variety—delivering the speech in a flat monotone. Also common are mannerisms, such as scratching your ear, and bad stage habits, like facing a blackboard with your back to the audience.

Avoiding such habits is best done by practicing repeatedly with a tape recorder or, better still, before a small audience of friends, colleagues, or family. These are the toughest audiences; if you excel in front of them, addressing a roomful of strangers is a cinch.

Preparing for a speech

According to Larson in *When It's Your Turn to Speak*, Daniel Webster, when asked how long he took to prepare his famous "Reply to [Senator Robert] Hayne" speech of 1830, replied, "Twenty years." In fact, he had about one day for his homework. Always assume that some day you will be asked to speak. It may be on the planning of acute-care hospital facilities; the engineer's role in air-pollution control; innovative zoning practices; or product packaging. Start a "speech file" now, making an occasional note—a telling point, an unusual piece of information, a happy phrase—in the area of your subject.

When the time comes, schedule a silent hour (after regular office hours or on a plane or train ride) and jot down *any* ideas, however remote, that enter your head on the assigned topic. Then review your speech file for nuggets. Enter all these on small index cards—one idea to a card. Arrange the cards in a sequence that allows a buildup. For example, if your theme is construction management, consider this outline:

1. The owner wants construction value for his money.

2. Traditional techniques often fail because design is divorced from construction and bidding is confined to a single package.

3. Construction management has the answers because a single professional represents the owner in dealings both with design professionals and contractor, and because it permits greater flexibility in the packaging of bids and phasing of construction.

4. As a result, construction management offers the owner more effective controls over quality, schedule, and costs.

Test out the outline with colleagues, and rearrange if need be. Next, expand it to full length and insert examples. Write out phrases for each subtopic on small cards, and underline key words. Except for quotes, *do not write out complete sentences*; the temptation to read them out to the audience is irresistible, and you cannot read and look out at the audience at the same time. With a very large (800 and up) audience, you can get by with fairly frequent glances at your cards. With a small group, avoid this. Make sure your notes are easy to focus on at a glance—triple space them with a pica typewriter or carefully hand letter them (see 7-1).

Rehearse the entire speech two or three times if you are new to speaking or have not spoken on this topic before. More rehearsals than that will take all spontaneity out of your speech.

Writing out the speech. Politicians and corporate executives (or their speech writers) usually write out the entire speech in advance. The main purpose is to preclude any loose word or phrasing that could embarrass the speaker, his government, agency, or company. That is also why such speeches are usually dull. As a professional, you need have no such great fears of misinterpretation, and the added spontaneity of speaking from notes is well worth the slight risk of saying the wrong thing.

Another major drawback of *writing* a speech is that, unless you take precautions, it will *sound* like a written speech. For, in speaking, one uses different vocabulary and terms of speech from the written. The following example shows the written form at left and the spoken at right:

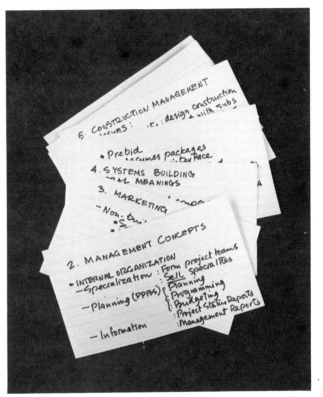

7-1 Write out key phrases for a speech boldly, on small index cards.

We must consider cost, schedule and quality control	We have to watch over cost control and schedule control and quality control.
The contractor went bankrupt since he lacked the capital to bridge the cash flow gap until the next contract.	The contractor went bankrupt because he didn't have the money to tide him over till the next job.
Architects, engineers and their consultants had a lot of commissions . . .	Architects were busy; engineers were busy; their consultants were busy . . .

If you *must* speak from a written text, dictate the speech from notes, and lightly edit the transcript to bring it in under the time limit. This will help ensure a spoken style.

How many words per minute? Your average convention speaker can deliver about 85 words per minute. That means a single, double-spaced page will take about 2½

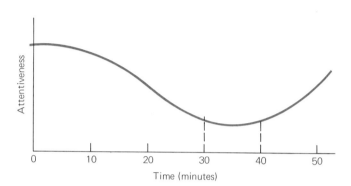

7-2 Classical attention curve for a 50-minute lecture. Keep heavy material out of the 30 to 40 minute slot.

minutes to read—in 25 minutes, you can cover ten such pages. Radio and television announcers are trained to utter about 120 words per minute, and hog callers have been known to top 200. If in doubt, slow down.

Other tips. As noted earlier, the main problem for listeners is to miss a key word and thereby lose the context. Use any means to make the task easier for the listener, such as what consultant Antony Jay calls "sign posting," or setting the scene at regular intervals:

> So here we were—the new site survey showed
> a high water table but the foundation had been
> designed to fit an earlier survey.

Avoid abstractions. This is important for written materials. It is doubly so in speaking:

> The uneven distribution of clinics throughout the community . . .

> Too many clinics in the Tremont area, not nearly enough in Morrisania . . .

Audience size. The larger it is, the more the audience reacts as one man, and the easier it is to influence. Also, the larger it is, the more it reacts to your personality and the less to your subject matter. Therefore (and your host should recognize this), the larger the group, the less intellectual content will you be able to put into your speech.

Attention span. Note the classic attention curve of the traditional 50-minute lecture (see 7-2)—insert your lightest material into the 30 to 40-minute slot, and the heavier points at the beginning and end.

Jokes. Avoid jokes with groups smaller than ten; you will only get embarrassed snickers. On the other hand, jokes are a good lubricant for getting larger audiences to your side at the start. If you cannot tell jokes, pass them up. A flat joke is worse than none at all. Make sure there is at least the thread of a connection between joke and subject and shun off-color jokes.

THE PANEL MODERATOR/CHAIRMAN

Serving as moderator of a conference panel or as chairman of a luncheon is a common experience for many design professionals. Moderating is not the same as giving a speech. You are no longer in the role of superstar but in that of host.

Tasks

Your main task is to see to the smooth running of the program's content. This covers many things.

Introductions. Make no speeches. Usher in the *context* of the topic in a half-dozen carefully chosen and rehearsed sentences. Introduce the speakers by giving only that much of their background as required to justify their presence on the panel. Obtain their biographies in advance, and underscore the most germane items. Throw out the obvious and the irrelevant. The audience does not really care that the expert on value engineering has six children, was born in Bent Fork, Montana, and likes to race sailing sloops.

Timing. Keep panelists or speakers to their assigned time limits. It is unfair to other panelists and to the audience to let a speaker encroach on their time. A slip of paper passed up to the speaker saying "You have 3 more minutes" usually does the trick. If not, more brutal measures are in order, such as a verbal admonition or even unhooking the microphone. Tact, yes, but firmness too are prerequisites for the good moderator.

The discussion/question period. A good, lively bout of questioning from the audience is often the icing that can make the panel cake memorable. There are pitfalls. If questions from the audience are long in coming, ask one or two of your own, prepared ahead of time; this usually serves to prime the pump, and others will follow. If a person in the audience makes a speech in lieu of asking a question, cut him off firmly and ask him point blank what his question is and who on the panel should respond. Always make the audience feel a part of the question phase—repeat aloud any questions that may be inaudible to the audience, as usually happens when asked from the first few rows.

If there is a lively question period, be happy, but be prepared to cut it off to stay within the schedule. Instead of a sudden break, promise two more questions, and do not give in to any more. When you in turn ask questions of the panelists, name him or her *before* you ask the question. It will give the panelist the extra few seconds to prepare a reply.

Seating. When moderating an active discussion among panel members, arrange to sit at the end of the row of seats rather than in the middle if you want to preserve an overview and do not want tennis-watcher's neck (7-3).

In general. Firmness from the very beginning will pay for itself in greater orderliness as your program proceeds. Never show irritation—it guarantees instant loss of authority. Use humor: the light touch is a potent oil for soothing troubled waters. Do not continually assert yourself; act as a catalyst, not as a boss.

THE BROADCAST INTERVIEW

The chief difference between a speech to a live audience and an interview on radio or TV is the size of the audience. A live speech may go to a gathering of from 8 to 8000. On radio or TV, you are talking to an audience of at most one or two, clustered around the living room set or near the car radio. Nor do you have a captive audience—if they do not like your message, they flip the knob and turn it off.

Accordingly, a more informal, fireside chat format is in order—no grand, oratorical gestures. The TV camera, focused mostly on your face, will cut them out anyway. And do not make exaggerated facial expressions—the camera will make you look like a caricature.

Unlike a speech, your broadcast interview time will be severely limited. There will be little or no chance to repeat or clarify statements. Therefore, make your key points first—you never know how much time you will have. I was once asked to discuss the subject of improved construction management procedures and what they will do for the general public on a news program. After about

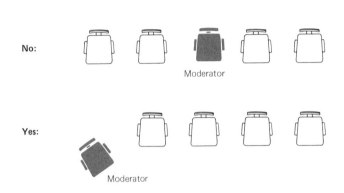

7-3 For good control, the moderator should sit at the end of a row of panelists.

15 minutes of video-taping, the news reporter said, "OK, let's do it in six." It is amazing what you can say in six minutes. At that point, the man said, "Fine, now let's cut it to 90 seconds—it's all we'll have." We did. It is amazing what you can say in 90 seconds.

It is tempting to direct short, furtive looks at the camera. Avoid it. Instead, be sure to look at the interviewer unless you are conducting your own talk show or are running for the presidency.

Radio broadcast

Radio has its own peculiar rules. Silences, for example, have their value on television, if there is time—they may show you as a deliberate, thoughtful person. Any silence on radio of over five seconds will tell your listeners that you just had a heart attack or the transmitter failed. Keep talking. A skillful or kindly interviewer will help bridge the awkward gaps, and, by his phrasing of the questions, will make it easier for you to reply. Homework on the topic, along with a written opening phrase or two, are vital to start the interview off right.

It is easier to get away with a typed text on radio, since no one can see you. Triple space all notes, and avoid rustling the paper. Gesture all you like—some experts advise it, claiming it shows up through an added animation creeping into your tone.

HANDLING THE PRESS INTERVIEW

If the point of the interview is to help a professional journal complete a profile of your firm or the story of a project, follow the procedures described in Chapter 9. Any mis-sayings can be easily corrected through a telephone call. If, however, your interview is with a reporter from a daily newspaper, you will not have that chance. To avoid the danger of being misquoted, answer questions with a complete sentence or rephrase them in your own terms instead of merely saying "yes," "no," or "you're right":

Question: Do you feel the changes in the city zoning law will end up driving out lower income families?

Answers:

No. There are safeguards built into it to stop this from happening.

The changes in the zoning law are part of an overall plan. The point of the plan is to encourage families of all incomes to make the most of the city. Safeguards have been built into the changes . . . etc.

The aim is to get a complete answer into the reporter's notes. Observe how seasoned politicians field questions from the press—it is a good lesson.

ADDRESSING THE COMMUNITY

With the growing stress on citizen participation, chances are you may be called upon to explain an urban design scheme or the plans for a new firehouse or elementary school to the community of which it will become a part. This should not be an encounter, but an excellent oppor-

tunity to get the community on your side for a scheme you have developed and feel strongly about.

It is good to try to program an early formal involvement of the local citizenry into the project development process, rather than presenting them with a scheme that is (or looks) frozen. This will not only tend to defuse opposition but also may contribute toward a better solution.

At the formal meeting, keep your standing as an expert constantly in mind, and confine what you have to say to your own area of expertise. Do not become embroiled in a discussion of the political issues—leave the handling of that aspect to the representative of the public agency.

Always be conscious of the special relationship between the community and those representatives. An ironic example of the need for this awareness occurred several years ago at a public presentation to a group of city officials. A four-person team from a major professional firm was outlining its approach to planning a local urban redevelopment project. Those in the unairconditioned meeting hall, which included over a hundred men and women from the community, sweltered in the airless August night. Inspired (so he thought) by an idea that would raise both the comfort and informality of the occasion, Bill, the head of the team, rose and jovially suggested to the officials that they shed their jackets and ties, and he himself ceremoniously set the example. He was met by a stony glare from the officials, and silence. Why? Despite the heat, he had neglected to see that here were city fathers on view before their constituents and that the officials would naturally see Bill's idea as an unpardonable affront to their dignity.

WORKING WITH AIDS

The most common aids you are likely to use for oral presentations to a client, to a class of architecture students, or to a neighborhood meeting are slides and charts.

Slides

Defeat Murphy's Law by reducing the number of things that can go wrong. As noted earlier, bring your own projector and spare lamps for simple presentations. Locate light switches and receptacles ahead of time, and arrange for an individual to control lights, or to lower blinds in the daytime. Consolidate the slides in one segment of your presentation to avoid a continual turning on and off of lights. Unless you are giving a lecture on the hill houses of northern Greece, where pictures are paramount, keep down the number of slides to the least possible needed to support your talk. Each time a slide is on the screen, you lose direct contact with the audience. Consider an electric pointer that casts a lighted arrow on to the screen for picking out details.

Determine if the setup is to be for front or rear projection, as it will make a difference in the way the slides are oriented in the tray. Indicate the correct orientation with a red mark in the corner of each slide.

When actually showing the slides, comment upon them as little as possible. Slides should be self-explanatory, and viewers will absorb the information much faster by seeing it on the slide than by listening to your explanation. How to plan and design slides for good viewing is covered in Chapter 6. A few pointers are worth adding here:

1. Do not make slides too "verbal"—the point of a slide is to complement, not replace what you (or a taped commentary) have to say.

2. Do not cram too much information on one slide—it is better to make five slides, each with a single message. This will prevent you from having to keep a slide on the screen too long, numbing the audience.

Charts

When showing a sequence from a stack of charts, confine one idea or concept to a chart. As with slides, five charts with one thought apiece are worth more than one chart crammed with five thoughts. Use color for emphasis, and test the lettering size beforehand for legibility from the most distant seat anticipated. (See Chapter 6 for a review of problems of letter size and legibility.)

If you plan to develop charts during the presentation, prepare a light, penciled outline on each sheet beforehand as a guide.

Conclusion

The spoken word is an important segment of every design professional's communications program. Because it helps to secure new work and to share your expertise with students and the community, and because it makes for better liaison with the client during the course of a project, the spoken word merits careful practice.

8

Photography

The purpose of this chapter is not to make the reader into a professional photographer, but to set out the issues every firm needs to consider before embarking on a photographic program.

Whether you design buildings, interiors, industrial products, or landscaping, photography serves to record the project before it is altered by the onslaughts of weather, owner changes, insurrection, and old age. It also saves you the trouble of transporting your client-prospect to each project you feel he should see.

This alone would perhaps not justify all the effort, were it not also for photography's other uses as a key tool in your firm's communications program. Brochures and portfolios, audiovisual presentations, news releases, client newsletters, design award submittals, and exhibit panels—all these hinge for success on the appropriateness and quality of your photography.

The basic purpose of your photography program should be to procure, within your budget, a basic selection of pictures that have the flexibility to be adapted to these various prospective uses.

INITIAL DECISIONS

Before sending out your best amateur house photographer or contacting a professional, it will help to make some initial planning decisions.

Choice of projects

The projects you choose to photograph should be tied in to your overall communications plan as discussed in Chapter 10. Only a limited number of projects will be at a stage or in a condition where they may be used for publicity purposes, and, you may wish to "push" only a handful of those that are. Consider the following criteria for photographing a project—neglecting any one of them may cause technical problems for the photographer.

Degree of completion. Photographing a facility during construction has merit on rare occasions—for example, for showing a "fast-tracked" school or office building—where a photographic record made at each completed stage may later be assembled into a powerful publication or slide show. Otherwise, wait.

Client approval. Do not make a move without it.

Season. Leaves on trees may be important or make no difference. Fall may be better than summer if reds or browns could enhance the look of the project. Early spring may be the best time if dense summer foliage con-

ceals parts of a project, but a winter shot through bare branches is considered too barren. If landscaping is incomplete, a snow-covered foreground safely conceals the problem. The time of year also influences the quality of natural light falling on the subject—harsh or soft, long shadows or short. If you prize views of buildings in use, avoid photographing schools or ski lodges in summer or northern coastal resorts in winter.

Weather. Being unpredictable, weather is a short-term planning problem. By and large, sunlight plays a major role in helping to define the various volumes and planes of a building, the textures of a landscaping design, or the daytime atmosphere of an interior (see 8-1 and 8-2). If a more somber mood is in order, an overcast or rainy sky offers the right quality of light. Projects are often enhanced by shooting after a rainstorm or by hosing down the foreground to allow reflections to enrich the image.

Time of day. This is the most crucial concern in exterior photography. It will in many cases influence the volume of street crowds and traffic or the crowdedness of a building's corridor, lobby, and parking lot, as well as the quality of natural light. For example, a major east-facing elevation must be shot before noon for modeling of planes and volumes by direct sunlight. Night views, usually shot at dusk, give luminous and revealing transparency to glass-walled structures (see 8-3).

Amateur or professional?

Perhaps one design firm in 500 has enough work to keep an in-house photographer busy year round taking shots of projects, models, and miscellaneous reproduction work. The remaining firms need to decide which photographic activities merit the decided advantages of professional help and which may safely be done in-house. Certain routine photography, such as the photographing of slides from artwork, the making of black and white working prints from models, and the visual recording of decisions made on paper or chalkboards at client conferences, may be competently done in-house with a little practice. Consult a reputable reference book for the technique, and use a good custom lab for developing and printing.

There are, on the other hand, projects that require a special kind of judgment—in such areas as the choice and arrangement of artificial lighting; use of larger format cameras; choice of lens and filters and positioning of the camera; choice of film and processing. Such occasions require, above all, intuitive feel and technical know-how

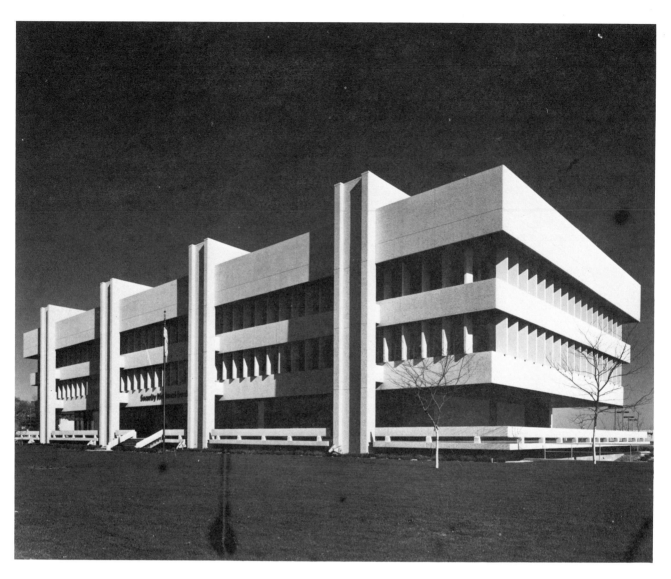

8-1 Sunlight as a definer of a building's various volumes and planes.

8-2 Sunlight enhances the daytime atmosphere of an interior.

8-3 Night views are usually shot at dusk to bring out the transparency of glass-walled buildings.

for achieving the kind of two-dimensional image that will best convey the three dimensions of the project and its setting to the lay viewer. In such cases, engage a professional photographer.

WORKING WITH THE PROFESSIONAL PHOTOGRAPHER

Two-thirds of success lies in the photographer you engage to do the work.

Choosing the photographer

The best way to select a photographer short of inviting a dozen candidates to show you their portfolios (a burden if you work in Tulsa and your favorite candidates are in Chicago, Boston, and Sausalito) is to assess their published work in the professional journals and consumer publications. Check them out for attitude and approach with the designers whose work is shown in the journals, and only then contact them directly. Before making a choice, satisfy yourself on the following points:

Philosophy. Does the photographer's philosophy of portraying a project agree with yours—does he want trick angles or literal representation; dramatic, high-contrast lighting, soft or hard contours; people in pictures or not? Is he meticulous in the arrangement of a scene or an apostle of materialism (i.e., shoot as it is)?

Reputation. Is his reputation in the field and among the professional press one that will smooth your route to publication? Does he shoot all projects himself, or will he lend his credit line but send only a staff man to do the actual photographing?

Personal attitude. Is he open to direction from you, or does he have strongly held ideas on how and when a building should be photographed?

One or many? Should you entrust all your projects to one photographer or spread the burden for variety's sake? This dilemma is often resolved by the cost factor of distance between photographer and project.

Working method. Does he shoot innumerable rolls of film and give you dozens of contact sheets from which to choose the final prints? Or, after he meticulously poses each shot, does his total daily production seldom reach ten exposures?

Cost Are his fees in line with your budget? (See below.)

Availability. Can he come when you need him?

Financial arrangements

Agreements vary widely from one photographer to the next. Before committing your firm to a program, you should look into these matters:

• What is the photographer's daily rate? What is included in the daily rate? Examples and variations include: one set of 8 x 10 black and white prints: contact sheets but no prints; one set of original 35mm color transparencies; one set of original 4 x 5 color transparencies.

• What are his fees for extra prints and duplicates of color transparencies?

• Does he offer the impressive 8½ x 11 black and white print size at no premium?

• What turn-around time can he commit to filling rush orders for prints? At what additional cost? (24-hour service can sometimes create a 100 to 200% surcharge.)

• Will he charge you for time he spends waiting for bad weather to change?

• What expenses will he charge you for? Travel expenses may be high if you want one particular photographer. Most photographers will gladly tell you of their travel plans, and, if a favorite project of yours can be combined with another's, then travel and subsistence expenses—often a major expense item—can be cut in half, or more. Will he bill you for film and processing, or even charge you a markup on those items? Will he bill you for bringing special props? (One well-known photographer was known to transport a rubber plant of a spectacular conformation on all his assignments, along with a trunkful of plastic flowers for exterior planting.)

• Will a journal or the client share in the costs? If so, be prepared to yield some control over selection of views and angles.

After obtaining numerical answers to these questions, you are in a position to work them into your communications plan and compare photographers on an equal basis. Actual dollar figures vary widely. Photographers charge from $150 to $500 per day. Some will work in half-day increments; others will not. Some charge $3.50 for an 8 x 10 print; others, $10; still others, $25. Consequently, a one-day shooting session for a new city hall, assuming no delays and based on a $300 daily fee that includes 10 original black and white prints and 10 transparencies, with additional black and white prints at $10 apiece plus $300 in travel and subsistence expenses, can quickly run the cost of a single project up to the $800 mark. Yet the benefits of having an exciting, professional package of illustrations to show your client-prospect and for other purposes may well outweigh the actual cost because of its marketing and publicity yield.

Rights

Under most arrangements, photographers retain negatives and all rights to publication. This is usually indicated in a credit note stamped on the backs of prints by prudent photographers. It is possible for a firm, client, or publication to buy the rights, but this will naturally lead to a higher fee schedule. Under the more common agreements, publications or product manufacturers who wish to use some of your firm's shots for advertising or other publicity must pay the photographer for that right. The rate varies with the types of user and use, and can range from $25 to as high as $400 per one-time use per print. Ask each photographer for his cost schedule.

Briefing and directing the photographer

The shooting session will be only as productive as the briefing you give the photographer. Before he even unpacks his tripod, he should walk through the project with your designer and someone with marketing or communications duties to absorb the design and note any special shooting requirements. Furnish the photographer with a set of floor plans, sections, and elevations ahead of time so he may get an early feel for the design.

Usually, the personal tour is not practical. In that case, a mailed set of plans and a telephone conversation with the designer are essential. Often, the client himself may offer the time of a senior facilities executive to accompany the photographer for part of the allocated time.

In any event, the effort must be scheduled and coordinated through a single individual in your firm. The aim is to see to such arrangements as access to the building and key spaces or rooms, the possible use of occupants as subjects, and any needed adjustments to the lighting system in the building and grounds.

FURTHER CONSIDERATIONS

A number of additional issues should be thought through as part of your photography planning effort.

People in pictures

Some photographers of interiors, and the journals that publish their work, dislike people in pictures because they get in the way of the furniture. Other photographers will reluctantly admit a person or two in front of a building or landscape scheme for scale.

This attitude ignores the underlying goals of most architectural photography, which is to show a client-prospect a building populated inside and out with happy users. It is true that, from a technical view, working with people can make for problems. You must obtain releases from the people photographed except when they are pictured in a public place. (Even then, lawyers recommend releases if there is any chance the picture will also be used for advertising purposes, such as by a supplier of materials.) You have to deal with the choreography of disposing groups larger than four or five in a space so they do not look stilted. And people do, indeed, hide the better part of a chair by sitting in it. On the other hand, the marketing purposes of photography must take first place.

As a not-so-last resort, you can get some excellent results by entrusting a project where informal people shots are especially important to a press or other photographer who does not specialize in architecture or interiors. These photographers tend to be at ease in crowds, and this is reflected in a fresh human quality of the photograph.

Photographing interiors

Photographing interiors requires special planning to achieve a coherent picture, due to the need for special accessories, furniture rearrangement, free and uninterrupted use of space, the need to control clutter, the special attention that must be given to lighting, and the prime importance of color. Make a special effort, when working with your photographer, to obtain cooperation from the client and users of the spaces. Compromises seldom make the grade when you photograph interiors.

Photographing the architectural model

Exterior and interior photographs of working and finished models are useful for explaining the concept for a project to the client and for marketing purposes. In skilled hands, the camera can produce images so lifelike that, once the building is up, only an insider can say which is the real building. For one thing, special periscopelike attachments for cameras are available for "moving" through the model's spaces.

Model photographs, oddly enough, have two advantages over viewing the actual model. First, pictures are easier to ship. Second, viewers who are laymen as a rule find it easier to identify with a model photograph (which, as noted, often looks like the actual project), than with the model itself, which always seems somehow small and a little bit cute (see 8-4).

Where else to find photographs

Besides arranging for photography of your own projects and models, you may sometimes need additional illustrations to round out a report or special study. For example, a feasibility report on civic centers may need to be illustrated with views of past civic centers, theaters, circuses, shots of happy audiences—some shots must even extend back to the age before photography. Rather than assigning a photographer, many of these shots may be bought ready-made. Examine at least these four good sources for such shots:

1. Stock photo houses or picture agencies, found in most large cities. From time to time, they issue illustrated catalogs of their wares. Black and white prints are paid for on a one-time use basis that can range from $35 to $100 for "inside the book" use to $100 to $200 for black and white cover use.

2. Photo files of your local newspaper. Some papers, such as the New York *Times*, maintain a very large photo library. Fees are about the same as at the stock photo houses. The wire services—such as Associated Press, United Press International, and Reuters—also have photo files.

3. Corporate files. These often carry views of engineering or industrial processes and products. These photographs usually cost far less than the ones from stock photo agencies. Sometimes they are free, as long as the company receives a credit line. Contact public relations or advertising departments of the companies.

4. The Bettman Archive. This New York City agency has a wealth of pictures from the prephotographic and early photographic eras. The archive has tens of thousands of prints and old engravings on almost any topic. Thus, to illustrate a report on solar energy applications, you may uncover some 40 different sun-based images—from a cherub using a lens to set a log on fire to a series of sun faces ranging from sad to happy. Dr. Bettman publishes, for about $20, a thick, illustrated catalog by subject matter of items in his files.

5. Government agencies are excellent sources—the Library of Congress for general subjects, and other agencies, such as the National Institutes of Health, for more specialized subjects.

8-4 Uncanny resemblance between the model and "as-built" photographs of Roosevelt Island, New York.

Conclusion

As noted earlier, this chapter is not intended to be a course on photography, but rather a guide to point up areas to consider before you begin a picture-taking program. If you are interested in exploring the potentials of that medium in greater detail, see the reference section. In addition, major film manufacturers such as Eastman Kodak publish specialized brochures on many topics, from photographing your drawings and other artwork, such as models and renderings in-house, to shooting 8 and 16mm movies.

The sources for commissioning or buying good, sharp photographs are without limit—there is seldom a reason for printing or sending to a client or award jury any but the best.

9

Reaching the media

As any baseball star knows, it is not enough to hit the ball regularly over the left field fence. The star's fame and his fortune are influenced by his public following, and that can be built up only by the power of the media.

However different the services provided by the baseball player and the design professional, the same principle applies. This chapter describes those elements of the nation's media that should interest the design professional, shows proven ways in which to reach them with your message, and lists other ways that are just as guaranteed to fail.

PRESS PROFILES

In different ways and using different tactics, the design office is interested in three classes of media. These are the *professional press*, the *business press*, and the *public media*.

The professional press

Think of the professional press as those journals which publish the work of your colleagues/competitors. In such a framework, an architectural journal is *professional press* to the architect. For the engineering consultant, however, to whom the architect is a major client to be courted, the same architectural journal becomes *business press*.

The indirect value in having your firm's project or profile or a signed technical article by a partner featured in the professional press is very large. Publication by a journal of your peers implies a judgment that can be won through few other channels. And it can bring with it many blessings. Design award juries read the professional journals, and their selection—no matter how glamorous and informative the submitted package on the table in front of them is—is made easier through prior exposure to, and, hence, awareness of the project. Their selection is subtly influenced by the approval implied in publication—editors tend to publish projects they like, and they ignore, rather than censure, those they dislike. Projects that boast a design award look good in your brochure, on slides at the interview, and as a casual mention in the newsletter you may send your clients.

Articles about your firm or written by a partner may be reprinted and included in your firm's brochure or portfolio. Reprints, too, reflect that third-party endorsement that is more valuable than self-praise.

At the national level, the professional press, locked in a struggle for a tight and, in some disciplines, dwindling pot of advertising, usually is hard put to find space for all the projects it would like to publish. This increases the amount of competition for publication of your work.

The regional, state, and local journals, on the other hand, are less limited, not because they have a glut of advertising revenues, but because they are less dependent on advertising and tend to be subsidized out of the dues of members of the local professional society. They vary widely in terms of writing quality, graphic design, and production, and should be scrutinized journal by journal before you cooperate with them in publishing your work.

The business press

The business press is where the clients are, and thus should be a key target of your communications efforts. (The term "business press" is accepted in publishing circles to mean all publications read by suppliers of a product or service. It is not limited to journals specifically for businessmen, such as *Fortune, Business Week, Forbes Magazine*, or the *Harvard Business Review*.)

From your standpoint, think of the business press in terms of what business journals your client is likely to read. These are made up of journals he needs for his job—*Hospitals* if he or she is a hospital administrator; *Appliance Manufacturer* if he is a buyer of industrial design services; *American School Board Journal* and *American School and University* if he is a school or university administrator.

Your client-prospect as a rule also reads another kind of journal—the very business publications in the narrow sense referred to above. Most potential clients are businessmen, and the *Wall Street Journal, Business Week, Fortune*, and other magazines in this group are likely to occupy their in-boxes alongside the more specialized journals.

How do you build up a list of these target journals? *Ullrich's International Periodicals Directory* and *Bacon's Publicity Checker* are a good start. They indicate, by category, the titles of journals, deadlines, names of editorial staff, and contact information. Some, such as Bacon, offer an updating service.

Even better is *Standard Rate and Data Service* (SRDS). SRDS is published in several volumes, one of which covers the business press. It costs some $70 a year, and each monthly issue has over 1300 pages. Do not buy it, but take notes at the public library or ask your friendly advertising agency for last month's copy. The purpose of SRDS is to give advertisers and advertising agencies the background information they need to help them in placing advertising. This helps you because, as a result, every business journal in the nation is listed, arranged into some 160 categories, and conveniently indexed by title and subject matter. Each entry provides generous data.

Especially helpful is the paragraph that sets down in detail each magazine's editorial aims. There is no better directory for getting an overview of the business press.

The public media

The public media are a less productive target for publicity. Aimed at the general public, they are less likely to publicize your new shopping center or calculator design, and when they do, it will be for the project's general news value rather than for its professional distinction. The general news media are also likely to leave out your firm's name if it is not germane to the point of the story.

The proportion of those who read the general media who are in a position to buy your services is very small compared to the general media's overall circulation, and your efforts will bring greater results for each telephone call, postage stamp, and martini that you buy if you direct them where the ratio is much higher—namely, the business press.

There are two exceptions to this rule. The first applies to the financial and real estate pages of the daily and weekly press. Both pages are read by (and hence edited for) the kinds of decision makers you need to reach if your are an architect, engineer, planner, or other professional concerned with the built environment.

The second exception concerns the smaller local newspapers. Suppose your firm has a practice concentrated in your city and its immediate environs, rather than in the state, region, or nation. If so, there is value in a mention of your project or firm even in the general news pages, since it will tend to bring or keep your name before the relatively tight knit circles that direct local business and development activities and control the hiring of professionals. *Ayer's Directory of Publications* lists all daily newspapers.

A growing phenomenon are the architectural critics writing for some of the country's big city newspapers. St. Louis, Boston, Washington, San Francisco, Los Angeles, New York, Chicago, and several other cities have, over the years, carried regular columns on architecture and its related disciplines of planning and landscape architecture. Your work described in such a column may bring you good publicity or bad—these critics are far more outspoken than editors of the professional journals. The audience reached by such columns is made up chiefly of your peers and a group of local interested laymen. But in that group may be the decisionmaker who hires you for the next project.

Broadcast media. Radio and television have the same drawback as general newspapers and the weekly news magazine—an audience that is too general and has a very low proportion of decisionmakers. Again, there are exceptions. An interview on a local station will provide useful visibility, with a good chance of being seen by a high proportion of local government and business people. But there is, of course, the inherent risk in such appearances of not making a good impression. This can happen if the person interviewed does not know how to handle himself well before the cameras or microphone.

Wire services. These are important as they supply the press, including much of the business press you need to reach, with a lot of its editorial fodder. Such companies as Associated Press, Dow Jones, United Press International, and Reuters tailor their services to the needs of their subscribers. Services are broken down into categories and include such areas as general news, sports, finance, and real estate. The wire services also carry regional and big city wires. They have local news bureaus, and a story transmitted in this manner can reach the business pages in papers all over the country. Several newspapers, including the New York and Los Angeles *Times*, also maintain commercial wire services.

UNDERSTANDING THE MEDIA

A basic part of communicating with the media is to understand how their writers and editors work and think. What motivates them? Why are they more likely to publish an article on that library in Milwaukee than a "how-we-conduct-our-interior-design practice" article? Or vice versa?

Following are several fallacies you should recognize—the fallacy is on the left, the truth on the right:

1. Editors eagerly await news of your projects, practice, and personnel.	Editors have their own editorial plans for the month and year. If what you send them fits, you are lucky. If not, be patient.
2. Take an editor to lunch. It will help clear space for you in his magazine.	Reputable editors are (rightly so) very sensitive to the implied obligation of the free lunch. Some have a fixed policy of paying their own way. By all means meet and discuss your practice. Do not push ideas (such as, "I think you might like to publish our new waste treatment plant . . .") Editors have their egos. Let them take the initiative as to what they want.
3. Once an editor has ignored an idea or overture, the case is hopeless.	Editors have long memories and bottomless files. An idea for an article on the relationship between the design of lamp posts and energy conservation may glean no response today, but may land you the main feature six months hence.
4. Editors are delighted to save time by having contributors (such as yourself) write the article for them.	Any journal with the budget to hire enough staff prefers to write its own articles, except for those on highly technical topics. Where editors accept a contributed article, they reserve the right to edit, sometimes heavily, as their job is to see each article communicates with their readers. Do not, therefore, insist on the last word. You may never be asked again.

5. The editor prefers to work with professional public relations people in gathering information, as they are more aware of his needs.

Editors want to go to the source. If the subject is right, they will find a way of making it intelligible.

6. Editors do not want to be bothered by firms seeking publicity for their work.

If you do not tell them, who will? (But see Fallacy No. 1).

7. The piece will appear in June, as promised.

Last minute advertising space cancellations, or a more lively story, may mean you will be bumped for July, or even August.

Reaching the press

How do you get the attention of the press? Public relations reputations have been made and lost over promises and guarantees to "place" an article. Such promises are a presumption and totally misread the way the press thinks and functions.

For a story or idea to be covered in the professional and business press, one or more of these conditions must prevail:

1. The topic is timely.

2. The topic fits the editor's plan. Normally, Nos. 1 and 2 should coincide, but not always. All journals have, and some disclose, the main theme of each issue 12 months ahead. Gear your approach to such a plan.

3. Your firm is well-known.

4. Your firm is not known at all but has achieved a breakthrough that will allow an editor to "scoop" his rivals.

5. You and the editor were classmates at Yale. This should make no difference, but, given two otherwise equally qualified firms for a story, it may swing the balance in your favor.

6. Your firm is prepared to write the article and has writing talent to do a good job. You also have a reputation for providing high-quality artwork.

The best way to start is to telephone or write a simple letter (maximum: half a page) to the editor-in-chief setting out the proposed topic and the reasons for its merit. Follow up ten days later. Another way to begin is by attending conventions. One reason editors attend, aside from covering the proceedings, is to meet just such firms as yours.

It has been said that firms that practice in the publication's home town have an unfair advantage. There is, indeed, some benefit in meeting editors face-to-face at exhibitions, lectures, and cocktail parties and in arranging lunch appointments with ease. On the other hand, most editors are acutely aware of this situation, and try consciously to serve up a geographically balanced fare.

WORKING WITH THE PRESS

Once you and an editor have come to an understanding that he will publish a piece describing some aspect of your firm's work, there are several paths the plan may take.

Written by the editor

If the piece is to be staff-written by the journal, you will have certain commitments:

Materials. The article will be based on interviews and background materials. If the article is about a project, provide the bones by presenting the basic statistics (see 10-5). Supply a selection of 8 x 10 photographs with glossy finish. If possible, send the editor a contact proof sheet so he has a broad range of photographs to choose from. Obtain clearances from the photographer. Negotiate with the editor as to who pays for prints and fees and for any new photography that must be made. In this last case, the journal will be prepared to share costs if the project is to be a major feature. Otherwise, you may have to pay. But if it is you who pays, you can call the tune and direct the photographic effort so you can use the results for other purposes, such as brochures and design award programs.

If the article is about a process, such as project management, value engineering, or cost control, interviews by the editor with the experts in your firm are the most efficient way of gathering the facts. Offer the editor reprints of past articles on the subject. This will save him the trouble of going over old ground. Also look for reports of related studies or investigations done for past clients.

If the article is a profile about the firm, select one staff member to coordinate the inevitable series of photographing sessions and of personal visits to the office and drafting room. Give the writer every bit of background information you feel he should see (personal résumés, office brochure, representative research reports, statements of philosophy), so he does not waste his time and that of others by asking questions to which there are printed answers. You are quite within your rights to ask to review the final manuscript for *factual* accuracy.

Be prepared not to like the outcome. As Fallacy No. 1 states, any invitation to write a firm profile is tied to the journal's own editorial plan. The journal is not doing it as a favor to you. Unless the article is very unfavorable—unlikely, under the circumstances—it should be useful for your firm's marketing program.

Deadlines. For an editor, due dates are holy. If the story is staff-written, the key deadline covers the delivery to the editor of background materials. Miss the date by more than a few days (for a weekly magazine by a few hours) and you risk being bumped or forgotten.

Clippings. If you are interviewed by a newspaper reporter, do not ask for a clipping when the story is published. He assumes you read his paper.

Credits and courtesies. Provide complete credits. Your client should be informed if a story is being prepared about his product or facility. Chances are he will be pleased. If he declines, you may still have the right to proceed. Check the original agreement, which should have spelled this issue out. Often, an owner will agree provided such statistics as cost figures are not cited. Others, especially in case of a residence, will agree so long as the name and exact location are omitted, to prevent a tide of visitors.

Some design firms limit credits to the name of the firm

1. Overture

Propose a topic to editor.

Determine the slant of editor's interest—technical, aesthetic, management, financial, or other.

Discuss honorarium but expect little, as publication is to your advantage.

2. Preliminary

Submit an outline. (Include, under each main heading, a descriptive sentence or two and an estimate of the number of words. Also identify the number and nature of proposed illustrations.)

Adjust the outline to editor's suggestions.

Establish deadlines for first draft and for the final manuscript and artwork.

3. Development

Conduct in-house and external research.

Prepare or assemble photographs, drawings, and other artwork.

Write a first draft.

Submit a first draft and proposed artwork (which need not be in final form at this stage).

4. Delivery

Incorporate revisions to the first draft.

Complete artwork in camera-ready form.

Prepare suggested captions for artwork (editors will usually rewrite these).

Assemble credits—author; photographers; project client; associated consultants; suppliers.

Prepare short (4-6 line) author's biography.

Submit combined materials to editor. Type the text double-spaced, with margins of at least 1 in./2.54 cm.

5. Final touches

Review type galleys for typographical and factual accuracy. The editor will no doubt have made some minor—even major changes—to improve the article's impact on his readers. Do not try to adjust text at this stage except on grounds of accuracy. Respond promptly.

Arrange for reprints.

9-1 Steps in developing an article for the press.

and the main outside consultants. You may have trouble persuading an editor to make such a policy stick, especially if the project team includes a well-known designer who is not a name partner. Other firms provide a list of all professional staff connected with the project, and still others list only those who led the major activities—for example, design, project management, and technical input. It is good to have a policy on this. It is another matter to enforce it.

Written by you

Many of the same precepts apply when you contribute a finished article. See 9-1 for an outline of steps in developing an article. The big distinction is that you, rather than the editor, will synthesize all the materials. When writing, follow the suggestions contained in Chapter 4. When preparing artwork, review relevant sections of Chapters 3 and 5. In addition, note the following tips:

Text. Type the manuscript in pica-sized type, double-spaced, with 1 in./2.54 cm margins all around. Avoid typewriters with proportional type—it makes it harder for the editor to compute length. Send two copies: one stays clean, the other is for editing.

Although editors in general prefer to write their own headlines, decks, subheads, and scans, they welcome suggestions.

A touchy issue is that of ghosting. Your expert on cost control or landfill management may know his topic a lot better than he can write about it. If the writing is then assigned to someone in your firm (or even to outside public relations counsel) who is more articulate, the editor may balk. In that case, it is better to submit a stodgy piece that tells the story, and leave it to the editor to clear up. Or else the expert may wish to tape his thoughts according to an agreed outline, and you can then edit the transcript.

Artwork. All artwork should be camera-ready. This means that the editor should only have to crop, reduce, or enlarge—not add titles or do any retouching. Avoid slides unless you have pretested them for conversion to black and white.

Some architectural journals redraw all floor plans, sections, and elevations for consistency, and add uniform titles. Be glad, as this is a thankless task.

Few editors will grant you more than 2500 words in which to tell the story. That is very scant—some ten double-spaced typewritten pages. As noted in Chapter 4, this requires tight control over content and style, paring away anything not in the scope of the outline.

Exclusives. Many journals, especially those which make a point of regularly presenting design projects in some detail, insist on exclusive rights to a project "in their field." That means that if *Progressive Architecture* wants to devote eight pages to your new fire station, you can also offer it to *Firefighting News*, but not to *Architectural Record*.

Exclusives are a legitimate form of self-protection for the press, if done within reason. If you commit your project to magazine A, and magazine A delays it for months without signs of publishing it, you should feel free to rescind the agreement and approach magazine B. Some journals with design award programs also require a first-publication rights commitment from the winners. It is best to go along with such arrangements unless the project is of such stature or import that you and your client can dictate the terms.

When to hold a press conference

Press conferences are costly to stage and quite hard to control. Therefore, at least the following conditions should exist before you hold one:

• The event is dramatic enough to attract a large body of reporters (this probably disqualifies staff promotions, a merger, a new branch office, a major design award, a $50 million hospital commission). A design or technical breakthrough that will cut the cost of ambulatory facilities in half is well worth a press conference.

• You can expect at least two dozen reporters, to justify the room rent and the caterer. This may mean holding the conference in a large city, with concomitant travel expenses on your part.

• You are prepared to pay for an elaborate press kit that all reporters expect to take with them, to free their time at the conference for asking questions and testing the canapes. The press kit may also be mailed to editors and reporters who do not attend.

It is not the aim of this work to deal further with the mechanics of press conferences. This is an art that requires a fine touch and much experience, and outside public relations counsel is usually in order to stage-manage the event (see 9–2).

SO YOU WANT TO WRITE A BOOK

We all, it is said, have one book in us. Some of us have more. A book may be an important sales tool for your practice.

What to consider

Before acting on impulse, you should consider a number of factors:

Time. Writing a book is not something that should be sandwiched in between regular activities. One or the other will suffer. One way to mitigate this conflict is to set aside a regular time each day, or day each week.

Funds. Until you are famous as a writer, and sometimes not even then, publishers will advance you only a modest sum against royalties while you are writing the manuscript. Some will advance nothing. You need, therefore, a reserve of dollars to tide you over, unless your partners or employer agree to keep you on salary or draw.

Topic. Ask yourself who but you cares about the subject? Are those who care necessarily the ones with the cash to buy your book after it is published?

Research. Is much of the material (content, photography, artwork) at your fingertips, or will you need to spend extra time, effort, and even travel to obtain it? Personal experience in the subject is a big asset, as it not only reduces research time but also tends to transmit itself subliminally to the reader.

Medium. Should it be a book at all? Would what you have to say be said better through a series of articles, a pamphlet, or a lecture series?

Facility of writing. Does writing come easily to you? This can mean two things. First, writing may *not* come easily, but once down on paper, it will require little editing. Fine. Second, whether it comes easily or not, is the writing turgid or dull, requiring major editing or perhaps a total rewrite by a professional writer before publication? In that case, embark on the project with great caution. Publishers are businessmen and will balk at committing themselves to a book that requires too much time from their in-house editors.

Fame or fortune? A book is a useful item to hand to prospective clients, especially if it is in an area of professional concern and not a study about the decline of the white moth in Western Utah. A book may also raise your standing with your peers. Do not, however, count on a book to make a major financial gain, unless the publisher feels it may become a universal handbook and textbook in the profession and beyond. Most publishers pay a royalty of about 10% on the first 5,000 to 10,000 copies sold, an extra 2½% on the next 5000, and a final further increment of 2½% on all additional copies. This is computed not on the list price but the so-called net selling price—the amount the publisher actually receives after subtracting the bookseller's discount. This amount is usually about 60% of the list price.

If, therefore, the list price of your book is pegged at $15, quick arithmetic will show that on the first 5000 copies sold, you will receive $4500; on the next 5000 copies, $5625; and on every additional 5000 copies, $6750. Nonfiction books that sell over 15,000 copies are rare.

What to do before you approach a publisher

If, after reviewing the foregoing questions, you decide to write a book, be prepared to develop certain documents to submit to prospective publishers.

A publisher will require at least three things: the *prospectus*, the *outline*, and a *typical chapter*.

The prospectus. The prospectus is a four to six-page memorandum that tells the publisher what your topic is and why he should take it seriously from a publishing viewpoint. Describe the intended audience in detail—its main subdivisions, what may motivate it to buy the book, its buying power, and its whereabouts. The last point is important because a large portion of book sales is by direct mail, and a publisher will smile more if he is assured that 95% of prospects may be reached through one or two easily rented mailing lists. Also, indicate the expected length (in words) of the book and the amount and type of artwork.

The prospectus is a tool you use to try to "sell" the publisher. It must be so written.

The outline. On three or four pages, list the title, the chapter titles, and the main points to be covered in each chapter. Assign a length in words to each chapter, and give a breakdown of proposed artwork.

Typical chapter. Select a chapter that is neither the introduction nor the conclusion, write, edit it, and polish it to a fine gloss. Add artwork as needed.

9–2 A typical press conference.

Approaching the publisher

There are three ways of getting your book published. The first is to publish it yourself, under your firm's imprint. This makes sense only for books of limited circulation. As a design professional, you are not geared to the business demands of publishing, such as printing, pricing, promotion, keeping records, and accounting. The task would quickly overload your staff and facilities.

The second course is to interest the so-called vanity press. A vanity press concern will publish your book under its imprint, handle the record keeping, and provide limited promotion in return for a commitment on your part to buy a minimum number of copies and, often, pay a substantial fee. The company then shares sales proceeds with you on a prearranged basis.

The third method is the most desirable and the hardest—namely, to interest a commercial publisher to take on your book. If you know or can get an introduction to an editor, write him or her a half-page letter describing your intent and your readiness to furnish a prospectus, outline, and typical chapter at once. Usually, you should receive a prompt reply, as publishing is a very competitive business and no editor wants to pass up an opportunity. If the editor accepts the idea, you negotiate an agreement and proceed with the manuscript. If not, approach a second, a third, a fourth publisher, until you get an acceptance. Be patient. Many best sellers are not accepted until the 17th try. Do not commit the faux pas of approaching two publishers at one time, unless you notify them to that effect.

Agreements

An agreement between author and publisher is a legal document. It is often longer and more complex than an architect/owner agreement to design a $50 million hospital. In essence, the agreement covers the rights retained by each party and the circumstances under which the book will be written, paid for, promoted, and reprinted. Agreements tend to have *standard* and *special* clauses.

Standard clauses. These cover such issues as rights at home and overseas—copyright is, as a rule, assigned to the publisher for convenience; manuscript delivery date; claims; royalties for bookstore, direct mail, and other kinds of sales; promotion; subsidiary rights by book clubs; foreign language editions, film, and television; new editions; and out-of-print rights.

Special clauses. These cover arrangements such as your rights to buy a certain number of copies at a price close to the publisher's manufacturing cost. This can be an advantage if you wish to use the book for marketing purposes. By agreeing to buy 1000 or 2000 copies, you can often obtain them at a very low cost. In that case, however, the publisher will need to satisfy himself that you will not be distributing the book free of charge to the very same market to which he is trying to sell it.

Conclusion

Writing a book can be an exciting venture, and a useful marketing tool. It does, however, require care, time, trouble, and funds, and should be entered upon only after a good, long look at the issues.

10

Organizing your communications effort

How a firm organizes its communications effort depends to some extent on such factors as size, geographical scope of the firm, and its marketing emphasis. Typical variations are indicated in 10-1.

OBJECTIVES AND FUNCTIONS OF THE COMMUNICATIONS EFFORT

Despite these variations, every firm's communications program has certain common objectives. These are *support of the direct marketing effort*; *public relations*; *development of publications*; and *information clearing house*. How these objectives may be translated into functions and activities is shown in 10-2.

Some of the activities will be carried out in-house, some through consultants. Unless your firm is very large, chances are that you will omit many of the activities listed, or conduct them on a more modest scale. As pointed out in Chapter 3, it is not necessary to order expensively produced brochure components when crisp, typewritten pages coupled with direct photographic prints are more in line with your budget and frequency of need. Nor, again, do you have to hire additional help or divert office personnel from fee-paying projects when properly directed and coordinated outside consultants and suppliers are available to handle graphic design, editorial work, presentation drawings, and so on.

The checklist points up how important an organized communications concept is to your firm. There are at least four ways to use the checklist:

1. To identify potential communications activities you are not now conducting.

2. To aggregate or group activities and relate them to efficient use of manpower in your office.

3. To identify and group those activities that could be assigned on either a per-project or a retainer basis to outside consultants or suppliers.

4. To help you prepare an annual communications plan and budget.

ORGANIZING AND MANAGING COMMUNICATIONS

Management and administration of the communications operation should be centered in or assigned to a single person, not necessarily on a full-time basis. Whether the responsibility includes communications *planning* or consists chiefly of the *carrying out* policies and procedures set by the principals, or is a combination of the two, depends

- Small firm (1–8 persons) with general, local/regional practice.
- Small to medium firm (4–35 persons) with specialized national practice (such as health facilities, construction management, systems building, or research).
- Medium-sized firm (9–50 persons) with general practice.
- Firm with high proportion of "interprofessional" work (engineers, landscape architects, interior designers, industrial designers, special consultants).
- Large firm (50 persons and up). Three variants include:
1. Multi-branch firm (branches autonomous or integrated)
2. Multi-specialty firm
3. High overseas volume

10-1 Typical breakdown of design firms by size and scope. Some types of firms often require a communications output well above the average.

on how each firm thinks about its communications. A number of typical patterns are shown in 10-3.

The coordinator's role may require him or her at various times to:

- Reconcile opposing views. Should the firm do a single brochure or a 6-module portfolio? Should it purchase equipment, lease equipment, or buy service from an outside supplier? Should it enter three design award programs this year, or nine?

- Move ahead rapidly with a communications project that has been approved.

- Become a reliable source of information so problems may quickly be related to practical issues of cost, time, and technical feasibility.

To succeed in that role, the person assigned to it must be granted a measure of authority. Small and medium-sized firms tend to allocate communications duties to a principal or associate, often combining them with direct market development functions.

In larger firms, a full-time individual should be retained as coordinator and manager—he or she should report to a senior or associate partner and derive required authority from such a partner. Such authority is essential, since an important duty is to extract information from project managers and department heads, who tend to balk at any diversions from fee-producing projects.

Activity	Examples	Function
Direct Marketing Support		
Market planning		Identify job sources (news clippings; *Commerce Business Daily;* various market letters)
		Contact and explore job sources
		Follow up (see: *Interview preparation, Proposal development)*
Interview preparation		Preliminary slide selection
		Preliminary selection of brochure components
		Bind brochure
Proposal development		Write/edit
		Design
		Produce
		Coordinate
		Deliver
Advertising (see p. 58)		Review candidate media
		Prepare budget
		Write/edit copy
		Design
		Produce
		Coordinate internally
		Coordinate with media
Public Relations		
Prepare design award submittals		Write/edit text
		Select, process illustrations
		Obtain client approvals
		Package
		Pay fees
		Mail
		Coordinate
Develop exhibit panels		Write/edit text
		Select, process illustrations
		Design
		Coordinate in-house
		Coordinate with processing/mounting shop
		Pay fees
		Ship
Develop client newsletter		Plan and coordinate
		Write/edit
		Design
		Produce
		Mail

10-2 Checklist of potential communications functions. Only the very largest firms carry on such a comprehensive range of activities.

Activity	Examples	Function	
Develop news releases		Identify need	Produce
		Write/edit	Distribute
		Design	Follow up
Media relations		Woo media	
		Furnish project data	
		Furnish office data	
		Check draft	
		Coordinate reprints	
Develop articles		Plan	
		Write	
		Illustrate	
		Edit	
		Coordinate with author	
		Coordinate with press	
		Coordinate reprints	
Clipping service		Engage service	
		Send news releases to service	
		Monitor	
		Disseminate clippings	

Publications Program

Activity	Examples	Function
Develop reports for clients	Planning	Edit
	Feasibility	Design
	Research	Produce
	Other	Coordinate
		Deliver
Develop portfolio/brochure system	Basic office promotional piece	Plan
	Specialization pieces (such as health facilities)	Write/edit
	Project fact sheets	Design
	Service fact sheets	Produce
	Client lists	Coordinate in-house
	Project lists	Coordinate with branch offices
	Lists of publications by staff	Coordinate with consultants
	Staff biographies	Coordinate with suppliers
	Reprints	
	Containers/binding system	
	Logo	
Special publications	Self-financed research reports	Edit
		Design
		Produce
		Coordinate with author
		Coordinate with consultant
		Coordinate with outside suppliers

Activity	Examples	Function
Financial reports (publicly owned firms)	Quarterly newsletter Annual report SEC 10-K report News releases	Plan Write/edit Design Produce Coordinate in-house Coordinate with legal counsel, auditor, designer Coordinate with outside suppliers Distribute
Internal communications	Stationery and memoranda Contract forms Project management forms House organ Bulletin boards	Design Produce Store Coordinate

Information Clearinghouse

Activity	Examples	Function
Visitors	Clients Professionals Students Consultants Branch office staff Press	Guide Furnish resources
Library	Books Periodicals Unclassified project reports Project files	Process Inventory

Marketing and public relations resources	Printed
	  Text
	  Photographic
	Audiovisual
	  Slides
	  Tapes
	  Films
	  Equipment
		Inventory
		Update/replace
		Secure

Personnel biographies	Biographical (listing) Biographical (narrative) Photographs	Update Coordinate
Mailing lists	Clients (past, current, prospects) Friends of the firm Media Financial Employees Clipping bureau	Develop Categorize Select format Update Coordinate
Branch office liaison		Fact finding Supply promotional materials

10-2 (Continued.)

SMALL FIRM WITH A LOCAL/REGIONAL/GENERAL PRACTICE (see 10-1)

Description. Over 90% of work as prime professional. Clients local, some statewide. Occasional association with out-of-state specialist firms. Over half of commissions traceable to local civic, social, and business contacts; a few to successful written proposals for federal work. Special communications effort needed to compete with larger, better known outside firms.

Communication products. One- or two-page project fact sheets, typewritten or typeset, illustrated. One- to two-page fact sheet on firm's organization, services, philosophy, partners. Cover sheet. Listing of past clients. Listing of awards and publications. Article reprints. 35 mm slides and glossy 8 by 10 photographic prints. Design award submittals. Government and corporate qualification forms. Appropriate elements assembled and bound according to need—mailed to client or left at interview.

Organization. No full-time communications staff. Heavy involvement by partner, especially planning, coordination, writing, and editing. Employee does presentation drafting and graphics after the initial guidelines are set up by a graphics consultant or advertising agency. Assembly of brochure by junior staff under partner's guidance. Photo files and project fact sheet inventory maintained by secretary. Many small firms seek and find secretaries who can draft; drafting personnel who can type; designers who can write/edit. Professional photographer retained for one to two key projects per year (see Chapter 8) balanced by in-house amateurs.

Budget for growth-oriented firm or firm with low work backlog: usually 7 to 12% of gross income covers the total marketing effort; 75 to 90% of this covers salaries; the balance goes for such expenses as travel, dues, typesetting, printing, limited outside photography, and consultants. Based on $300,000 in gross fees, $21,000 to $36,000 would be allotted to total marketing, with perhaps 20% of this amount allocated to production of communication materials and 80% to direct marketing. Percentages do not include reports, shared photography, and presentation drafting chargeable to client.

For a stable firm or firm with high work backlog, the budget could be approximately one-half of above percentage, or 4 to 6% of gross income.

SMALL TO MEDIUM FIRM WITH A SPECIALIZED NATIONAL PRACTICE (see 10-1)

Description. Nationwide clientele. Firm specializes in such areas as health facilities, educational facilities, systems building, or construction management. Commissions traceable to strong promotional effort, including printed and audiovisual materials and participation at specialized conventions. Firm usually serves as prime professional or in association with a second firm.

Communications products. Detailed, carefully structured project fact sheets, usually typeset and illustrated. Firm's services fact sheet, more elaborate, may run to eight pages or more. Other fact sheets list past clients, publications, and awards. Sizable inventory of 35 mm slides and glossy 8 x 10 photographic prints. Heavy stress on article writing in specialty journals, design award submittals to specialized client associations, and preparation of exhibit panels. Two to three news releases per year. One to two self-financed research publications per year. Formal reports for clients.

Organization. No full-time communications staff until firm reaches 15–25 persons. While office is small, one partner coordinates development of materials, coordinates work of "borrowed" draftsman, does limited public relations, and sets criteria for development and upkeep of promotional resource files, slides, photographs. Resource files under stewardship of versatile assistant. As firm grows above 20, a full-time manager in charge of communications effort spends most of the time on coordination of materials preparation, press relations, support of search effort, response to leads.

Budget. From 8 to as high as 15% of gross income goes into marketing, and as much as 30% of that into development of promotional materials and public relations oriented travel (speeches, lectures, and panels). 75 to 90% of these outlays are for personnel time, the rest for out-of-pocket expenses.

MEDIUM-SIZED FIRM WITH GENERAL PRACTICE (see 10-1)

Description. 90% of work as prime professional. Practice concentrated in city and region, with occasional commissions beyond it. No specialization, but commissions fall into prestige institutional and some high-quality commercial. Personalized approach by the marketing partner and associates is a major factor in job development.

Communications products. Project fact sheets, combined with a typeset, printed, illustrated 8-page, saddle-stitched basic brochure that is updated every two years. Project fact sheets assembled as needed, by building type (like schools) and services (such as master planning); each category has introductory sheet listing clients, awards, and publications. Two to three news releases per year. Eight-page client newsletter issued every six months. Strong stress on design awards (six to eight submittals per year). Government and corporate qualification forms. Proposals (six to eight per year). Formal reports for clients.

Organization. One full-time person plans and coordinates production of communications elements; uncovers and explores job leads; administers inventory of promotional resources; contacts media; and edits proposals. Assisted by a half-time clerk/typist. Reports to marketing partner. Presentation drafting by employees borrowed from project work. Three projects per year photographed professionally for a total cost of $1000–$1200. Graphic consultant used to develop first-time format and procedures for different types of communications products; execution is by employees.

Budget. 6 to 8% of gross income allocated to marketing including communications. Marketing dollars first come out of a general promotion budget from which funds are assigned to each project sought; if it wins, a separate account is set up within project to build up communications fact and photo file.

FIRM WITH HIGH PROPORTION OF "INTERPROFESSIONAL" WORK (see 10-1)

Description. 50% of work is as prime professional, 50% as consultant to other professionals, mostly architects. The firm, therefore, has a two-pronged effort. As the "prime," the firm needs a full range of promotional materials. As consultant, the firms relies on referrals and needs a reduced range of materials Such firms, because of special technical expertise (engineering firms, industrial design firms), also promote directly to manufacturers.

10-3 Various approaches to organizing the communications effort. Five general models that each firm must adjust to its own goals and circumstances are shown. Size of work backlog, state of the economy, desire for growth, type of client, and specialization must be considered.

Communications products. Basic 12-page brochure describes services, past clients, and projects. Larger engineering firms also prepare smaller brochures on subspecialties (like transportation planning, materials handling, and building management). Updated every two to five years. Series of project fact sheets supplement base brochure. Heavy stress on published technical articles. Larger firms issue a regular technical letter (see 10-6) mailed to prospects among prime professionals. When the latter is choosing a team to promote a project, team member firms furnish credentials which are recast into an umbrella proposal package; hence, such credentials should be kept very simple, typed. Good photography is crucial. Heavy on reports (mostly typewritten) for clients.

Organization. Even in medium-size firms, if they have a high (over 50%) ratio of referral work, there is minimum in-house involvement with communications. The basic brochure is assigned to outside editorial and graphic consultants and photographers. As firm's prime professional workload rises, firm's organization takes on profile of firms with general practice (above).

Budget. Wide range (5–12%) of gross fees allotted to marketing. The amount varies with ratio of referrals: a high ratio requires fewer publications, less travel, and less time of marketing personnel. Much repeat work also lowers outlays.

LARGE FIRM

Description. Three variants of the single office large firm include: the multi-branch firm, with branches either autonomous or integrated; the multi-specialty firm; and the firm with a high volume of overseas business.

Communications products. Several variations possible for brochure/portfolio system: basic family of fact sheets describes the firm and key projects; is augmented by appropriate fact sheets and a cover that stress identity of the branch that is promoting new project. Parts are assembled by mechanical binder into single package. Fact sheets may also be divided according to specialty, with identifying covers or binding, stressing identity of specialty rather than that of the firm. Firms with much overseas business consider one to two-page general fact sheets in key foreign languages as a supplement to English materials; they also include metric dimensioning of project illustrations.

Other products. Formal reports for clients. News releases as needed. Frequent entry into design award and exhibit programs. Client newsletter issued quarterly. Annual financial report (publicly owned firms). In-house newsletter as liaison between branches. Special self-financed study reports. Active media relations.

Organization. Overall policy typically set by principals' management committee. Office policy may range from heavy reliance on outside writing/editing, graphics, and photography, with planning and coordination in-house; or else total in-house performance. Either course requires a senior full-time person (occasionally at the associate or partner level), often with a full-time assistant, to plan and coordinate effort within large single-office firm or among branches of multi-branch practice. Full-time individuals for graphics, editorial, and photography come only in firms in the 200-persons-and-over range. Even then, presentation drafting, special maps, and so on usually are done by borrowed project draftsman. For the brochure system, numbered master fact sheets are stored in the central office and assembled to fit the type of client. Assembled and bound copies reflective of general work of firm are kept on hand in all branches. Full-time associate's functions include search for and follow up of job leads; may include direct promotion activity.

Budget. Averages 5–10% of firm's income depending on circumstances. Thus, for firm with $3 million in billings, $150,000 to $300,000 might be allocated to all marketing, including salaries; about 20% of this, or $30,000 to $60,000, may be assigned to developing marketing communications products. This must cover salaries of full-time communications manager and staff and of part-time involvement of assistants in the branches. Salary of the full-time partner or associate is apportioned among communications and direct promotion activities.

General budget note. The 20% of total marketing outlays assigned to communications reflects typical practice but is open to review, as no clear dividing line exists between direct promotion and communications or marketing support. The high proportion of senior principals' time and the expenses of travel for direct promotion accounts in large part for the 80% to 20% ratio of direct promotion expense to communications expense.

10-3 (Continued.)

Another route is to supplement the coordinator's duties with major communications planning and even direct marketing responsibilities, along with partner or associate status. The need for swift decisions will quickly be resolved by means of such added formal authority.

Staffing requirements

As indicated in 10-3, the smaller firm's communications effort may be carried out through a principal allocating part of his time to this duty and working with an administrative assistant who has some editorial background. The actual work of writing, design, and production is assigned to employees temporarily taken off their regular duties for that purpose. Other needed services are bought outside.

As a firm expands beyond about the 25 employee mark or opens a branch office, a full-time manager should be considered to pull together the many strings of the communications operation. And as a firm expands further (into specializations and/or a national practice), the manager may find the workload will also require a full-time writer/editor, and perhaps a graphic designer (who would also prepare mechanicals and supervise typesetting and printing).

By this time, there begins to evolve a full-fledged development resource center (DRC). Library functions are not usually part of a DRC; nor are project and personnel records, although these are useful sources of information for some activities, such as the preparation of proposals.

Every office needs to develop a "least-cost" balance between the three methods of getting the work done—drawing on available office talent on an on-loan basis; buying outside; and, finally, hiring full-time.

As a rule, outside consultants, such as graphic designers, will tend to deliver the finished product somewhat faster than an internal staff-on-loan operation that draws experts from all parts of the firm—to the outside consultants, you are—after all—a client who must be kept happy.

On the other hand, a fat backlog of project report writing and encouraging market estimates for the coming year, may show that dollars spent on a consultant's fees (including his profit) and expenses (including his mark-up), could be used instead to hire the services of a qualified, full-time graphic designer, cutting back the need for outside coordination. A similar analysis may suggest the need for a full-time writer/editor.

Borrowing project staff. The practice of borrowing regular draftsmen and other project personnel for communications tasks must be handled with kid gloves, as no firm likes to see fee-producing labor diverted to overhead-type duties. Also, it helps to know in advance what staff will be needed. As soon as you make a communications plan for each coming year, you will be able clearly to foresee the need for such borrowing of staff. Project staff should be alerted in good time so the extra effort may be worked into their regular project schedules.

The annual communications plan

Every firm, but especially, perhaps, the smaller firm, should prepare an annual communications plan and budget. This will help avoid surprises in the shape of sudden unexpected outlays and staffing needs. The plan should list all projects and activities for the coming year that will require communications input. Items may be identified as "definite," "probable," and "other," and duration times and due dates should be assigned to each product (see 10-4).

Here are some suggestions for developing the annual plan:

Preparation of text and artwork. As soon as a project is placed on the list, it should trigger an effort to make sure needed art and text materials are ready on time, based on estimated lead times required for writing and editorial reviews, drafting, photography, and audiovisuals.

Cultivation of sources. Your communications effort will starve unless linked to the network of in-house and outside sources that will feed it a regular diet of facts on projects, people, and services. The problem is manageable in the smaller firm due to proximity of the sources. In the larger or geographically dispersed firms, the communications manager may develop the network in the following ways:

• Prepare a simple project data questionnaire, and ask project managers to fill in the information for each of their projects (see 10-5). The form should ask for completion dates for key phases of each such project, whether it is a master plan, a building project, or a research report. A partial alternative for gathering such information is to obtain a copy of the firm's weekly or monthly project status report, and transfer the relevant data to your own planning file.

• The smaller firm, with fewer staff and fewer projects, should also make a point of recording information it will need for promotion purposes using the kind of standard reporting format suggested in 10-5. It is easier to record the information when it is fresh than to try to dig it out of project files nine months later.

For news of design award and exhibit programs, firms should contact the local, state, regional, and national professional societies for a listing of such programs and their due dates. Many product manufacturers and institutional client associations sponsor such programs. The national society will normally keep an overall listing. And many sponsors put all eligible firms on their regular mailing lists.

Partners' secretaries are an invaluable source for updating clients' titles and addresses to help keep mailing lists up to date, and partners' biographical fact sheets for proposal writing.

Schedule. Some items have an elaborate series of interim and final due dates. Design award programs, for example, have dates for mailing entry fees and registration forms, submitting materials for judging, registering for the ensuing exhibit (if any), and delivering the panels. It is easy to miss these dates if they are not clearly tabulated.

Priorities. Concentrate on documenting those projects (through text, drafting, and photography) that will have the widest use. For example, choose an office building that can become not only a fact sheet, but also a slide sequence for use at interviews, the subject of a news release, the basis for submittal to three national and one local design award program, and the subject of a long article in your local paper.

Organization and storage of resources

Whether your firm is small or large, it is important to organize and store your communications resources so they can be easily reached, used, updated, displayed, and protected against unauthorized removal. The following discussion pinpoints some of those concerns. The smaller but growing firm should plan for a modular resource storage system that will allow it to begin modestly and add units as needed.

Project files. These are vital sources for developing portfolio project fact sheets and for preparing design award submittal packages. They are best kept in hanging files, each identified with a project or client name and number. Divide each file into two folders, one for descriptive information and project statistics, the other for ready-to-use prints of drawings and photographs. Keep office-owned negatives separately under lock and key. A clerical staff person should review the print file regularly, and reorder prints as needed. Arrange projects alphabetically by project or client name, by location, or numerically. In large or specialized offices, break down the classification further by building type or specialty. Biographical source materials and photos belong in a separate set of hanging files.

Slides. Slides deteriorate about 5% for each new "generation" made. Therefore, do not let go of the original under any circumstances—like photo negatives, they should be kept under lock and key or so arranged for viewing that they cannot be removed. Keep in mind that it is usually less costly to make several originals during the shooting phase than to order duplicates. Since slides are standard fare at most interviews and for many design award submittals, and because any office after even a few years in practice will have slides in the thousands, it is impor-

Item	Deadlines	Candidate projects	Costs	Special work required	Remarks
Design awards:					
American Hospital Association	Fees: 3/29 ($40) Submittal: 4/15	St. Mary's Hospital Williams Clinic	$300	Photography, presentation drawings	Exhibit panels required if accepted
City Club	Fees: none Registration form: 9/1 Submittal: 9/20	Elm St. fire station	$300		
Brochure components:					
Revised client listing	5/1		$ 40		
New project fact sheets (3)	5/1	Elm St. fire station Williams Clinic County airport hangar	$125 $125 $400	Photography	
Client reports:					
Jackson Developers Inc.	3/15	Shopping center feasibility report	$100	Writing Editing	Cost is for copies for own use
Canfield Community College	7/15	Master plan report	$100	Writing Editing Special drafting	Cost is for copies for own use
Exhibit panels:					
Community show at Southside Shopping Mall	6/7	Beason Elementary School	$350	Presentation drawings Photography Produce two panels	Crate for re-use
American Hospital Association	7/9	See entries under Design awards		Depends on outcome of design awards	
Miscellaneous items:					
Article for American School Board Journal	7/5		$ 35		Cost of reprints
News release (office move)	10/2		$100	Update mailing lists	

10-4 Typical annual communications plan for a small (8-person) office. Update this monthly and prepare a detailed budget for each entry on a separate sheet and include estimated in-house labor requirements. Figures in the *Costs* column are estimated, nonreimbursable costs, and do not include labor. In larger firms, add a column designating names of individuals with main responsibility for each task.

tant to organize them early. Some manufacturers supply integrated systems that comprise storage and secure viewing (same size or enlarged) of original slides, storage of duplicates, and sorting and editing accessories. Systems come with varying capacities, from a few hundred up to as high as 10,000 35mm slides. One manufacturer's system inserts slides into roughly 3 x 2 ft./91.44 x 60.96 cm transparent screens with about 200 slides to a screen. These are stacked upright up to 20 deep and slide out as needed in front of a vertical light table for initial selection. Drawers under the unit store duplicates. For the best and most economical arrangement that also has room to grow, consult local suppliers.

Components of the portfolio system. Reports, article reprints, and so on are best stored flat on shelves in individual, labeled piles with fold-over door for cleanliness and control. Mechanicals of reports and brochure components are usually best stored with the printer, for ease of reordering.

Reports and reprints. These may be displayed on a slanted shelf, with additional copies stored behind provided in many shelf models. The same unit may be ordered for the library to display and store periodicals.

Control over loss

Access to photo negatives, original slides, and other costly or hard-to-replace items should be controlled to avoid dispersion or loss. Keep these resources in locked cabinets. Maintain an inventory of high-priced printed reports, slides, photoprints, and portfolio components.

CONTROLLING QUALITY AND CONSISTENCY

Without proper controls, your firm's communications can easily lapse into a series of uncoordinated efforts, some of which may stand out but will develop no overall, combined impact.

BASIC DATA

Name, location, status and estimated completion date of project. Name of client, associated architects or engineers, outside consultants.

BUILDING, PLANT OR OTHER STRUCTURE

General information on site development. Site dimensions, location, access. General dimensions of building or plant, number of stories. Parking capacity. Orientation. Unusual building code or zoning provisions influencing solution.

General project design features. Principal program requirements. Gross and net square foot areas. Disposition of main plan elements; horizontal and vertical space relationships; brief reasons for these relationships. Planning module. Use of building systems.

Landscape design. Concept. Special ecological factors.

Materials. Principal interior and exterior facing materials.

Interiors. Color. Texture. Lighting. Furnishings. Special program and design features.

Graphics. Building signage—interior, exterior. Colors.

Structural system. Type of system used; spans; unusual problems. How system is integrated with mechanical, lighting, partition, and other subsystems. Integration with industrial process, if any. Departures from structural system in auxiliary areas, if any. Degree of prefabrication. Type of foundation system and unusual conditions.

Mechanical system. Concise description of HVAC system. Equipment used, where located; design temperatures. Type of control system. Heating and cooling distribution system and zones. Type of space supply and return outlets. Unconventional conditions and energy sources. Fire protection system. Special provisions for energy conservation.

Electrical system. Type of primary service. Emergency system, if any. Type of primary and secondary substations and where located. Transformer sizes and voltage. Type of building service for power, lighting, and miscellaneous equipment. Internal communication and security systems.

Lighting system. Description of system including general and task-oriented illumination; any unusual effects. External and floodlighting, if any.

Vertical transportation. Number and types of passenger and freight elevators and escalators. Pneumatic tube and other special materials handling systems, if any.

Cost information. Itemize, if possible, according to costs for: total project; construction only; fixed equipment; furnishings; special equipment; landscaping; site development; design fees; contingencies.

Special project delivery procedures. Construction management. Design-build. Fast-track. Computer-aided techniques. Other time or cost saving procedures.

SPECIAL ITEMS

Project report. Topic (planning; urban design; research; feasibility; other). Scope and concept.

Industrial design. Name and type of product. Type of service (product design; packaging; signage; other).

ILLUSTRATIONS

Photo of project, model or rendering (exterior; interior; close ups). Drawing of ground floor and typical floor plan. Simple site plan. Flow diagram of process, if any. Slides.

Controls should deal both with individual quality and overall consistency. Control over quality is best obtained by designating in every office (and, in case of very large or dispersed organizations, each autonomous division or specialty), a partner or a small two to three-person quality-control panel that regularly reviews the latest communications products of the firm, as well as samples of correspondence. Look for appropriateness and clarity, both verbal and visual (for yardsticks, see Chapters 4 and 5). Stick to finished products, not work-in-progress. After each formal evaluation, develop a verbal or written appraisal, with recommendations. This kind of evaluation is desirable as much in the small office as the large.

In addition to individual quality control, the review panel should also look for consistency among your various communications products. Do this once or twice a year. All the firm's recent communications products should be displayed as a group and judged for their overall quality level and consistency. It is an excellent opportunity to step back and gauge the firm's visual and written output.

10-6 A program of occasional technical newsletters is a good way to impress prospective clients.

10-5 (Left) Checklist for developing a project publicity source file. Obtain this information from in-house sources while the project is still fresh in their minds.

11

Communications:
a time for change

As noted in the first chapter, the design professions are in a high state of flux. The 1975 recession, the intensified search by clients for comprehensive packages of services under single-responsibility management, and the growing specialization of services, continue to tax the competitive position of the smaller general practice firms. A rising proportion of work is to be found overseas. Increasingly sophisticated clients are insisting on getting from their professionals thorough controls over project costs and time schedules, coupled with efficient long-term performance of the facility or product. Many firms (for the first time) have been selling stock to the public for operating and acquisition capital. And the public is more and more, by law and in fact, becoming a factor in decisionmaking in matters that shape the built environment.

All these factors have sharply intensified the climate of competition among professional firms, and led to the need for far better, more effective communications programs.

What is more, traditional professional ethics are being increasingly eroded under the pressures of government intervention. A higher degree of price competition on public work and the prospects of a blessing on advertising and on expanded use of direct mail marketing are opening up radical new opportunities for firms to tell their story.

To succeed in the face of such sharpened competition, professional design firms will need to focus on good performance and good communications as never before. One goes with the other—strong performance is the meat of fine communications, and skilled communications are the spearhead of new commissions.

The attitudes and tools of communications, too, are changing. There is a growing, if belated, acceptance that brevity is the soul of good writing. Likewise, in graphic design, the narrow-minded search for effect for its own sake is giving way to a focus on performance-oriented graphics.

In the technical area, industry is working hard on increasing the sophistication and reducing the cost of word processing and typesetting equipment; facsimile transmission of reports, brochures, and other kinds of text and images to clients, branch offices, and consultants; computer generation of drawings; and the storage of records in a minimum of space through microfilm technology.

When the price of an electronic table calculator was lowered from $2000 to $200 in ten years, it revolutionized certain aspects of engineering practice. So, too, in communications. It is not unlikely that by the end of this century, proposals will be mailed on microfilm or even transmitted via satellite and evaluated on a screen. Firms may keep their office and staff qualifications on a central computer, update it from an office terminal as needed, and arrange to incorporate it automatically with other promotional materials in the desired paper, film, tape or disc mode or for facsimile transmission to the client's terminal by telephone or satellite.

Design award programs—instead of being linked to a burdensome process of sorting, selecting, making prints, adding descriptive text, and using uncertain mail services—would merely beam a series of televised sequences directly from the building or engineering project to a jury sitting before a receiver screen in the jury room.

The care (and feeding) of promotional mailing lists will be made less awesome by the progressively lower cost of storing short lists on the computer along with a broad choice of print-out formats.

The need for laborious writing of proposal letters and other correspondence may disappear as machines pick up speech and convert it to a printed text, which is edited and read back to the unit for final print-out or facsimile transmission.

The cost of direct telephone lines connecting remote branch offices will be reduced through such means as Western Union's Westar satellites, at the same time reducing the danger of distortion or interruption.

Many of these developments are still in their infancy. Some are with us, but only the large and the wealthy firms can afford to use them. But we can all look forward to the day when the combined labors of science and industry will place at every design professional's beck and call the means that will make today's techniques seem fossilized by comparison.

This will lift from the professional's shoulders all burdens but one—namely, *how to use* the new tools so they will best communicate the right message.

Appendix

Exercises

The following assignments are arranged to correspond roughly to sections of the book. In each example, a background statement is followed by a specific assignment and a suggested approach. There are no one-of-a-kind solutions: each reader must take into account the objectives and characteristics of his own organization.

BROCHURE/PORTFOLIO

Problem 1.

Background

Your firm, Barton and Williams, has been in practice for two years. You have a combined staff of six. Your practice is local—architectural, with some interiors work. Barton and Williams met at a major national firm, where they gained considerable experience in many building types. Each has published one article in a major architectural magazine and both are active on national and local AIA committees—Barton in Health Facilities, Williams in Historic Preservation. You have associated with several well-known firms on specific local projects.

Assignment

Develop a concept for a brochure.

Approach

1. With a small local practice, the bulk of your communications effort would be through civic, social, and business contacts, along with aggressive efforts for articles on your projects and firm in local and national professional and business journals.

2. Your brochure/portfolio effort should be modest until you accumulate a greater volume of work. Meanwhile, include work you designed or managed in other firms, but so indicate.

3. Determine how many copies or sets you will need over two years. Chances are this will not exceed 250. Therefore, put the bulk of your budget into a good simple two- to four-page printed piece. Supplement it with actual photographic prints, article reprints, and typed, offset-reproduced lists of major projects and clients. Assemble *as needed*, using commercial mechanical or plastic spiral binders.

[For a more detailed discussion, see pp. 27–33.]

Problem 2.

Background

Your firm, Nichols, Nickel and Nidecker (3N), has been in practice for 25 years and now has offices in Chicago and St. Louis. The Chicago office has 85 staff; the St. Louis office has 20. Your practice is institutional, mostly in educational and health care facilities. You have done a few moderate-sized office buildings, which have been published and given design awards. You offer construction management services and intend to expand this and give it separate status over the next two years. You do not provide in-house engineering services, but have a long-time, happy relationship with three Chicago-based engineering firms.

Assignment

You are head of communications for 3N and have been directed to prepare a prospectus for a brochure system for submittal to the firm's three "name" principals.

Approach

1. You obviously have a large record of produced work. Break it down by building type, and select those projects which deserve a separate fact sheet due to evidence of special client satisfaction and peer recognition.

2. If your two offices or building type specialties also market independently, arrange fact sheets of projects and key personnel so they can be assembled—by office or specialty—in a suitably identified container or with a separate cover.

3. Your consumption of brochures will certainly exceed 500 over two years. This would justify a high-quality printed output.

4. For presentation to your principals, indicate the main categories of informational fact sheets (projects, people, special services, lists of published works, and reprints) and which ones should be developed first.

5. Indicate how the brochure will be produced (writing, editing, design, production). State which of these efforts will be performed in-house and which by outside consultants and suppliers. Provide cost-benefit data (cost, delivery times, quality).

6. Estimate total budget (labor and expenses) and time schedule.

7. Prepare a simple mock-up of a typical package.

[For a detailed discussion, see pp. 27–33.]

PROPOSAL

Background

The architectural and planning firm of Environmental Design Associates (EDA) has asked your 8-person landscape architecture firm to join it in submitting a proposal to a government agency to develop a series of guidelines for making barrier-free the exterior approaches to different types of facilities.

Assignment

Prepare materials that EDA can incorporate in its proposal.

Approach

1. Agree with EDA on a clear-cut theme, or "parti," around which to organize the proposal, such as, the adaptability of your design solutions to various kinds of client construction budgets.

2. Submit to EDA a draft statement spelling out the scope of the problem of landscaping the approaches to buildings for various kinds of access situations (automobile, pedestrian, mass-transit, marine).

3. Submit to EDA biographical fact sheets on your staff to be assigned to the project. Update existing materials as needed but do not retype, as this should be done by the prime proposor for consistency of style.

4. Submit to EDA photographs of applicable past projects, enlarged if possible to the intended format of the final proposal, along with a brief description. In lieu of photoprints, submit printed project fact sheets if you have them.

5. Submit a man-hour and expense estimate for your involvement.

6. Play down the identity of architectural or planning firms you have associated with in the past, as this may weaken the standing and chances of your present associate.

[For a more detailed discussion, see p. 33.]

NEWS RELEASE

Problem 1.

Background

After several months of tough negotiating, your 50-person architectural firm, Jones, Jones and McRae, has agreed to acquire, through merger, the 10-person firm of Higginbotham and Brown, located in a city in another state. This is the first step in a planned program of expansion through acquisition. The basis of your growth plan is to acquire firms with expertise that will complement yours, either in terms of services (such as structural engineering) or building type (like health facilities). Both firms are partnerships.

Assignment

Prepare a news release announcing the merger. Limit it to 300 words.

Approach

1. Write a strong headline, and an opening sentence that would contain the message even if the rest of the news release were scrapped. Include the timing of the merger and the new name of the firm (if changed). Point up the importance of the merger to the public.

2. Include this additional information: circumstances of the merger; background information on both firms; appropriate quotes by a principal.

3. Indicate release time and contact information.

4. Prepare a distribution breakdown. Divide into printed and broadcast media; past and present clients.

[For one solution, including distribution list, see 3-5.]

Problem 2.

Background

You are a 12-person firm in Centerville, a large mid-western city. You have just been awarded a commission to plan and design a new community college in the southwest. Because of the size of the project and the prospects of additional work in the region, you have decided to open a branch office in Southtown.

Assignment

Prepare a news release announcing this development. Limit to 300 words.

Approach

The news release should include the following information in the order stated:

1. Timing and location of the new office.

2. Rationale for opening the office.

3. Details of the new project.

4. Background information on your firm, including data on the principals.

5. Quote by a partner (optional).

6. Date that the information may be released, and the name and telephones of sources of more information.

Problem 3.

Background

You are a large firm with branches in four U. S. and two overseas cities, with numerous partners in three categories. Once a year, new partners are created, and you take advantage of these promotions to publicize—to clients and prospects known to you—the current activities of your firm and main accomplishments during the past year. This year you have created one new general partner, three associate partners, and five associates.

Assignment

Write a 300-word news release announcing the promotions.

Approach

The release could include the following information:

1. Names, branch office and background of promotees. Mugshots are optional.

2. Background of firm.

3. Key firm accomplishments during the past year.

4. Quote by a partner (optional).

5. Time of release and telephone contact.

NEWSLETTER

Background

Your firm, Booth and Babcock, has a highly regarded consulting engineering practice with 10-person branch offices on the two coasts and one in Texas. Over half your work comes to you through referrals from architects. As a way of disseminating your qualifications, you have decided to issue an occasional newsletter.

Assignment

Develop a scope and direction for your planned newsletter.

Approach

1. You have two choices. A "newsy" letter, with short reports on new projects, professional activities by your principals, and news of awards; or a "technical" letter, with each issue centered around one or two topics discussed in depth. As an engineering firm with unique experience in advanced energy conservation design, you should probably consider the second option. This will keep your name regularly before potential clients; if you include professional journals on your mailing list, it may yield you many useful articles based on your newsletter.

2. Limit this newsletter to four pages, and consider a publishing frequency not higher than three to four times per year. Anything greater risks overtaxing your resources as well as the reader's patience.

[For a detailed discussion, see pp. 40–43.]

PLANNING REPORT

Background

The University of East Dakota (Deaton Campus) has asked you to prepare a development plan that will guide its growth over the next decade. The plan will determine the status of numerous existing buildings; the need (tied to enrollment projections) for new buildings; their type and location; and the development of the campus circulation pattern, mechanical infrastructure, landscaping, and parking.

Assignment

You are to prepare a report (not to exceed 40 pages) detailing the present status, current and anticipated influences, and the recommended development plan.

Approach

Follow steps beginning on p. 44.

LETTER OF INTEREST

Background

Your city has just completed a new city hall. The old hall, an ornate structure built in 1875 and in fair condition, has been sold to William Newsome, an entrepreneur. Mr. Newsome intends to recycle the old hall into offices, preserving the exterior and the more memorable interior spaces. You are interested in the project but have few similar projects to point to.

Assignment

Write a letter of interest to Mr. Newsome, indicating your interest in being considered and reasons why he should select your firm. Maximum length: 250–300 words.

Approach

1. Point to your firm's consistent record in bringing in work on time and in the money.

2. Point out also that before you opened your firm, you worked for the Office of Preservation Services of the National Trust for Historic Preservation; that three of the general contractors you have worked with in the past have considerable experience in renovation work; and that you have worked for other developers before, with good results.

3. Stress that you have designed many small office buildings.

[For detailed discussion of letters of interest, see p. 46.]

DESIGN AWARD SUBMITTAL

Background

The City Club in the community of Christopher, Indiana, sponsors an annual design award program for civic architecture. The contest is national in scope and has a very high prestige value, in part because the dissemination of winning designs is backed by a generous publicity budget. Limit: two projects per firm. Your 10-person, 6-year-old firm has produced a number of public libraries, fire stations, and jails.

Assignment

Prepare a submittal package.

Approach

1. For each of your two projects, include a finely honed statement that sets out not only the design *solution* but the design *problem*. Check and recheck the statements to eliminate trade jargon.

2. Select photographs that show the facility in use. That means people—not merely a solitary figure to show scale.

3. Keep drawings simple. Make sure that titles are still legible after photostatic reduction.

4. Throughout, gear your written information and drawings to the level of understanding of the lay majority on the jury.

[For a more detailed discussion, see pp. 49–53.]

CONVENTION EXHIBIT PANELS

Background

Your firm has been invited to submit two panels for exhibit at the 1977 Convention of the American Hospital Association. You have selected a 100,000 sq. ft. ambulatory care facility that was completed in record time and within the budget due to your use of phased construction, system building, and construction management. It was reviewed favorably in several major city dailies and won a preconstruction design award from *Progressive Architectural Record Journal* magazine. The facility is in a single one-story structure on a mostly sloping, suburban site, with plentiful parking on the flat portion of the site and many trees throughout.

Assignment

1. Prepare the concept for the pair of panels.

2. Prepare a writing, graphic design, and production plan, listing which functions are to be done in-house and which outside.

3. Select illustrations and drawings you feel will show the concept to best advantage.

4. Write a careful 250-word statement describing the project, bearing in mind the type of audience and the limited viewing time available to the convention-goer.

Approach

1. Emphasize not only your *solution*, but also the client's *problem* that you helped to solve.

2. Use a large illustration (50% of a panel, minimum) to bring viewers "into the picture."

3. Select mainly those photographs that show people using the facility, inside and out.

4. Prepare a simplified flow chart showing how good management led to on-time completion of the project within the client's budget.

5. Include a capsule box with area, construction, equipment, and other project statistics that the interested viewer may study.

6. Print your firm's name as large as regulations permit.

7. Wet-mount on sturdy material and protect the surface so you can reuse the panels at local and regional conventions.

[For a more detailed discussion, see pp. 53–58.]

SLIDE SHOW

Problem 1.

Background

Your firm is completing a schematic design for a new high school for the town of Overton. Overton's city fathers have scheduled a town meeting four weeks hence at which the community will vote on the design and the budget. You have been asked to prepare a 20-minute slide show, with live commentary by your principal-in-charge. The purpose of the slide show is to explain features of the project, its flexibility to accommodate changes in enrollment, its use by the community at large, and measures being taken to obtain the most school for the money. The meeting will be held in the auditorium at the town hall, which seats 400 and has its own projection booth with standard equipment.

Assignment

1. Prepare a concept for the show.

2. Prepare a script and storyboard.

3. Develop selected artwork.

Approach

Consider the following sequences:

1. Attractive views of the community.

2. Views of crowded classrooms and deteriorating structure in the existing high school.

3. Views of women's clubs, youth groups, and the elderly meeting in a crowded basement room of the 75-year-old public library.

4. Charts of enrollment projections and the city's population projections.

5. Views of the proposed school. Use realistic model photos and simplified floor plans and sections.

6. Simplified tables of cost figures tied to various project delivery systems, showing how the ones you propose (phased construction and construction management) are likely to produce the lowest and most controllable contract cost.

[For a more detailed discussion, see Chapter 6.]

Problem 2.

Background

Your firm has a national reputation for the design of low-cost housing that has yielded high resident satisfaction and minimal crime. The Department of State has asked you to prepare a self-contained slide-talk show for dissemination overseas. The slide show is to stress user-oriented planning and design, concern for quality, cost and schedule control, and use of modern building technology. The show should range between 15 and 20 minutes of running time.

Assignment

1. Prepare a concept for the show.

2. Develop a plan, budget, and time table for producing the visual and audio elements of the show, indicating parts to be done in-house and outside.

3. Prepare a script and storyboard.

4. Prepare selected artwork.

Approach

Consider the following order of sequences:

1. Views of dirty, crowded, noisy housing, both low-rise and high-rise. Include tapes of background noise.

2. Shots of evening discussion meetings with low-income families, public officials, and lending institutions, indicating a hammering out of user needs for typical low-income project designed by your firm. Include taped pieces of dialogue. Assume that overseas viewers (public officials, architects, developers, and builders) will understand English.

3. Shots of selected passages from typical user requirement and space program documents.

4. Flow charts recording development process of a typical project.

5. Chart showing economic analysis of typical project.

6. Series of progressive views of a project under construction.

7. Series of views of several completed projects showing residential areas, as well as evidence of easy access to shopping, schools, recreation, and health care. Views should be well studded with people of all ages.

[For a full discussion, see Chapter 6.]

SPEECH

Background

As principal of an innovative 12-person structural engineering firm, you have been invited by the organization representing the nation's concrete product manufacturers to deliver a 30-minute keynote speech at its July annual convention in Cincinnati. Convention theme: Structure 2001.

Assignment

Select a speech concept and break down into principal sections or sequences.

Approach

1. Review new directions in structural engineering technology, including suspended structures, air-supported structures, very large spans, and so on.

2. Point out that the yardstick for acceptance of a structural material is strength-to-weight ratio combined with cost.

3. Note that cost criteria now include amount of energy used in material's manufacture, installation, and maintenance.

4. Point out where your host's material (concrete) does and does not meet the criteria of strength, economy, flexibility, and energy conservation.

5. Discuss design potential of the material for the short and long term.

6. Remember that your host does not expect you to be an expert on the marketing aspects of his material. He does, however, expect you to tell the members some of its long-term engineering prospects, from your vantage point as a pioneering structural designer.

7. Prepare a short summary of your speech (taken from your cue index cards) for publicity by the sponsor and yourself.

[For a fuller discussion, see Chapter 7.]

EVALUATING A TEXT

1. Read the following text:

"The services offered by the design professional have expanded beyond those traditionally required for the design of simple individual buildings. This expansion has been the response of talented and versatile professionals to new demands by the owners, operators, and users of facilities and by the public agencies regulating the environmental design and construction process, as well as to the increasing complexities of the built environment in this technological age. With the combination of greatly increased responsibilities and static levels of remuneration, many professional firms have been caught in a profit squeeze, which is disadvantageous both to the client and to themselves."

2. Apply the *Fog Index* and *Difficulty Score* (see 4-7).

3. Edit and retype.

4. Repeat Step 2 to measure improvement.

EVALUATING TOTAL IMPACT

1. Select a recent report prepared for a client.

2. Convene a jury consisting of yourself and two other members of the firm.

3. Apply the criteria of 4-8 and compute a score.

4. Repeat with a different item.

References

Note: Several cited publications are issued by the major paper manufacturers. These companies are listed, along with addresses, at the end of this reference section.

GENERAL

The Annual Report. S. D. Warren Co., Div. of Scott Paper Co. History, purpose, design, and production of the annual report.

Annual Report Guidebook, Potlatch Corp. Brief, brisk look at planning, scheduling, contents, and graphics. Includes excerpts from SEC rules on type sizes for annual reports of public corporations.

Architectural Presentation series. *Architectural Drawing and Planning* by William T. Goodban and Jack J. Hayslett; *Professional Perspective Drawing for Architects and Engineers* by William W. Capelle; *Architectural Rendering* by Albert O. Halse; *Model Building for Architects and Engineers* by John R. Taylor. New York: McGraw-Hill Book Co.

Confessions of an Advertising Man by David Ogilvie. New York: Ballantine, 1972. Distributed by Random House. Paperback. Tells it like it is. Fresh, crisp style.

How to Market Professional Design Services by Gerre Jones. New York: McGraw-Hill, 1973.

How to Prepare Professional Design Brochures by Gerre Jones. New York: McGraw-Hill, 1976.

Information Sources on Business Writing and Speaking. *Harvard Business Review*, May-June 1976. Reviews series of eleven works. Typical titles: "Effective Business Report Writing"; "Writing Reports for Management Decisions"; "Presentational Speaking for Business and the Professions."

Marketing Architectural and Engineering Services by Weld Coxe. New York: Van Nostrand Reinhold, 1971.

Pocket Pal, 11th edition, 1974. International Paper Co. Order from International Paper Co., P. O. Box 100, Church Street Station, New York, New York 10046. Treasure-house of information on art and copy preparation, typography, paper, ink, printing. The best $2 you will ever spend on the ins and outs of printed matter.

WRITING/EDITING/STYLE

The Art of Plain Talk by Rudolph Flesch. New York: Collier (Macmillan), 1951 (8th printing, 1974). Paperback dealing mostly with writing, despite the title.

A Civil Tongue by Edwin Newman. Indianapolis/New York: Bobbs-Merrill, 1976. A sequel to *Strictly Speaking* (see below). Takes another lethal scalpel to sloppy, artificial, pompous English.

A Dictionary of Modern English Usage, 2nd ed. by Henry Fowler. Oxford: Clarendon Press, 1965. Opinionated but useful.

The Elements of Style by William Strunk, Jr. and E. B. White. New York: Macmillan Paperbacks, 1962. A classic on how to write and not to write good, readable English. Read once a year to stay in shape.

How to Take the Fog out of Writing by Robert Gunning. Chicago: Dartnell Corp., 4660 Ravenswood Avenue, Chicago, Illinois 60640. 1964. Paperback. Good basic rules.

A Manual of Style, 12th ed. University of Chicago Press, 1969. A classic guide.

The New York Times Manual of Style and Usage. New York: McGraw-Hill Book Co., 1962.

Roget's International Thesaurus, 3rd edition. New York: Thomas Y. Crowell, 1962. Synonyms for every occasion, especially when replacing multi-syllables with good, simple words.

Strictly Speaking by Edwin Newman. New York: Warner Communications, 1975. Paperback. Merciless dissection of verbal fads and fancies.

Style Manual. U.S. Government Printing Office, 1973. Order from Public Documents Distribution Center, 5801 Tabor Avenue, Philadelphia, Pennsylvania 19120. Note also *Word Division*, a slim supplement to the *Style Manual*, which divides 12,000 words.

Words into Type, 3rd Edition. Marjorie E. Skillin et al, ed. Englewood Cliffs, New Jersey: Prentice Hall, 1974. A detailed, practical guide to manuscript preparation, copy editing, style, grammar, and typography.

GRAPHICS AND TYPOGRAPHY

Designing with Type by James Craig. New York: Watson-Guptill Publications, 1971.

Graphic Communication Standards Manual. U.S. Department of Labor, 1975. Division of Graphic Services, Auditors Building, 14th & Independence Avenue, S.W., Washington, D. C. 20210.

Graphic Design Manual by Arman Hoffman. New York: Van Nostrand Press, 1965.

"How to Design Your Publication for Readability" by Stephen A. Kliment. Article in May 1974 issue of *Association Management* Magazine, Washington, D. C. 20036.

How to do Pasteups and Mechanicals by Ralph S. Maurello. New York: Tudor, 1960.

IBM Selectric Composer Type Designs. IBM Office Products Division. A 16-page guide to company's office typesetting equipment, with available typefaces. Obtain from nearest branch office or independent type supplier.

Legibility of Print by Miles Tinker. Ames: Iowa State University Press, 1969. Conscientious look at elusive topic. Research findings.

Publication Design by Allen Hurlburt. New York: Van Nostrand Press, 1976. A guide to page layout, typography, format, and style.

Techniques of Typography by Cal Swann. New York: Watson-Guptill Publications, 1969.

PRODUCTION

The Fundamentals of Photoengraving. American Photoplatemakers Association, 166 West Van Buren Street, Chicago, Illinois 60604. 1966. Does just what it says, and well.

General Appearance, Typography and *Photography in Commercial Printing.* Series of 3 booklets by Chillicothe Paper Co. Series illustrates quality standards and offers hints on how to reach them.

Paper n' Graphics, a mini-guide. International Paper Co., 220 East 42 Street, New York, New York 10017. Covers the intricacies of color printing in vivid color. Contains useful guide to fitting copy, a guide to proofreading marks, and a proportional wheel for scaling photographs.

"Printing." A special issue of *Folio* Magazine, 125 Elm Street, New Canaan, Connecticut 06840. Useful series of articles on printing quality and the state of the graphic arts.

Production for the Graphic Designer by James Craig. New York: Watson-Guptill Publications, 1974. A thorough look at the way printed matter is readied for production. Very helpful chapter on mechanicals and how to prepare them.

MAILING

"Direct Mail for Architects" by Martin McElroy. *AIA Journal*, November 1974.

Memo to Mailers. U.S. Postal Service. P.O. Box 6400, Arlington, Virginia 22206.

AUDIOVISUAL

Basic Production Techniques for Motion Pictures. Eastman Kodak Co. Publication P-18, 1971. Write to Dept. 454, 343 State Street, Rochester, New York 14650. How to make films, with emphasis on 16mm.

Basic Titling and Animation for Motion Pictures. Eastman Kodak Co. Publication S-21, 1972. Shows how to make titles, mostly for 16mm films. Includes sources of equipment.

Copying. Eastman Kodak Co. Publication M-1, 1974. Shows how to copy drawings and other artwork. Covers lighting, exposure, and processing.

Planning and Producing Slide Programs. Eastman Kodak Co. Publication S-30, 1975. This superb guide covers planning, preparation, selection of equipment, and film for slide photography; preparation and photographing of artwork; and provision for sound. Also describes packaged slide preparation kit made by manufacturer.

"*She Teaches Talk-show Guests How to Bubble*" by Dan Greenburg. *New York Times*, May 30, 1976. Article covers some do's and don'ts when appearing on television.

Videofilm Notes. Pamphlet series H-40-1 through 8. Eastman Kodak Co. Series covers preparation of color slides for television, television program assembly, television film editing and splicing, sound production, and some basic questions and answers about television.

Visual Presentation Workshop Handbook by Ernest Burden. Published by author, 20 Waterside Plaza, New York, New York 10010. 1977. Based on workshops by author. Covers planning, preparation, presentation, and follow-up.

THE SPOKEN WORD

The Art of Speaking by Millett Wood. New York: Drake, 1971.

"How to Run a Meeting" by Antony Jay. *Harvard Business Review*, March-April 1976. What to do before, during, and afterward.

Moving Mountains or the art of letting others see things your way by Henry M. Boettinger. New York: Collier (Macmillan), 1969. Paperback with shrewd insights into the psychology of influencing people in groups.

The New Oratory by Antony Jay. New York: American Management Association. Step-by-step guide for mounting a major presentation, but full of hints for all levels of effort.

Problem Seeking, New Directions in Architectural Programming by William M. Pena and John W. Focke. Caudill Rowlett Scott, 1111 West Loop South, Houston, Texas 77027. 1969. Useful section on communication between designer and client covers use of various visual aids, questionnaires, interviews, and gaming.

Public Speaking by Jane Blankenship. Englewood Cliffs, New Jersey: Prentice-Hall, 1972. Chapters 7–9 contain good, practical hints.

"Saratoga's the Name of the Game" by Ben Griffin and Tom Moyer. *Planning* (Journal of American Society of Planning Officials), Chicago, Illinois. September 12, 1975 issue. How planners can make use of gaming techniques.

"Saratoga Springs Plan of Action: Citizen Participation in Urban Planning" by Robert E. Bristol and Donna E. Wardlaw. "Citizens Can Participate—a Demonstration of Actionplan" by Gregory M. Frech. Two articles in *Intersections*, Vol. 2, No. 1, Spring 1975. Center for Urban and Environmental Studies, Rennselaer Polytechnic Institute, Troy, New York 12181. How you can use gaming. No jargon.

"Toward a Design Process that Reenfranchizes Citizens and Consumers" by David Lewis and Raymond Gindroz. *AIA Journal*, Washington, D.C. November 1974. Walks you through process of how to use gaming in dealing with your client. Offers ideas on how to use in your own practice.

When It's Your Turn to Speak by Orvin Larson. New York: Harper and Row, 1971. Down to earth, full of practical hints.

PHOTOGRAPHY

Architectural Photography by Joachim Giebelhausen. English edition tr. E. F. Linssen. Munich: Verlag Grossbild-Technik GMBH, 1965. Aimed mostly at photographers.

Photographing Architecture and Interiors by Julius Shulman. New York: Whitney Library of Design, 1960. Still the basic book for designers and photographers. Emphasis is on approach to the subject, less on technique.

Photography and the Law by George Chernoff and Herschel Sarbin. Garden City, New York: Amphoto. What you and your photographer may and may not do.

MEDIA DIRECTORIES

Ayer's Directory of Publications. Philadelphia: Ayer Press. Reissued annually. Detailed guide to the nation's magazines and newspapers, including editorial staff, publishing scope, circulation, and deadlines.

Bacon's Publicity Checker. Chicago: Bacon's Publishing Co. Reissued annually. Loose-leaf guide to periodicals. All you need to know about editorial staff, scope, and deadlines.

Business Publication Rates and Data. Standard Rate and Data Services, 5201 Old Orchard Road, Skokie, Illinois 60076. Issued monthly. The advertiser's bible. Detailed information on circulation, advertising rates, and format of the nation's business periodicals. Each entry contains succinct paragraph on magazine's editorial scope.

Ullrich's International Periodicals Directory. New York: R. R. Bowker Publishing Co. Reissued annually. Arranged alphabetically and by subject. Short paragraph on each of 57,000 domestic and overseas periodicals.

PAPER COMPANIES

Selected major paper manufacturers that publish useful guides on paper, graphics, production, and related topics:

Champion Papers, Knightsbridge, Hamilton, Ohio 45020.

Chillicothe Paper Co., Division of the Mead Corp., Chillicothe, Ohio 45601.

Consolidated Papers Inc., 135 South LaSalle Street, Chicago, Illinois 60603.

International Paper Co., 220 East 42nd Street, New York, New York 10017.

Potlatch Corp., Northwest Paper Division, Cloquet, Minnesota 55720.

S. D. Warren Co., Division of Scott Paper Co., 225 Franklin Street, Boston, Massachusetts 02101.

Credits

1-1 Wide World Photos.

3-1 (Page 29) Clockwise: Weiskopf & Pickworth (Page, Arbitrio & Resen, graphic consultants); Syska & Hennessy, Inc., engineers, New York, Washington, D.C., Los Angeles, San Francisco, Paris, Tehran; Hellmuth, Obata and Kassabaum, architects; Venturi and Rauch.

3-1 (Page 30) Right: Geddes Brecher Qualls Cunningham: architects, Philadelphia, Pennsylvania and Princeton, New Jersey. Above: Caudill Rowlett Scott.

3-1 (Page 31) Above right: Caudill Rowlett Scott, architects, engineers, planners. Above left: Touche Ross & Co., New York, New York. Top: Fred Bassetti & Company, architects (upper brochure); Harry Weese & Associates (lower brochure).

3-4. Above: Caudill Rowlett Scott. Below: Reid and Tarics Associates.

3-7 Top to bottom: Hellmuth, Obata and Kassabaum; Bolt Beranek and Newman, consultants, Cambridge, Massachusetts; Haines Lundberg Waehler (HLW) Graphics Department.

3-10 Top three sheets: The American Institute of Architects. Bottom sheet: Caudill Rowlett Scott. Right sheet: National Bureau of Standards/Center for Building Technology.

3-16 Drawings reprinted from *Architectural Record*, July 1976, © 1976 by McGraw-Hill, Inc., with all rights reserved.

3-17 Photo courtesy of the American Institute of Architects.

3-18 Reid and Tarics Associates.

3-20 Photograph courtesy of Stone's, Cambridge, Massachusetts.

4-4 Permission to adapt from original letter, courtesy of William W. Caudill FAIA.

4-5 From *Architectural & Engineering News*, May 1969, © 1969 by the Chilton Company.

4-6 Top: reprinted from the *AIA Journal*. Above: copyright 1973, Folio Magazine Publishing Corp.

4-7 Description of Fog Index from *How to Take the Fog Out of Writing* by Robert Gunning, courtesy of the Dartnell Corporation. Discussion of "Difficulty Score" and "Average Sentence Length in Words" from pages 58 and 38, respectively, of hardcover edition of *The Art of Plain Talk* by Rudolf Flesch. Copyright 1946 by Rudolf Flesch. Reprinted by permission of Harper & Row, Publishers, Inc.

5-1 Above: Weiskopf & Pickworth (Page, Arbitrio & Resen, graphic designers). Below: Copyright Chrome Yellow Films 1973 (Stephanie Tevonian, graphic designer).

5-3 Below: from *Automotive Engineering*, copyright 1974 by the Society of Automotive Engineers, Inc. All rights reserved. (Design by Stephen A. Kliment).

5-5 Reproduced by permission from May 1974 issue of *Association Management*. Copyright 1974 by the American Society of Association Executives.

5-10, 5-11 Courtesy of TypoGraphics Communications, Inc.

5-12 Reprinted by permission from *Legibility of Print* by Miles Tinker © 1976 by Iowa State University Press, Ames, Iowa.

5-13, 5-14 Courtesy of TypoGraphics Communications, Inc.

5-16 Text from publication "Housing in Extreme Winds," prepared by Stephen A. Kliment for National Bureau of Standards/Center for Building Technology.

5-18 Courtesy Raymond International, Inc.

5-19 Above: American Institute of Architects. Below: reprinted from *Engineering News Record*, December 2, 1976, © 1976 by McGraw-Hill, Inc., with all rights reserved.

5-22 Above: offices of Caudill Rowlett Scott, Houston, Caudill Rowlett Scott, architect. Photo by Rondal Partridge. Below: Science Center, Harvard University, Cambridge, Massachusetts, Sert, Jackson and Associates, architect. Photo by Steve Rosenthal. Opposite page above: drafting room, Cambridge Seven Associates, Inc., Cambridge, Massachusetts, Cambridge Seven Associates, Inc., architect. Photo by Steve Rosenthal. Opposite page below: Lincoln Park Elementary School, Somerville, Massachusetts, The Architects Collaborative, architect. Photo by Steve Rosenthal.

5-25, 5-26 International Monetary Fund Headquarters, Washington, D.C., The Kling Partnership, architect. Dan Peter Kopple, partner-in-charge. Photo by Stephen A. Kliment.

5-27 "The Retail Life Cycle" by William R. Davidson, Albert D. Bates, and Stephen J. Bass, November-December 1976, *Harvard Business Review*. Copyright © 1976 by the President and Fellows of Harvard College; all rights reserved.

5-28 *Technology Review*, copyright 1976 by the Alumni Association of M.I.T. Graph © 1975; Table © 1976.

5-29 Right: Courtesy, Heinz Jaster. Above: same as 5-27.

5-30 From American Institute of Architects report "Into the Mainstream," by Stephen A. Kliment, June 1975.

5-33 Upper example: Richard G. Stein and Associates.

5-34 Top left: Haines Lundberg Waehler (HLW) Graphics Department. Top middle: Battelle Memorial Institute. Top right: The Stetson Partnership. Bottom left and middle: Caudill Rowlett Scott-CRS Interior/ Graphic Division. Bottom right: Valk & Keown Architects (Cook & Shanosky Associates, Inc., Graphic Designers).

5-36 Same as 5-16.

5-38 Letratone self-adhesive tone and shading patterns by Letraset.

5-40 Daly/Ehrenkrantz Joint Venture, for the General Services Administration. Graphic consultant: Lawrence Ratzkin.

5-43 From Corporate Communication: Champion Papers.

5-44 Illustrations courtesy S.D. Warren Company.

5-46 Same as 5-16.

5-47 From Corporate Communications: Champion Papers.

6-1 Reprinted by permission of 3M Co. from the Wollensak Multi-Image Production Manual.

6-2 (Page 128) Information courtesy Cambridge Seven Associates.

6-3, 6-4, 6-5 Daly/Ehrenkrantz Joint Venture, for the General Services Administration. Script by Stephen A. Kliment. Audiovisual consultant: Robert Eckholm.

8-1 Security National Bank, Melville, New York. The Eggers Partnership, architect. Photo by James Brett.

8-2 Lincoln Park Elementary School, Somerville, Massachusetts, The Architects Collaborative, architect. Photo by Steve Rosenthal.

8-3 Dance Building, State University of New York at Purchase, Gunnar Birkerts, architect. Photo by James Brett.

8-4 Residential buildings, Roosevelt Island, New York, Sert, Jackson and Associates, architect. Photos by Steve Rosenthal.

9-2 Wide World Photos.

10-6 Syska & Hennessy, Inc., engineers, New York, Washington, D.C., Los Angeles, San Francisco, Paris, Tehran.

Index

Type: faces, 28, 42, 77, 79, 80, 86, 94, 99, 120, 121; sizes, 44, 53, 82, 83, 98, 109, 112, 121, 154

Typesetter, 75, 82, 98, 101, 109, 112, 114; working with, 120–121, 122, 123

Typesetting, 32, 44, 64, 67, 75, 79, 99, 101, 109, 117, 120, 125; costs of, 32; photo-, 81; variations in, 82, 83, 86

Typewriter, as a form of typography, 40, 42, 43, 44, 75, 79, 80, 82, 85

Typography, 79–82; appropriateness of, 75, 76; cold type, 79, 120; composing machines for, 121; computing length of, 115; costs of, 78, 117, 121; hot type, 79, 81, 120, 121; legibility of, 79–82, 128; specifying, 80–82, 83, 84, 112, 117, 121

Ullrich's International Periodicals Directory, 151

U.S. Department of Housing and Urban Development, 45

U.S. Department of Labor, 76

U.S. Postal Service, 109

Victoria, Queen, 135

Wall Street Journal, 58, 151

Webster, Daniel, 136

When It's Your Turn to Speak (Larson), 136

White space, 79, 83, 94–98, 99, 109, 112

Wire services, 36, 147, 152

Writing, 61–63, 155, 165; aids for the reader, 66–73; Anglo-Saxon, 61; archaic, 45; colloquial, 45–46; density of, 61; formal, 45, 63, 76; French-Latin, 61; goals in, 61; how to measure quality of, 67–73; jargon in, 21, 27, 35, 53, 61, 62; pitfalls in, 27; style of, 21, 61–64; titles in, 28, 65, 66–67, 77, 79, 101, 104. *See also* separate entries

Edited by Susan Braybrooke, Susan Davis, and
Ellen Zeifer
Design by James Craig